The IT Professional's Business and Communications Guide

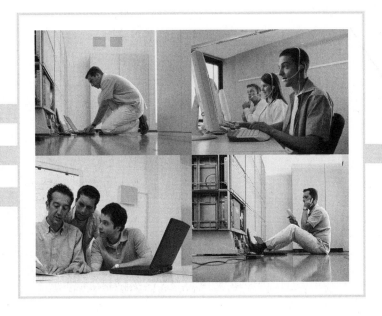

The IT Professional's Business and Communications Guide

A Real-World Approach to Comp TIA A+® Soft Skills

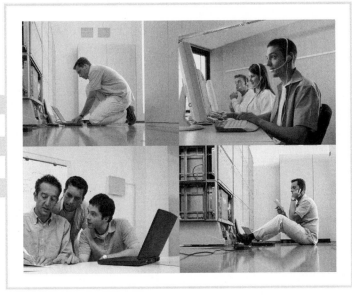

Steven Johnson

Wiley Publishing, Inc.

Acquisitions Editor: Jeff Kellum
Development Editor: Toni Zuccarini Ackley
Production Editor: Christine O'Connor
Copy Editor: Elizabeth Welch
Production Manager: Tim Tate
Vice President and Executive Group Publisher: Richard Swadley
Vice President and Executive Publisher: Joseph B. Wikert
Vice President and Publisher: Neil Edde
Book Designers: Judy Fung and Bill Gibson
Compositor: Craig Woods, Happenstance Type-O-Rama
Proofreader: James Brook, Word One
Indexer: Ted Laux
Anniversary Logo Design: Richard Pacifico
Cover Designer: Ryan Sneed
Cover Image: © Image Source, getty images

Copyright © 2007 by Wiley Publishing, Inc., Indianapolis, Indiana

Published simultaneously in Canada

ISBN: 978-0-470-12635-6

For general information on our other products and services or to obtain technical support, please contact our Customer Care Department within the U.S. at (800) 762-2974, outside the U.S. at (317) 572-3993 or fax (317) 572-4002.

Wiley also publishes its books in a variety of electronic formats. Some content that appears in print may not be available in electronic books.

Library of Congress Cataloging-in-Publication Data

Johnson, Steven, 1981-
  The IT professional's business and communications guide : a real-world approach to Comp TIA A+ soft skills / Steven Johnson.
       p. cm.
  Includes index.
  ISBN 978-0-470-12635-6 (pbk.)
  1. Electronic data processing personnel--Certification. 2. Computer technicians--Certification--Study guides. I. Title.
  QA76.3.J6535 2007
  004--dc22
                                    2007011149

10 9 8 7 6 5 4 3 2

Sybex®
An Imprint of
WILEY

To Our Valued Readers:

Thank you for looking to Sybex for your CompTIA A+ exam prep needs. The Sybex team at Wiley is proud of its reputation for providing certification candidates with the practical knowledge and skills needed to succeed in the highly competitive IT workplace. Just as the CompTIA is committed to establishing measurable standards for certifying IT professionals, Sybex is committed to providing those individuals with the skills needed to meet those standards.

The author and editors have worked hard to ensure that the book you hold in your hands is comprehensive, in-depth, and pedagogically sound. We're confident that this book will exceed the demanding standards of the certification marketplace and help you, the CompTIA A+ certification candidate, succeed in your endeavors.

As always, your feedback is important to us. If you believe you've identified an error in the book, please visit Wiley's Technical Support web site at `wiley.custhelp.com`. If you have general comments or suggestions, feel free to drop me a line directly at nedde@wiley.com. At Sybex we're continually striving to meet the needs of individuals preparing for certification exams.

Good luck in pursuit of your CompTIA A+ certification!

Neil Edde
Vice President & Publisher
Sybex, an Imprint of Wiley

For Tracy,
who told me I could,
and for John,
who made me believe it

Acknowledgments

This book would not have been possible without the careful guidance of dozens of people, all of them having affected my life in some positive way. Most especially, I'd like to thank Jay Gandee and Jeff D'Adamo, who provided me with the opportunity to be in a position to write such a book.

Moreover, I'd like to thank the incredible editorial team at Sybex, including Jeff Kellum, Toni Ackley, Neil Edde, and Christine O'Connor. Their courtesy, encouragement, belief, and support have been more than I ever could have asked for during the periods of reevaluation and questioning, and even doubt. Any author should be honored to work with such a group of talented individuals.

Another big help along the way has been some of my colleagues: Brian Harkins, Todd Lammle, Justin Korelc, Christopher Parker, Lou Rossi, and James Stanger. They've not only been an inspiration but also friends and counselors along the way.

Last, I'd like to thank the Computing Technology Industry Association (CompTIA) as a whole. Were it not for their amazing certification programs, hundreds of thousands of dedicated information technology professionals would be without a way to verify their capabilities and show their worth.

About the Author

Steven Johnson is the managing editor for PrepLogic, a leading IT training and preparation company, and he has been involved with IT for more years than he'd care to admit. In addition to being "Triple A+" Certified (Remote Support, Depot Technician, and IT Technician), Steve holds many other certifications and is a graduate of Texas Tech University. Steve got his start in IT as a sales associate for RadioShack Corporation, which he credits as the single greatest business inspiration in his life and the greatest teacher of true customer service that he's ever known. When he isn't doing IT support for his work, friends, family, or associates, he spends most of his time in the air as an ambitious private pilot dreaming of one day soaring the skies as an airline captain.

Contents at a Glance

The IT Professional's Business and Communications Guide

Table of Contents

Introduction

Welcome to *The IT Professional's Guide to Business and Communications*. Whether you are new to the field, an IT professional looking to bone up on your communication skills, or a seasoned pro looking to arm yourself for your upcoming exam, you've come to the right place. This book is a tool that you can use to understand business communication as a whole and particularly the important role that communication plays in IT. By reading this book, you will not only improve your personal and business-related communication skills but also your general IT skills.

The Purpose of This Book

The IT world has changed a great deal since its inception. At the dawn of the computing era, you could possess absolutely no social skills whatsoever but could still be highly technical and expect to receive a job with a major corporation commanding a high salary. Today, however, this is no longer the case. Now, companies have begun to require that IT personnel, in addition to possessing specific technical requirements, maintain a high level of social and communication skills.

In 2006 CompTIA reacted to this industry demand by making the biggest change that had ever been made to the A+ exam. Rather than testing technical knowledge and ability only, it became a test of IT business aptitude as well. CompTIA achieved this by implementing two things: soft skills and customer interaction questions. The reason this book is so valuable to you as an IT professional is because you need to have the knowledge and ability to deal with customers, coworkers, consultants, and other businesses as an IT technician. Without a lot of training and experience, you simply cannot understand it unless you've seen it in action!

Who Should Read This Book

You should read this book if you are new to the computing industry, have never worked in a business environment, have never worked in a situation that involved much communication, or are generally interested in improving your communication and customer interaction skills. You probably don't need to read this book if you are an experienced businessperson, skilled orator, or communication expert. The approach is high level, general, and designed for those transitioning into the professional world.

How This Book Is Organized

Unlike a textbook, this book is broken into case scenarios. There are a total of 49 scenarios, each involving some of the most important points in customer interaction and business communication. You will be able to jump into each topic headfirst and observe both mock and actual situations that are either likely to occur or have occurred in the real world. The major topics covered in this book are:

Customer Interaction   How to treat, respect, understand, and assist your customer in a retail, corporate, or other business environment

Professional Behavior   Understanding the proper way to conduct yourself in a business environment as an IT professional

Proper Phone Techniques   Basic phone communication procedures, including transferring calls, treating callers with respect, and conducting yourself professionally in a phone center environment

Communication Security   In-depth analysis of common communication security issues, such as privileged information, social engineering, and user privacy

Workplace Communication   Communicating with other professionals in the workplace in a clear, direct, and easy-to-understand manner

Leadership   How to present yourself as a leader in an IT environment

Communication in the Real World   Actual historical scenarios pulling from the preceding six subjects to give you a real-world perspective of the IT business environment

Study Tips and Best Wishes

Jumping into IT is not an easy thing to do. It's common to get bogged down or intimidated by the sheer amount of paths, information, and technical capabilities that some of the people in the world possess. As you start down this road, you're going to feel a bit torn as you feel your technical interests pull toward one specific area or another, but don't fret—this is normal. When you're reviewing this book, just keep in mind that while the technology may change, the business world may adapt, and the industry as a whole may have a different face in the future, good communication practices aren't going anywhere.

After reading this book, if you aren't already a business-savvy professional you should be well on your way. Or if you struggle with communication, you will understand the actions and intentions of your coworkers much more than you would have without reading this book. As you're reading, mark for future reference those scenarios that occur frequently in your own life. If you still have difficulty, turn back to the situations you struggle with in real life and read the /Key Concepts/ and /Resolution/ sections once again—after all, practice makes perfect.

Chapter

1

Interacting with Customers

Before I can begin discussing any type of interoffice, general, or business communication, I have to point out one very important fact. This fact is that, whether you realize it or not, the foundation of all IT and general communication in the professional world is based on customer interaction. This is because a customer is much more than just a person you deal with in a retail environment. A customer is any person you interact with who could stand to grant you and your company potential benefits. This includes consumers, other businesses, service providers, consultants, and a myriad of other individuals.

Remember: A large potion of your exam is going to be on customer interaction, and it will probably involve situations that are similar to those listed here. It's a good idea to read about the interaction, collect your own thoughts on how the situation could best be resolved, and then take the suggestions and analysis into consideration.

This chapter breaks down into the following seven different scenarios, each dealing with some of the most commonly occurring issues in professional communication:

Scenario 1: The Angry Customer
Scenario 2: Rude and Ruder
Scenario 3: Impatience: Not Quite a Virtue
Scenario 4: Assertive Intelligence
Scenario 5: The Challenged Customer[
Scenario 6: A Quiet Case
Scenario 7: Easing Tension

The Angry Customer

Here's the hard-and-fast truth: no matter what you're doing, whether you're in information technology, business, support, engineering, or working at a fast-food restaurant, chances are that you're going to run into an angry customer. As much as we don't like to deal with angry people, they are just one of those tough facts of life that we as IT technicians have to learn to deal with. Fortunately, the trick to dealing with angry people is that most of the time they are upset, frustrated, angry, or just generally agitated, but not with us. They are agitated with the *situation*. In this scenario, you're going to see what it's like to deal with an angry customer, how best to resolve the situation, and how you can turn an angry customer into a friend of your organization for life.

Scenario

It's 9 A.M. and you've just opened the gates to a local computer store where you have recently been placed into a position of authority. As the sole A+ Certified Technician, not only are you in charge of ensuring that all of your technical tickets and requests are fulfilled, but you are also responsible for customer support issues involving technical matters that the normal customer service representatives cannot field.

After setting up your work area and greeting two of your newly arriving coworkers, you are disturbed from the assembly room by a frantic and frightened coworker who bursts into your back room, breathlessly saying, "There's someone at the front counter screaming at the top of his lungs and demanding to speak with a person who 'knows what he's doing!'" Surprised, you walk out to the sales floor to investigate.

Upon arriving at the sales floor, you immediately notice an incredibly large and furious-looking man, hunching over a sales terminal and glaring at your second coworker. This coworker, equally as frightened as the first, turns to you for support with a pleading look on his face. The customer catches on to this instantly and turns to address you, yelling, "You better know what the heck you're talking about!"

Stunned, you stammer for just a second, but you are able to get out, "Yes, sir. How is it that I can help you?"

Barely allowing you to get your statement out, the customer yells, "I've had a really bad night and your piece of junk computer is broken. What are you going to do about it?" He then stares at you directly, further urging on a confrontation and intimidating other coworkers in your store.

Background

Although we'd like them to be the exception, angry customers in the modern workplace have become sort of the norm. When unfortunate events happen to people, they tend to react negatively toward the people is closest to them. In this particular case, it's happening in a retail or personal contact–oriented business. However, this happens even more often on the phone or via distance (as in an e-mail), because although only a few people might have the courage to approach you with an "I'm angry!" attitude, many more people feel that not seeing someone face to face allows them to vent their anger at will. Therefore, it's important to remember that while customers like this might require the most attention and the gentlest of kid gloves when you're interacting with them, these ideas should be put into practice when you're dealing with all of your customers. It will help your customer performance evaluations and might just make someone who's boiling on the inside feel a bit better.

Overview

Before I talk about being in the position of dealing with an angry person, put yourself in the shoes of Fred, the angry customer. Fred has just bought a brand-new laptop from Super Company X. The laptop is fast and stylish, and it's got every new feature Fred could ever ask for. To top it off, this laptop even comes with a nice briefcase he can use to carry it back and forth to work.

Unfortunately, last night Fred spent his entire night preparing a business presentation for his company. After he had spent three hours writing the presentation, the computer screen went blank and the computer refused to turn back on. Panicked, Fred has come to your computer store. At this point, his hardware, work, and job are on the line. He's tired, scared, and more than a little frustrated.

As stated before, Fred is not necessarily angry with you or your company. In fact, it's the opposite of that. Fred is actually hopeful that your company will be able to help him with this problem that he has encountered. In reality, Fred is angry with the company that manufactured the product and is upset with said product's usability. He has the sincerest hope that your company, and more importantly you, will be able to help him. That's the first thing you have to reassure him about.

Key Concepts

When most people without certification training are presented with this situation, they naturally respond with one of four options. These options generally depend on the type of person, but they can be broken down into:

- Lecturing
- Fighting
- Resolving
- Helping

None of these thoughts is necessarily illogical, but one of them is certainly the best approach for dealing with an angry person. Let's consider all these options and discuss why each of them is or is not a good idea.

Lecturing Fred About His Tone

Of all the options presented here, this is by far the worst one. When people are angry, they don't want to hear that they are sounding angry. They want to hear that their anger has gotten the attention that they desire and that you are going to help them with their problem. Furthermore, this doesn't let the customer know that you're going to try to help him, which is what he really wants.

Fighting Fire with Fire

If you respond to rudeness with rudeness, you're not going to help anyone, especially yourself. Most people who respond with this attitude to a situation believe that whoever is addressing them in this fashion is insulting them. This isn't necessarily true. One could actually argue that when someone is angry with an employee in a retail or remote situation it is because the person believes that the employee is capable of helping them but unwilling. This indicates a great deal of unspoken respect.

Getting Straight to the Issue

Of the options discussed so far, this would seem like the most appropriate one; however, it has some flaws. First, it doesn't necessarily tell the customer that you are going to help him out. In fact, it indicates to the customer that you are already classifying him along with hundreds of other cases you have already seen. Second, the customer hasn't explained the problem yet. He's barely begun to discuss it. Already asking questions indicates that you believe you have already solved the problem and, in his view, are insulting his intelligence.

Telling Him You'll Help

Although it may seem fairly obvious, the best thing you can tell an angry person is that his problem is going to be fixed. Truth be told, he does not want to be there and you do not want him to be upset. After you've established this, the customer can feel comforted in you as a person and begin to tell you what you need to know to help him.

Resolution

Most frustrated and angry customers just want to have their issue resolved. Furthermore, they want you to address them in a way that they find comforting and to investigate their issue with concern. This simple tactic and mind-set can save you hundreds of hours of argument, frustration, headaches, and annoyance, as well as making someone a friendly customer of yours for life. However, there are a lot of additional tactics you can use, including using passive voice and speaking in a pleasant tone.

Passive Voice

The simplest way to remove blame from any situation is to discuss the problem as if it just happened by chance. This is accomplished by using passive voice. Simply defined, passive voice is voice that is not active but acted upon.

Although that may not seem immediately clear, it's actually fairly simple to understand. It means that whenever you speak about action involving a subject, you speak as if the subject has had an action impressed upon it, versus making the action itself. To clarify, consider these few examples:

Active (Normal) Voice
"So, you disconnected the motherboard from the power supply?"

Passive Voice
"So, the power supply was disconnected from the motherboard?"

Active (Normal) Voice
"Did you buy the right type of DIMM for your motherboard?"

Passive Voice
"Is the DIMM that was bought the correct type?"

This tactic succeeds in removing any type of personal blame and instead places the blame on an unknown entity. Although in reality it's normally still the user's fault or issue, the language used removes any personal liability.

Pleasant Tone

Remember the old saying, "You can catch more flies with honey than you can with vinegar"? It's true. Customers who are angry always respond better to people who are polite and courteous. It takes away any ammo they have to become angrier. If you think back to the times when you were extremely irate and were calmed down, chances are that the person you were dealing with was very understanding and spoke in a way that you found soothing in some form or another. It's important to understand the effect this can have on customers in a retail or remote environment and to effect a semblance of it on a day-to-day basis. You'll find that it goes a long way toward making not only your customers a bit easier to deal with, but also your friends and family.

Skills for the A+ Exam

Here's an example of the type of questions you will see about angry customers on the A+ exam:

1. A furious customer slams his hands down on the desk in front of you and demands that you pay for the computer that he believes you broke. Which of the following is the best statement to calm the customer?

   A. OK, sir. Let me see if it's broken and we'll go from there.

   B. I'll be certain to let my management know to help you.

   C. OK, sir. How much does that product cost? Maybe we could help.

   D. Sir, I'm more than willing to help. Let me see what I can do to fix the situation.

   Answer A: Incorrect. This answer leads the customer to become angry. He will think, "What do you mean you'll CHECK to see if it's broken?"

   Answer B: Incorrect. This answer makes the customer believe that you can't help him with anything and that he should be speaking with your manager.

   Answer C: Incorrect. This answer makes the customer think that your company is cheap and will only help him if it's in the budget.

   Answer D: Correct. This informs the customer that you are willing to help and try your best. That's all the customer can really ever hope for.

Rude and Ruder

I don't know about you, but I really just don't like rude people. I don't think anybody actually does. They're not the sort of people you want to have over for dinner, or the sort of folks you'd like to call friend. Unfortunately, whether or not we want to associate with them, rude people have a weird habit of just showing up where we don't want them. Take this real-life scenario as an example. The names, places, and people have been changed to protect the innocent (or perhaps I should say the guilty), but the truth is still intact.

Scenario

You've been working at your retail computer business for six months and you think you've finally started to get a grip on how things work. You're familiar with the inventory, you've gotten to know your coworkers on a more personal level, and you think that your manager approves of your performance up to today.

Today, in order to get ahead on the business inventory that is going to be conducted at the end of this month, you've decided to start counting some of the currently existing parts and computers that are normally not used and then place them into a safer area where they will not be exposed to the potential of theft or misplacement. This way, you can cut down on the time you're going to have to spend on your inventory management later.

Suddenly, just as you've begun your project and started to unpack a great many boxes onto the main floor, the door to the front office opens and an older-looking man in his late 60s walks into the store. He then makes his way directly up to the front counter, looks you in the eye, and says, "This place looks like a complete mess. Don't you know how to run a business?"

You immediately apologize for the situation and ask how you can help. He then responds by saying, "I'll tell you how you can help—you can clean up this mess. Until then, I'm not sure if I really want to be caught shopping here. This place isn't up to my standards, and I don't think it's up to yours, either."

Slightly frustrated, you nod but maintain a professional appearance. You then say, "OK, sir. Well, I'm sorry for the appearance of the store, but do you think that you could still give me an idea of what you're looking for? After all, you're already here and I'm willing to help."

Chuckling, the man says, "Trying to sales pitch me now, huh? Fat chance of that happening, punk."

Background

One of the more "interesting" things about working in support, customer service, or anything involving the service industry is that we as professionals are exposed to a wide variety of people from an uncountable number of backgrounds. This is important to note because while you might find the behavior of others to be rude, it may not be intended that way. Granted, in this case it's pretty obvious—the customer has a fairly large chip on his shoulder. However, that isn't always the case.

In some places in the United States, a common way to joke is by complaining about situations. It doesn't matter if something is perfect or if they don't have any real complaints at all, they will still complain. Because of this, it's important that you weave an aura of complete and total understanding about you before you begin to deal with any sort of customer. If they do something that is rude or upsetting, don't fret. After all, you're only going to be dealing with them for a limited amount of time. Furthermore, you can also consider that this might just be their way of expressing their beliefs and, by their standards, may not be rude.

Overview

The first thing I have to point out in this situation is that your customer is obviously upset. The right thing was done here, in that before the actual situation of the customer was dealt with, an apology was made. But even after that apology was made, the customer continued to complain and make acid remarks.

Personally, I find situations like this fairly tough to deal with. You almost want to go up to them and say, "What is it that you WANT!?" In fact, I've even seen someone do that at the workplace. And while I wouldn't recommend it, it actually had pretty good results.

In the section that follows, you're going to see some of the basic temptations to avoid in this situation (such as raising your voice and asking them what they want) and then look at some of the reasons that they have this demeanor. By reviewing these facts, you should be fairly well armed to deal with a customer who makes you as upset as this one. But be warned, there is no easy fix-all for dealing with different types of people; there are only general guidelines. Each situation is unique, and you have to use your best judgment of what will and will not work.

Key Concepts

Although it would normally be a good idea to understand your customer's perspective, in this case the customer is openly hostile. With an openly hostile customer, it's going to become extremely difficult to obtain information from them. Therefore, you have to consider the possible avenues of approach you have to communicate with them.

Temptations to Avoid

People like this customer can bring out the worst in us. Because of that, it's important to remember that there are certain temptations that should just be avoided. In particular, you should make sure that you do not ask someone to calm down, and that you do not refuse service or become equally argumentative. The following will explain how these concepts can turn a bad situation into an even worse one very quickly:

Asking Them to Calm Down   This is a *bad* idea. Have you ever had someone ask you to calm down when you're angry? Did it work? When people are angry and you ask them to calm down they just instantly think, "Hey! Aren't you listening to me? I'm angry! I want attention."

In the real world (that is, the nonbusiness world) you don't really have to placate everyone you meet. If someone wants attention when they're angry, you can always choose to ignore them or just wait until they've calmed down after an indeterminate period of time. In business, you don't have that choice, especially in retail.

Refusal   Boy, it would be great if you could just say, "I don't feel like dealing with you today, Mr. Customer. Thank you and have a very nice day." I think it would save everyone a lot of headaches. Truth be told, I've actually seen people do this. They get to the point where they don't want to deal with a customer and then they simply tell the customer to go away.

There's a simple reason you can't do this: collateral damage. If you allow one individual to walk away angry, that customer creates 10 more who will not want to deal with you in the future. People like to talk, and you deciding that you don't want to deal with a person could be just about the worst event in that person's day—and you'd better be darn sure that they're going to want to tell someone about it.

Being Rude Back   You know, I don't think I need to get into this one. But, just in case, it almost goes without saying that you can't be rude to customers—no matter what they do. If you're like me, you've actually been the rude customer once or twice in your life and dealt with someone who was rude back. You've also probably dealt with someone who remained professional and calm throughout the entire incident.

To this day, I can still remember walking into an unnamed cell phone store and chewing out the manager. He stood there and took every bad name, insult, and angry complaint I could throw out and just responded with kindness and understanding. It really took the wind out of my sails. On the other hand, just the other day I went to go buy a pretzel at another unnamed business and I wasn't served. After two minutes of that, I asked for service. The attendant responded with "Yeah," and then continued to baste and ready a fresh garlic pretzel (which happened to be the exact one I wanted at that moment). Things like that stick with you. The bottom line is don't be rude, no matter what somebody else does.

Remember, these are things to be avoided at all cost. No matter how upset you get, don't give in to these temptations! Not only are they damaging to your customer, but they also can be damaging to you and your business. Instead, consider the discussion in the following section.

Resolution

There are a lot of reasons why people tend to be rude, but they usually boil down to one of these two things:

- Frustrated
- Culturally different

Frustrated

Of the two problems, frustrated is by far the easiest one to handle. Frustrated people just want their problem to be fixed! Remain calm, do your best to help the customer, and know that you're going to make them have a good day if you fix their issue.

Focus on the customer. Let the customer know that you're concerned about their problem. They will think better of you and appreciate that you're doing everything you can to help them.

Culturally Different

You don't need someone like me to tell you that there are a lot of different types of people out there. In the United States alone, people in the South tend to think and act differently than people in the North. People from California don't usually vote the same way as people from Texas. The trick is that you can do a few things to make sure that everybody stays happy:

Use acceptable language.   There are certain things you can and cannot say to people. Some of the language that you need to avoid using are slang words or phrases, derogatory terms, acronyms, and just about anything that would make someone who doesn't come from the same background as you feel uncomfortable.

Avoid excessive body language.   It's always a safe bet to not make many hand movements when dealing with a customer. Unless you're a master of empathy (which most of us aren't), you can't say for certain how someone is going to react to a particular gesture. They could feel threatened, insulted, or even sexually harassed by an action you make. Consider that while such expressions as a good old-fashioned "thumbs up" might be considered friendly and encouraging in the United States, it is considered to be one of the rudest gestures on the planet in many other cultures.

Skills for the A+ Exam

Here's an example of the type of questions you will see about rude customers on the A+ exam:

2.   A user informs you that he has been waiting on hold for a very long time and wants to be spoken to immediately. You currently have three other customers who have been holding longer and are also reading an e-mail saying that you have to log out of your workstation in five minutes, forcing you to place your current customers back into the hold queue. What is your best response?

A.   I'll be glad to help you immediately, sir.

B.   I apologize, sir. We will be with you as soon as we can. It shouldn't be much longer. Again, I apologize for the inconvenience.

C.   OK, no problem. I have to leave in just a few minutes, but is there a chance that it's a tiny problem? I'd like to help.

D.   Sir, I'm more than willing to help. Let me see what I can do to fix the situation. Or if I can't fix it, I'll get you to someone who can.

Answer A: Incorrect. You can't do this. If you start, you probably won't be able to finish this in five minutes and won't be able to log out of your terminal.

Answer B: Correct. Sometimes you have to tell a customer the hard truth, even if they're rude or upset.

Answer C: Incorrect. I have a bit of a soft heart, so I've tried to do this more than once. Unfortunately, it never works. The problem is *always* a big problem. But even if it isn't, it's not a good practice to get into. The A+ exam is going to ask you questions like this. Be prepared.

Answer D: Incorrect. This is a great distracter. You're being polite, kind, and very helpful. Unfortunately, this response doesn't account for the fact that you have people currently holding and that all your other associates are busy. Be sure to watch out for this type of thing on the real exam.

Impatience: Not Quite a Virtue

I bet if I were to sit down and have a one-on-one talk with you about being impatient, you'd probably confess to me that there's been at least one time in your social or working life that you've been anxious about *something*. For most people, it's been a lot more than just once. In fact, it's probably happened a couple of hundred times.

Patience is a hard thing to master. Even for the most calm, confident, and level-headed people you will ever meet, patience is just one of those things in life that takes a lifetime to be able to control and two lifetimes to master. One of the "joys" of IT is that you have to learn how to do it as soon as you start your position. Unfortunately, your customers don't exactly have to share your state of mind.

Scenario

It's Christmas, the busiest time of the year at your small office. Everyone has built up a good share of vacation, personal leave, and even a little sick time that they've been talking about using now for the past month. Truth be told, you've even arranged to take some time off yourself. After all, what good is having paid vacation if you don't use it?

As a result of the upcoming vacation, everyone is in a hurry to pack things up and get ready to leave the office. Employees have been submitting jobs to the servers, locking down workstations, and doing their best to get documents signed off by the boss before their leave begins.

On the morning of your last day in the office before your vacation starts, you receive an early phone call from your supervisor, notifying you that the office Exchange server has just gone down and you need to rush to the office immediately. Upon your arrival, you quickly realize that the server has been infected with an extremely malicious virus and that it's going to take you hours to fix. To top it off, most of the crew is planning on taking a half day today and needs the equipment.

As soon as you finish the diagnosis, you receive another phone call from your supervisor: "Hey, it's Alan. Can you have that server back up in 30 minutes?"

Background

Someone once told me that if you want to get into IT to give yourself more free time, you're getting into the wrong business. I thought he was kidding at the time, but he turned out to be almost completely correct. IT is one of those businesses that, just like being a doctor or a lawyer, may require you to work at some very odd hours. Problems happen and they don't normally tend to just resolve themselves. Because of this, it's important to remember that there are going to be times when things go wrong. Unfortunately, they always seem to come at the wrong times, like holidays, weekends, or other times that we'd like to think about anything other than work.

As you read over this analysis, I encourage you to put yourself in a particular mind-set before you begin to think it over. That mind-set is that you are going to have to work very hard in IT and there are just times when work is going to take a long time. As simple as it sounds, that frame of thought will save you a lot of time and frustration if you can get yourself mentally prepared for it before it happens.

Overview

From the description of the condition of the office, you can easily tell that most people are anxious to have all their problems solved and be under way with the rest of the day. Just like it says in the beginning, who can really blame them? It's the holidays and they're all ready to take a break. The problem is, problems don't take breaks.

When you're involved with a situation like this in your business, you're going to need to consider a lot of factors: elements like time, complexity, workload, and just how generally difficult a problem is going to be to fix. You should take all of these factors into account and present your supervisor with what you consider to be a fairly reasonable timeframe. However, when you do that, you should also consider some of the key concepts listed next in this scenario when you're speaking to someone about a problem that won't just quickly disappear.

Key Concepts

There are many sides to the practice of being patient. Some of them come from the perspective of the customer/coworker and some from the perspective of the employee. The important thing to remember is that, as far as you are concerned, there is only one side that you have to worry about—yours.

Granted, you're going to have to be concerned with the customer's state of mind. You can't just ignore their feelings and continue on with the workday. (Since you've made it to this point of the chapter, you probably already understand that.) But the main idea is that customers are always going to have problems. Being impatient and in a hurry is just one of those problems that you have to learn to deal with for their benefit. Let's now take a look at a few things to keep in mind as you deal with an impatient customer.

The Problem Isn't Going Away

Just because a customer may want a problem to be instantly fixed, it doesn't mean that it's going to happen. Because of this, it's a good idea to let people know the severity of their problems. In the previous scenario, you were dealing with a complex server that had an extremely urgent and complex problem. Although the manager may want it done in 30 minutes, it probably isn't feasible. Furthermore, if you try to do what you can in 30 minutes and just turn the server back on, the problem will still be there.

Whenever possible, be up-front with your customer. If they ask for the unreasonable, professionally tell them that it's unreasonable. If someone came to you and said, "I need you to overhaul this V-8 engine in 10 minutes," you could easily tell them that you don't believe that you can overhaul the engine in 10 minutes. Instead, you'd need somewhere around a week (assuming, of course, you could work on cars in the first place).

Doing a Half-Job Will Be Worse Than Not Doing It at All

It's easy to tempt yourself into committing one of the cardinal sins of IT and, more importantly, one of the cardinal sins of business. The best advice you will probably ever receive in business is the following: never do a half-job. Don't just patch something together. Don't get something to the point that it works, but not very well. Get your task done to the point that what you were supposed to do was done *great*.

Your goal in everything you do in business is to get people to say, "Wow." If you don't accomplish that every single time you set out, it's not the end of the world. However, not trying to shoot for that goal every time you go out is just letting yourself down. If you fully grasp your potential and do everything you were gifted with, you will be able to churn out some amazing results. If something's worth doing, it's worth doing well.

Resolution

When dealing with impatient people, just remember that the key is to be polite and to do the best you can to solve their problem as quickly as possible, whether that involves abstract ideas or the traditional method of just working your way through their issue. At the end of the day, they are people just like you and they just want to have their situation taken care of. Remember that every time you deal with someone who is anxious or impatient about something, you have the opportunity to be the hero and solve problem quickly. Along the way, here are some good practices to keep in mind as you're solving these problems.

Be Extremely Polite

Being polite can go a long way to diffusing an impatient customer. As you've seen in previous scenarios, it's a disarming tactic to someone who is openly hostile or confrontational. In the case of someone who is extremely impatient, it is an almost miraculous tactic, and in the case of your superiors, it can actually score you a lot of brownie points.

If someone is anxious and ready to have something done immediately, they're most likely not going to act adversely if you say one of the following easy-to-memorize quotes:

- "I'll do my very best to get to you [or your problem] as soon as I can. Thank you for your patience."
- "Thank you, sir/ma'am. I'll be with you in just a moment."

Offer Alternatives

One of the most interesting things about the social issue of patience is that it only occurs if someone has a problem that they want attended to immediately. Whether that problem is personal or work related, it can be quickly diffused by thinking of a solution that the individual may not have considered.

When you have a customer or coworker who appears to be concerned about a particular issue, the best advice is to quickly ask them about their situation and see if you can think of any alternative solutions they may not have considered.

- "Mr. Boss, I think the server is going to be down for quite a while. Do you think it might be a better idea for us to queue up the e-mails on the backup Exchange server while I repair this one?"

- Or, in the retail world, "I'm currently with another customer, Mr. Customer. I'll be with you as soon as I can, but if you need immediate assistance I can call a coworker from the back to come and help you."

Skills for the A+ Exam

Here's an example of the type of questions you will see about impatient customers on the A+ exam:

3. You are working on one of three priority help desk tickets when your supervisor calls and says that he has another priority ticket that has to be taken care of immediately. The tickets you currently have will probably already take you several hours. What is your best action?

    A. Stop what you're doing and take care of the ticket your supervisor has.

    B. Stop what you're doing and inform the supervisor of your situation.

    C. Continue working on the ticket and suggest that it might be a better idea to hand the ticket to the second team; your office is at its max.

    D. Continue working on the ticket and tell your supervisor that you think you can handle the situation, but make him aware that there is an issue.

    Answer A: Incorrect. It's a good idea to do what your boss tells you, but not at the sacrifice of your performance. You should also never stop working on an issue when you can continue diagnosing it.

    Answer B: Incorrect. You should always keep your supervisor informed, but you shouldn't stop working just to do that.

    Answer C: Correct. This answer not only informs your supervisor of the situation, but also suggests an alternative for him. Your superiors will appreciate your understanding of their situation, and this will help them remember that you can handle difficult situations well.

    Answer D: Incorrect. You should never tell a supervisor that you can do something but there may be problems attached to it. Supervisors want to hear that something either can or cannot be done.

Assertive Intelligence

Have you ever noticed how most of the people you meet in this world tend to be a little less smart than you? Most IT people know the feeling. It's not exactly an industry that attracts people who dislike an intellectual challenge. In fact, some of the smartest people you will ever meet are in this field . . . which is actually the problem.

A good portion of the time you'll be administering, assisting, or troubleshooting an issue with someone, they'll be a lot smarter than you are. On top of that, they'll probably be older, more experienced, and a great deal more connected. That makes it pretty tough to be the new IT guy sometimes.

Scenario

You're working in a call center environment for a local cable company and have just been promoted from a Level 1 support technician to a Level 2 support technician, and you couldn't be happier. Finally, you've stopped receiving phone calls that involve trivial things like unplugging the cable modem and plugging it back in. Now, you're starting to get involved with actual technical issues like subnetting, driver conflicts, failed hardware issues, and the sorts of thing that tech geeks just love! You're on the top of the company's tech food chain.

Sometime during the day you receive a phone call and you answer with a standard greeting. The customer responds with:

"Hi. I'm a consultant working for SmallBus, Inc. and it looks like their 2600 is having QoS issues. I'd like to set it up to be fed in from our backup cable modem here, but your DHCP server seems to keep assigning us new IP addresses every hour. Can you give us something static for a day until I can figure out what the issue is?"

Background

Most companies that you will work for in your career will have a whole range of employees with different skill levels. Because of this, there's a strong chance that you'll have someone else in your organization who is much more experienced in IT than you—or, if not more experienced, who will certainly have a larger knowledge base.

However, this isn't always the case. Many small companies will hire just one IT person, who will be in charge of virtually the entire business. This is a difficult situation to be in, because IT is so broad and the expectations of a sole IT person are extremely high. So, for those of you who are planning on working for a smaller company, pay especially close attention to this scenario—chances are that you will encounter it a lot as you deal with other companies that interact with your own.

Overview

There are a couple dead giveaways that you can look for regarding problems of a complex nature that have extremely experienced professionals asking about them:

- They immediately identify the problem without hesitation.
- The problem is narrow and self-contained, not broad and overarching.
- There is usually a specific request.

This makes it fairly easy to identify exactly what is wrong (assuming you can understand the technology) and move on to some of the tactics you can use to resolve the problem.

Key Concepts

First off, let's say you don't even know what a 2600 is. (I know that some of you might be saying, "Hey, Steve, it's a Cisco router. I know this stuff," but bear with me.) Second, let's also say that you're not familiar with IOS and how to configure Cisco networks. In case you don't know what IOS is in the first place, don't worry; you'll be fine. Now, let's analyze the conversation and take a look at the things you know before you even start to deal with the customer.

Someone who throws around Cisco terminology and consults for a living is probably a pretty intelligent, or at least technically experienced, person. Some key things to listen for in your customer or coworker's language are:

- Length of words
- Acronyms
- Technical terms
- Jargon usage

If the person consults for a living, they're going to know their way around the IT field, whether or not they've got all the certifications in the world. Make sure you avoid the following when dealing with a smart, experienced person:

- Avoid explaining the basics.
- Avoid overly long explanations.

Resolution

Since you'll come across this scenario pretty often, it's a good idea to prepare yourself for exactly what to do when and not if it presents itself. As a general guideline, you can get past the situation by doing two things: Concentrating on what they need and not using technical terms back.

Concentrate on What They Need

Experienced professionals are going to have a good idea of what they want before you even start diagnosing their issue. One of the best things you can do early in your evaluation is to find out exactly what they want from you. The more you understand what they want, the better you are going to be able to help them.

Don't Use Technical Terms Back

This one goes against what you might normally think. The guy called up, started spouting off terms, and is asking for something very technical. This is all true, but it doesn't necessarily mean that the person is going to understand everything you throw back at them. In this particular case, the person seems to be a Cisco expert. Say your DHCP server used Juniper technology, instead. Or, in the worst case, say the problem is actually because the person did something wrong in the first place.

Assume They're Dumb; Act Like They're Smart

This sounds mean and deceitful and, well, it sort of is. *However*, it's a good philosophy to adopt. People *really* like to feel as if they're intelligent, well spoken, and an absolute expert on the subject. Making them think otherwise can result in a lot of negative emotions, such as anger, sadness, or maybe even a little anxiety.

Furthermore, the person might know a little about a particular field, but that doesn't necessarily mean that they're an expert. For the moment, you can feel safe to use some more technical terms and treat the person with a little more credit than you would a normal user, but it's best to stick to a common playing field.

Skills for the A+ Exam

Here's an example of the type of questions you will see about technically proficient customers on the A+ exam:

4.   How should you respond to a customer who uses jargon?

   A.   Use the jargon back moderately.

   B.   Don't use it in return at all.

   C.   Use it heavily in return.

   D.   Ask the customer if they understand the terms, then use them heavily.

   Answer A: Incorrect. While this might be appealing, jargon is just not a good idea in technical support. It can really confuse the issue.

   Answer B: Correct. When in doubt, don't use it. That's the first rule of jargon, acronyms, and special terms. Whenever you're in technical support, you have to resort to the least common denominator.

   Answer C: Incorrect. Young Skywalker, this is not the way of the Force. Never use acronyms, jargon, or special terms heavily!

   Answer D: Incorrect. This is an interesting idea, but still not a good one. If you asked a customer about every single term, the two of you would be on the phone or talking together for a *very* long time.

The Challenged Customer

Dealing with a disability is difficult for both the person with the disability and the person who has to adjust their behavior because of it. Whether the problem is physical, mental, or emotional, a disability can often imply some type of communication issue that inhibits your ability to understand the customer's needs. However, as an IT professional, it's your responsibility to overcome that problem and understand what the needs of the individual actually are. The only problem is that doing so can prove to be quite difficult.

Scenario

In the middle of the day a customer walks into your retail store and indicates with her hands that she would like to speak with you. This is odd, because most customers usually indicate to you that they would like to speak by calling out your name or saying "Excuse me." Furthermore, you've been working underneath the counter arranging some of the inventory and you couldn't see the person waving at you, so she must have been waving for at least a few seconds, if not a few minutes. Regardless, you immediately make your way over to the customer and greet her professionally with a polite "Good afternoon, ma'am, how can I help you?"

The customer responds with a polite nod and then begins to wave her hands in odd directions again. At first, you aren't sure what she's indicating, so you interrupt with a brief "Pardon, ma'am? I'm not sure I understand."

Then, as soon as you say that, the customer screams in an almost piercingly loud voice and yells out something absolutely unintelligible. After recoiling from the impact of the sound, you ask the customer to politely repeat her request, and she again screams something that you do not understand.

A bit intimidated, you ask her to repeat herself one more time. Unfortunately, she doesn't respond to this well. She begins to look very upset and starts waving her hands even more frantically, continuing to scream.

Background

It's a bit hard when you don't have a disability to remember that there are literally millions of people in this world who live day to day with a life-altering illness, infirmity, or impairment. However, in the workplace, disability is an important factor to consider when you're providing customer service, because it is your duty to provide service not just to healthy and fully functioning people but to people who are challenged as well.

What this means to you as an IT professional is that you need to be able to easily identify when someone has a disability and you need to know the ways to cope with it—and there are many. Although you may not be intimately familiar with all of them, this scenario will familiarize you with some of the most common ways to communicate to someone who has a disability that presents a barrier to their communication.

Overview

Some of the indications that you can look for to determine whether a customer has a disability are as follows:

Physical Movements   Does the person have a limp? Is there some impediment in their motor functions that is recurring?

Visual Comprehension Levels   Does the person you're dealing with seem to understand everything you're telling them?

Inanimate Accompaniments   Does the person have a hearing aid? A cane? Are they in a wheelchair?

These are just a few of the things you can look for. Table 1.1 in the next section will further illustrate some of the communicative techniques that you can use when you're communicating with individuals who have easily diagnosable problems.

Key Concepts

This is a tough situation. The customer obviously wants something and it is your inability to understand, not her inability to communicate, that is causing the issue. Fortunately, there are some pretty safe procedures that you can use to deal with this sort of scenario.

Step 1: Diagnose the Disability Sensitively

Believe me when I say that this is a very difficult thing to do politically. What you are doing in this first step is trying to discover what the customer's disability is and figure out ways to overcome it in a way that doesn't make the customer feel embarrassed. Here are some of the best ways to determine the nature of a customer's disability:

Body Language

Customers who are deaf or hard of hearing will usually try to make sudden movements to attempt to convey their meaning. Additionally, people who are incapable of speech will generally use more refined movements to indicate what it is that they desire. In this case, a customer is moving her hands rapidly and seemingly randomly, which usually indicates that the customer is hearing-impaired.

Speech Patterns

People who have disabilities tend to speak in different manners. Some people have difficulty enunciating terms or speaking in complex sentences. Sometimes people who are hearing-impaired will speak in unusual tones because they don't know what their voice truly sounds like. Understanding what to look for in these types of disabilities is key to discovering how to communicate.

Step 2: Attempt a New Mode of Communication

This is the easy part. Once you have diagnosed someone's problem, it's fairly easy to find a way to communicate with them. Check out Table 1.1 for a list of good communication recommendations for disabled customers.

TABLE 1.1   Communication Methods for Disabled Customers

Disability	Communication Method
Hearing-impaired	Use illustrations and written communication.
Visually impaired/blind	Use descriptive language and the sense of touch.
Mentally disabled	Be patient and understanding, and try to make things simple to understand.
Physically disabled	Don't ask to assist; just assist with moving and finding things as if it were standard customer service.

Resolution

When dealing with disabled individuals, it's important to remember to be patient and understand that they are not stupid or inept; they are simply disabled. The best thing you can do as an IT professional in a difficult situation like this is to remember that it is your job to communicate. It is your job to make the customer pleased with your service and responsibility.

Watching their body language, understanding their alternative forms of communication, and readily keeping communication tools, such as a pad and paper, at your disposal to help with the occasional situation not only will help you quickly diagnose their problem, but also will quickly impress the person and maybe even impress your superiors.

Skills for the A+ Exam

Here's an example of the type of questions you will see about disabled customers on the A+ exam:

5. A customer who happens to be visually impaired asks you if you can help him identify what is wrong with his laptop computer. Immediately upon inspection of his laptop, you realize that the plastic has been broken on the bottom of the computer and exposed to the elements, ruining the equipment. What is the best procedure?

   A. Inform the customer of the broken plastic professionally and offer alternatives.

   B. Attempt to make light of the situation and say that it looks like something accidentally broke the computer.

C. Speak very slowly to the customer and ask him if he understands.

D. Apologize repeatedly and say that the problem will never happen again.

Answer A: Correct. This is the absolute best thing you can do. You need to be straightforward, honest, and professional in a situation like this, just as you would be for someone who isn't visually impaired.

Answer B: Incorrect. You should *never* make light of a customer's disability. It is rude and insulting, and will probably result in disciplinary action.

Answer C: Incorrect. The customer is not hearing-impaired, and it isn't a good tactic to use, even if he were.

Answer D: Incorrect. You have nothing to apologize for. You did nothing wrong.

A Quiet Case

There's something that is both really likable and really irritating about people who are very quiet. They're likable, because we don't feel intimidated or judged by them. If you don't say anything, no one really knows what you think. Therefore, we automatically assume that they're probably not thinking anything too negative. Unfortunately, the fact that they don't say much at all has a tendency to make most of us nervous.

In IT, you will run into a lot of cases of quiet people who have technical issues. They present an extremely interesting scenario, because you have to not only be able to diagnose their issue, but also do it with barely any information whatsoever. Let's look at a typical case of a quiet customer and examine some of the tactics you can use to overcome their naturally shy nature.

Scenario

Your company is running a huge promotional sale on computer memory. For the first time ever, system RAM is half price and every DIMM that you sell includes a free 32MB Compact Flash card. It's a heck of a deal, and you've managed to pick up a few DIMMs and cards yourself.

While you're near the front counter, an individual approaches you with a copy of a magazine in hand. Without saying hello, he motions you to look at his magazine, and then indicates a bright red advertisement for your company and for your sale. Afterward, he gestures for you to follow him and leads you toward a specific brand of memory. He points, mumbles something under his breath, and then indicates back toward your memory stick again.

Background

In the real world, most corporations outline a pretty firm policy that they like you to take when it concerns their customers. They believe there is one way that will suit every single customer you will ever have, and it will make everyone match up into a perfect little row that works just the way they want. Unfortunately, the real world doesn't work like that (although it sure would be nice if it did).

Whenever you're dealing with an "unusual" customer, whether that customer is quiet, quirky, or just strange, you should keep your company's view in mind, but you should also be aware that not everyone fits into a "one size fits all" box. You're going to have to adjust. Now, I'm not saying that you should go in the opposite direction from what your company has been teaching you, but you can do well by keeping your company's viewpoints in mind and following the spirit of them while embracing your own sense of customer service. The A+ exam encourages you to do this by asking a few out-of-the-ordinary questions, and the real world will do the same by presenting situations just like this one.

Overview

This situation is actually inspired by something that happened to me once in the real world. All too often, people will approach you with written material that they think will convey information better than they are able to verbally, and they will place it in front of you as if to say, "Here, read this and understand what I want." Personally, I find it kind of frustrating, but I had to place myself in the shoes of someone in just this sort of situation. Specifically, this person probably:

- Has poor communication skills
- Doesn't like to interact with sales or service people
- Has done a lot of research on the subject
- Would like to see this transaction taken care of as quickly as possible

With these things in mind, you can really put yourself into the mind-set of being a helper. Never forget—understanding your customer is the key to understanding what you have to do to complete a successful transaction. The next section offers some tips on how to do that.

Key Concepts

I don't know about you, but when I think about situations like this (which are all too real), I find it hard not to laugh. I mean, really, I don't think most people act that way. But occasionally, folks just like to act a bit differently than the norm. And, at the end of the day, it takes a lot of different types of people to make the world work. Let's take a look and see if we can figure out the tactics for dealing with someone like this.

Do the Talking for Them

When someone won't talk, do it for them! Talk about the product, talk about the store, talk about anything professional or promotional about your company. The more you say, the more likely that the person will acknowledge what you say or feel compelled to comment, whether that be through verbal or physical language.

In this case, you could say something along the lines of, "Oh, so you're interested in applying our sales toward this particular stick of memory. Is that correct?"

Feel Free to Suggest

Most people who don't talk a lot have a lot to say; they just don't choose or know how to voice it. Instead, you can let people know exactly what you think they are trying to indicate.

- "Are you interested in this promotion?"
- "Are you looking for a replacement DIMM?"
- "Is this what you're looking for?

This sort of forceful, yet respectful communication engenders trust in people and helps them understand that you're not a stranger; you're someone who is there to help them. People tend to be a lot more communicative with helpers than they are with strangers.

Resolution

OK, now for the good part. How to fix it! The best thing about this type of person is that it's not all that hard to fix. You just have to be a little creative, and a little excited about doing it. Let's go into a little bit more detail on how to do that.

Be Excited!

Don't ever feel afraid to be energetic about your job and your company. When someone seems quiet, docile, or uninterested in your company, it's not going to hurt to be excited about what you do. People *like* enthusiasm. It doesn't matter if it's enthusiasm that is in their field or not; they just like it. But you should always remember that you're a professional, not a cheerleader. Getting a reputation as someone more excited about their company than Steve Ballmer may not be a good idea. Just remember to be open and encouraging, and be the one who takes the first step.

Be Creative

Another thing you shouldn't be afraid to be when dealing with quiet people is creative. While someone quiet may not like to be outspoken or unusual themselves, that doesn't mean they're not going to respond well to someone whom they view as insightful. Keep a good attitude, don't be embarrassed to embrace new ideas, and always be the first one to provide a suggestion.

Skills for the A+ Exam

Here's an example of the type of questions you will see about quiet customers on the A+ exam:

6. What is the *best* solution for dealing with a customer who is not very communicative about her problem?

   A. Repeat your questions, ensuring she understands.

   B. Repeatedly ask for clarification of her issues.

   C. Speak very softly, concentrating on her issue.

   D. Speak very passionately, concentrating on what you need to understand about her problem.

Answer A: Incorrect. Chances are that she already understands your question; she is just having difficulty getting you to understand her response.

Answer B: Incorrect. It's not a good idea to continuously repeat information until you hear an answer that you either like or understand. You're likely to upset your customer.

Answer C: Incorrect. You should only speak softly in an office environment if someone appears adverse to your loud tone.

Answer D: Correct. Speaking passionately and concentrating on what you need to understand about her problem is a surefire way to get someone to open up.

Easing Tension

You wouldn't believe how stressful computers and technology can be to some people. When you tell them that they have to own, operate, and even maintain a computer, you might as well be telling them that they are going to have to spend their day filing tax returns that are inevitably going to be audited. They're tired, frightened, and more than a little nervous about the machine they're going to get or the problem that they've come across.

Scenario

Halfway through your day, you take the time to assist a customer who has been staring at your new computer systems for over an hour. You introduce yourself, tell him your position, and ask if there is any way that you can help him. After a little visible reticence, the customer informs you that he's looking for a computer that ensures that "No one can spy on him or give viruses."

After explaining to the customer that viruses and spyware are more of a software issue than a hardware one, he tells you that he thinks it just doesn't make sense that there isn't a single computer on the market that can be completely resistant to malware. He then asks you to get your manager or someone who knows more about the subject so that he can consult them.

Background

If you work in any sort of customer service, which, as you can certainly tell by now, we do, you're going to hear the words "I'd like to speak to your manager" a lot. Be prepared for this. It's not anything to be ashamed of. Sometimes people will ask to speak to your manager for the oddest reasons. They may have a complaint. They may think that your service has been so admirable that they'd like to ask if there's a way you could receive a bonus for it. Or they could just be curious about a factor that's totally unrelated to you.

This is worth mentioning because hearing that someone wants to speak to your manager can make you nervous. It immediately brings to mind questions like "Am I in trouble?" or "Did I do something wrong?" But what you should keep in mind is that you shouldn't be afraid. Even if it is the worst possible case, the situation won't be that bad. Chances are that, even if you get a bad review, your company is not going to fire you or get you in a lot of trouble over a single incident. At the end of the day, things will be what they will be. Now, let's move on to how to deal with easing the obvious tension in this situation.

Overview

What lets us know that there's a problem with this customer's state of mind and situation is that the customer is asking a specific question about security. In general, whenever this topic comes up, it's a good idea to put yourself in the mind-set that you're going to have to ease someone's worry. In fact, there are a lot more dead giveaway subjects that let you know you're going to have to do this. For instance, there are subjects such as:

- Broken hardware
- Malfunctioning software
- Quality problems
- End-user difficulties
- Customer service issues

While there are a lot more than these few subjects, these first concepts give you a good idea of just how many problems there are that have to be handled with care. In fact, it's a good idea when you're dealing with a customer to automatically put yourself in the mind-set that you are going to have to ease some tension. People are nervous about a lot of things, and your confident words can go a long way to making them feel better. Be sure to layer your words with kindness and don't spare the simple explanations; they can go a long way. Beyond that, let's take a look at the next section for more questions to ask about a customer's condition.

Key Concepts

The first thing you can tell with someone who behaves in this manner is that something has happened. Regardless of how, when, or why, the person has been led to believe something by someone else. There are a lot of rumors in the IT industry, and there's a lot of confusion. Close to 99 percent of all problems involving anxiety, tension, or fear in the IT industry originate from one thing: ignorance. As IT professionals, we have to discover the source of this ignorance and see what we can do to remedy it.

Why Does the Customer Feel So Nervous/Have This Problem?

People can be told some pretty incredible things. One technique that can help you get to the bottom of whatever it is that they have learned is by simply inquiring about what the customer knows. Has he or she been told something that is complete nonsense? Are they confusing technologies? Is there a way that they may just have been given some inappropriate advice? By asking a simple question, you can understand a lot about the person you're dealing with and what you're going to need to do to help them.

What Is the Customer's Goal?

There has to be some reason the person is anxious enough about whatever their situation is that they've felt motivated to do something about it. Once you understand what that is, you'll be better suited to help him or her out of the bad situation.

Resolution

Once you've clearly defined the the customer's situation, understood their goal, and realized what has caused them so much tension, you're in a good spot. Chances are that once you understand their mind-set you'll be able to help them out. However, there are two tactics that you can put into play: are being confident and being informative.

Be Confident

A good friend of mine once told me that 99 percent of the things that we worry about the most never happen. Some people just need to be told that in a bit more detail. Remember that when you're dealing with someone who is ignorant of a field it's important to be logical and reasonable, as well as to appear to be an authority on the subject. Nothing cures concern quite as much as confidence.

Be Informative

Nothing tops off the concept of being confident like the idea of being confident *and* being informative. If you're just purely confident and don't know what you're talking about, you're going to make someone more nervous. However, if you are confident and you're informed, you're going to be a valuable resource to the person with the problem. Stay calm, keep yourself in the know, and always remember—chances are that you know a lot more about the subject than the person you're dealing with.

Skills for the A+ Exam

Here's an example of the type of questions you will see about stressed-out customers on the A+ exam:

7. What is the best way to calm an apprehensive customer?

    A. Be as technical as possible.

    B. Ask for clarification of their issues.

    C. Speak very slowly, calming them to the best of your ability.

    D. Speak in a calm tone of voice, appearing concerned about their issue.

    Answer A: Incorrect. This is probably just going to make them more nervous. It's best to err on the side of plain speech.

    Answer B: Incorrect. If you choose this method, chances are that the customer is going to get frustrated on top of being nervous—not exactly a good combination.

Answer C: Incorrect. If there's one surefire way to make someone even *more* nervous, it's to speak to them like they're a child. In addition to making them feel awkward about an issue, you'll make them feel insulted.

Answer D: Correct. Speaking in a calm tone of voice always goes a long way in communication. However, the key is to appear extremely concerned about their issue. An understanding person is a good person in the eyes of the customer.

Summary

One of the greatest, if not the greatest, concepts in modern economics is the idea of supply and demand. If something is in great supply and low demand, it will economically fail. And vice versa if something is in great demand and low supply, it will succeed. The key is that creating demand in any given market is necessary in order to have a viable business. Part of the process of creating that demand is ensuring that you not only have great products but also excellent service.

Every moment that you neglect a customer, fail to utilize skills that you've been taught, or don't capitalize on the fact that you could enhance the mood and experience of a consumer is a moment that will cost either you or your industry vast amounts of time, money, and effort. Because of this, we as professionals in the IT support industry have to be aware that we must take into account the effect everything we say and do will have on the image of the company we represent. If you're ever having trouble along the way, keep a copy of this book nearby and review some of the encounters we've gone over. If you're still lost, take comfort in the fact that if your mind is in the right place, you're most likely going to succeed. But if you fail, there will always be ways to recover in the eyes of the customer.

Chapter 2

Working with Professionals

As an A+ Certified help desk technician, you're going to be entering a world you've probably never encountered before—the world of business. And, as I'm sure you already know, the world of business can be a difficult place in which to function because there are so many different types of people with whom you interact. For almost every type of person you have to communicate in a different way. Some people will like things spelled out explicitly; others will just want a rough overview. Some workers will prefer to never be spoken to, and some will simply never be quiet.

Given that, there are several ways you can adapt to the professional environment and succeed in your new career. You can start by being aware of some of the most common personality types you will deal with in your workplace activities. This chapter will go into the personalities in detail and explain how you can interact with a variety of individuals.

- Scenario 1: The Inquisitive Coworker
- Scenario 2: Dealing with Sexual Harassment
- Scenario 3: The Lazy Worker
- Scenario 4: An Issue of Trust
- Scenario 5: Working with Your Manager
- Scenario 6: The Technical Professional
- Scenario 7: The Business Professional

The Inquisitive Coworker

Some people are just curious. More often than not, you'll run into someone who will ask you about your day, your family, your activities, or a variety of other aspects of your day-to-day life. Most of the time, their interest is purely innocent. People have a generally curious nature and normally believe that any inquiries they make into your personal business are just indications that they have a certain amount of concern for you and your well-being. There are occasions, however, when someone appears to be innocently curious but, in fact, is being exceptionally deceptive.

Scenario

You've been working on a project for your boss for the past several weeks. The project involves cleaning out your company's inventory warehouse and reorganizing it from a system that relies on ID tags into an alphabetical system. Halfway through the project, you realize that you have made a mistake in the "B" section and that you have placed them in reverse order.

As you begin to rearrange things, a coworker approaches you from behind and asks, "Hey, what are you doing?"

Stopping your work for the moment, you take the time to turn around and explain the situation to your coworker and then continue to arrange the inventory appropriately. The next day, you receive a notice from your supervisor that he would like to have a meeting about the organization of the inventory room.

At this meeting, he specifically mentions that he noticed an error yesterday in the "B" section of the boxes you've been organizing, and asks if this duty is something you don't feel comfortable with. It is extremely unlikely that your superior could have noticed this on his own and you suspect that he was informed about it by your coworker.

Background

It's time for another hard-and-fast truth: people can be sneaky in the workplace. It sounds very harsh, but I don't think I can write this book without telling you that you should be careful of whom you trust in an office or retail environment. This isn't to say that there aren't good bosses, good coworkers, and good customers, but there are so many bad ones that it's difficult to tell the good from the bad.

The second part of this hard-and-fast truth is that people are normally out for themselves. It's unfortunate that all too many people believe that by making another person look bad they can make themselves look better. Again, this isn't always the case, but nine times out of ten, it is. You simply have to be careful and be wary of anyone who wants to know something out of the ordinary.

Overview

Something else I should make clear about this situation is that what your coworker did in this situation (or at least we presume he did) is something that you should never do. You may remember your parents telling you this when you were growing up: nobody likes a rat, and this includes managers. The reason that you should never do this is because it shows little loyalty to the people you are associated and working with. If you're willing to expose someone's mistakes for your own personal gain, you're probably not someone who is worth being trusted.

However, as you saw earlier, rats do exist and they seem to pop their heads up in business environments very frequently. If you're in a situation where you're dealing with someone who shows that they are obviously untrustworthy after one or two circumstances, it's best to adjust your interactions with that person to protect yourself. Don't associate with someone whom you know has acted against you in the past; it's just not a good idea.

Now, we aren't always granted this luxury. There's a time period before you really get to know someone in the office when you're not sure what their beliefs are. Therefore, it's a good idea to have a strategy for how to deal with someone who is overly inquisitive or just generally involved in business you don't want them to know about. In the following section, I've outlined some of my best suggestions of how to implement these protections. Take a look and see if they might work for you. They might very well save you a possible loss in reputation, just as in the current scenario.

Key Concepts

There are several tactics for avoiding someone who is overly inquisitive. They are (in no particular order):

- Avoidance
- Answering by omission
- Playing dumb

Tactic 1: Avoidance

The best way to deal with a problem is to avoid it in the first place. When someone you know to be inquisitive approaches you with what you believe to be a detrimental question, avoid it. Say that you have somewhere to be or that you don't think that now is the appropriate time to deal with that. You can also simply say that you're very busy and can deal with them later.

Most inquisitive people won't have the nerve to continue their line of questioning if you try to dodge it in the first place. However, you will occasionally see a random person who simply refuses to go away until their question is answered. In this case, you can simply say something noncommittal but informative—in this case, "I'm fixing a problem with these boxes." By doing this, you're giving an answer and at the same time forcing that person to dig even further for a simple truth. Chances are it simply won't happen. And, if it does, just do it again.

Tactic 2: Answering by Omission

This tactic is what is colloquially known as "a car salesman's best friend." Answering by omission is a trick that works well against people who are inquisitive and rarely requires any work by you. The method is simple. You answer the question, but you leave detailed portions of it out. In this case, consider a full answer:

Full Answer: "I am rearranging these boxes because I accidentally placed them in reverse order."

An alternative to this answer would be:

Omission: "I am rearranging these boxes for <your boss>."

Do you see the beauty of this? It's very subtle. If the employee asks you why you are rearranging the boxes, not only will they be challenging the authority of your boss, but they will also be forcing you to give the inevitable answer. What's that answer? The truth: "I'm not sure why he wants the inventory in alphabetical order, perhaps you could ask him."

With this scenario, you have diffused the situation by taking out the most damaging element—the fact that you made a mistake. The truth is that mistakes happen; you just don't have to let everyone know about it.

Tactic 3: Playing Dumb

Playing dumb involves not owning up to what the problem is. It's not necessarily lying, but it's a bit of an ethical fine line. A dumb answer to your inquisitive worker's question would be something along the lines of "Well, I gotta move these boxes."

It not only sounds ignorant but it also discourages further inquiry. Normally, people don't want to pick the brain of someone who either doesn't know a lot about a subject or is just too uncaring to know the difference. Be cautious with this one, however. If you're not careful, it can get you in a little trouble. Consider what would happen if you played dumb in front of a superior. That could result in your losing face, and that's never a good thing.

Resolution

The best solution to dealing with a person like this is to not use just one of the resolution tactics I just listed , but to combine all of them into a series of diverted questions, omitted answers, and lack of information. There are a lot of ways to deal with this situation, but I'd like to repeat my bottom-line advice once again: be cautious when dealing with people who are too curious. They're usually not in it for your benefit.

Skills for the A+ Exam

Here is an example of a question involving the use of the word manipulation that you might see on the A+ exam:

1. A coworker asks you how it is that you manage to stay so unoccupied most of the time. What should your response be?

    A. Sometimes I just take an occasional break.

    B. I like to make use of time management; would you like some tips?

    C. There's a pretty simple way to look busy; let me show you.

    D. After you've been here a while you'll get the hang of how to do it, too.

    Answer A: Incorrect. This is something that can be used against you, and it's never a good idea to reveal that sort of information in an office or retail environment.

    Answer B: Correct. This answer makes you seem informed and willing to help.

    Answer C: Incorrect. Confirming that you are indeed trying to "look busy" most of the time is ammo that another employee can use against you.

    Answer D: Incorrect. Although this does divert attention from you, it also confirms to the coworker that you know how to stay unoccupied most of the time; this is not a good impression to make on someone who is overly curious.

Dealing with Sexual Harassment

It's hard to handle harassment when it happens. What makes it even harder is that it takes so many forms. Harassment can be physical, verbal, sexual, racial, or even religious. When you combine this with the fact that an all-too-alarming number of people view even the grossest aspects of harassment as mundane and insignificant forms of human behavior and communication, you can see how it can quickly become a large problem.

In this scenario, I'm going to concentrate on a particularly uncomfortable form of harassment: sexual harassment. The reason I'm going to focus on this as opposed to any other form of harassment is twofold. First, it is the most prevalent form of harassment in the workplace, and second, it is one of the most difficult to deal with. Most importantly (and surprisingly to some people), sexual harassment can occur to both men and women.

Scenario

You've been working in your new office for several days and you feel as if you're starting to fit in well. You know your job duties, the technical level you are expected to adhere to is within your capabilities, and you believe there is a lot of opportunity for advancement within the organization. Furthermore, you've been able to make a lot of new friends through the company's matriculation program and it looks like you're set for a long-term career.

However, there is something that isn't to your liking. In the cubicle across from you, your two coworkers, Sarah and Dan, talk almost all day long about material that isn't related to work. They discuss the weather, politics, or anything that suits them at the moment. Furthermore, they have a terrible habit of telling extremely inappropriate jokes that you find very offensive.

Today, Sarah and Dan have been up to their usual shenanigans and have begun to speak inappropriately once again. However, today they've decided to involve you in their discussions. In a joking manner, Sarah turns from her conversation and says to you, "So what about you, newbie? When's the last time you got laid?"

Background

Sexual harassment has existed for centuries. Unfortunately, it hasn't been much of an issue until recently. This is mostly because people's feelings about the subject haven't been very understanding until the development of several lawsuits involving hostile work environments and harassing behavior.

The term sexual harassment wasn't coined until 1974, when it was created at Cornell University. It became truly famous when Anita Hill, a former associate of Supreme Court Justice Clarence Thomas, accused him of sexual harassment and brought the issue to the world's attention.

Since then, many other cases of sexual harassment have been brought to the attention of the world. Most recently, a previously unknown subject called "hostile work environments" was brought into daylight in the movie North Country, which depicted a dramatic interpretation of the events in the legal case Jenson v. Eveleth Taconite Co. that involved pranks, inappropriate remarks, and physical abuse.

Almost every day, more is being learned about sexual harassment. There are more situations, circumstances, and unusual scenarios that need to be brought to the world's attention. Thankfully, the world is certainly now listening.

In your workplace, you need to be aware of the consequences of sexual harassment and actions you should take to avoid being part of it. It should be clear that this book in no way provides sexual harassment legal advice, and you are strongly encouraged (if you feel harassed) to bring it to the attention of your superior. Otherwise, you may hinder the legal process. Instead, the purpose of this section is to guide you to a calm and rational approach to the situation, making you aware that consequences exist for both those who sexually harass and, unfortunately, those who report the sexual harassment.

Overview

A couple things to remember when dealing with harassment:

- Intent does not matter.
- Specific words do not matter, but interpretations do. If a comment is made that is not technically offensive, human resources personnel can still claim that it was an offensive topic because it was viewed as offensive to that individual.

You have the right to work in a comfortable environment. Just because someone may behave a certain way, it doesn't mean you can't ask them to stop.

Key Concepts

Just as I said in the beginning of this scenario, harassment can take many, many forms. This goes further in that sexual harassment can take many forms of its own. Specifically, sexual harassment is defined by the Equal Employment Opportunity Commission as:

> Unwelcome sexual advances, requests for sexual favors, and other verbal or physical conduct of a sexual nature constitute sexual harassment when:
>
> 1. submission to such conduct is made either explicitly or implicitly a term or condition of an individual's employment,
>
> 2. submission to or rejection of such conduct by an individual is used as the basis for employment decisions affecting such individual, or
>
> 3. such conduct has the purpose or effect of unreasonably interfering with an individual's work performance or creating an intimidating, hostile or offensive working environment. Title VII. The EEOC Guidelines, 29 C.F.R. Section 1604.11

This basically means that sexual harassment can be interpreted as almost any sexual action that is done to curry favor, make employment decisions, or create a hostile work environment. Essentially, sexual harassment can be broken down into almost any action that is sexual in nature. This is why almost every single sexual harassment coach who's worth a darn will tell you that sex is not a subject you discuss, think about, or even bring up at all in the office environment! It's not going to be good for your career or anyone else's. With that said, let's now take a look at some of the specifics in this scenario.

Hostile Environment and Actions

A hostile work environment, as far as sexual harassment is concerned, is an environment where actions or comments are egregious and frequent. While there are no generalities where the law or harassment are concerned, it's safe to say that a work environment will not be defined as a legally hostile work area by a single action, unless it is particularly offensive.

In this case, you could make a fairly clear argument that this environment is hostile, because of the comments that are being made repeatedly. However, in any event, they are certainly considered hostile actions in and of themselves because they provide an uncomfortable workplace. This alone would give you grounds to inform your supervisor if you felt the need. However, the comment regarding "getting laid" is a clear case of a comment that is sexual in nature and violates your rights to work in a harassment-free workplace.

Resolution

Step 1: Weigh Whether or Not It's Worth It

Try to forgive and forget. This is almost always the best solution to dealing with any form of harassment. Try not to disagree, respond, or get in an argument. In fact, if you find yourself able, don't even report it.

The reason behind this is that reporting it can sometimes hurt you in the long run. Consider that whenever you report something to human resources or a superior, they're going to remember it. Human resources writes everything down and will mention this fact to whomever they are speaking with every single time that there is an evaluation of your performance. If it comes out that you seem to be someone who is a tattletale, or just someone who is picked on a lot, people are not going to believe that you are the best person for the job.

Now, I should point out that this sort of action by your superiors, colleagues, or human resources department is called "retaliation" and it is very illegal. However, it's very difficult to prove. And the fact is that people will tend to behave the way they want to behave, whether or not it is the right thing to do.

Once you've weighed whether reporting the issue is worth it in the long run, you can finally move to step 2.

Step 2: Obey the Chain of Command

Obeying the chain of command is a phrase they like to use in the military. It basically means that you shouldn't connect directly to someone who can make the most broad and aggressive action without first explaining the situation to your direct superiors. For IT personnel, this means that before you report anything to human resources, you should first speak to your supervisor about the problem.

 Notice that your first step is to speak to your supervisor, not the individual you have the disagreement with. You should never, under any circumstances, confront someone directly with a problem in a large-scale business environment. Instead, you should rely on the skill and discretion of your superiors.

Once you have brought the problem before your supervisor, they should handle the problem according to your company's guidelines. The process may end at this step and not go any further. Even though you may not see anything happening, chances are that the offending person has been properly informed of your displeasure.

Step 3: Elevate the Severity

If your supervisor decides that they cannot handle the problem alone, they will involve either their superior or the human resources department. At this stage, your direct involvement will probably end. The key thing to remember is that you have to have faith in your coworkers and superiors. If they need to speak to you about a subject, they will bring it to your attention. They might interview you about the situation or ask for further explanation at some point during the process. However, at this point, the problem has been handled and the higher levels of authority will dispense what judgment they view as appropriate.

If your harassment case has reached this level, it may be advisable to consult an attorney. Only a licensed practitioner of law can give you the specific details regarding legal advice, your situation, and proper procedures you should follow.

Skills for the A+ Exam

Here is an example of a typical question you might see on the A+ exam involving how to deal with harassment in the workplace:

2. You have been working at a company for four months when a coworker says something very insulting to you. What should you do?

A. Report the situation to the human resources department.

B. Calmly tell your supervisor.

C. Inform a coworker, so they can know to watch out for the person.

D. Confront the individual.

Answer A: Incorrect. This step comes after you have reported the situation to your supervisor.

Answer B: Correct. A supervisor is the best person to handle this situation. They will understand the complaint, decide the best way to handle it, and consider your words when they evaluate their next opinion of this person and any further incidents.

Answer C: Incorrect. Under no circumstances should you do this. Informing a coworker of a problem creates unnecessary dissension in the workplace and can cause people's opinions to shift wildly in a short amount of time.

Answer D: Incorrect. Of all the choices listed here, this is the one that you must understand is unacceptable. Confronting an individual can result in scenes of emotion, violence, and further incidents that will need to be properly tossed up the chain of command.

The Lazy Worker

There has been at least one point in everyone's life when they were too tired, busy, uninterested, or simply unwilling to do a task that they have agreed to do in the first place. The strange thing is that even though this is by far the most common negative character trait in the office, it s also perhaps the single most loathed. There are lots of reasons for this, but the most glaring is that laziness in the office keeps work from getting done and hinders production, thereby hindering a company. Therefore, it is vital that we as IT professionals know how to combat laziness in all its forms and understand what it takes to create action out of inaction.

Scenario

Early this morning, a small business owner with two broken computers came into your store and asked that they be taken care of immediately. The computers contain vital information, such as the company's payroll, inventory, and sales numbers for the current fiscal year. In order to operate, the business owner needs the machines to be able to keep things running.

Understanding that this task was extremely important and needed priority attention, you suggested that you should handle one of the desktop computers while your coworker, Jason, would handle the other.

Three hours later, you have fixed the problem with the first computer by replacing the Windows mandatory boot files and cleaning the computer of a malicious virus that was designed to keep the computer from doing any of its dedicated tasks. On the other hand, your coworker, Jason, still has not begun working on the project. Instead, Jason claims that he needed to assist with another customer's issue. However, the issue was an extremely low-priority consultation on picking the correct form of backup media for a new computer. Knowing this, what is the best way to handle the situation with your coworker?

Background

Before you can begin to think about how to deal with laziness, you have to understand where laziness actually comes from. Surprisingly, most of the time laziness in the workplace does not occur because someone is inherently lazy or averse to work. The two primary causes of laziness are actually apathy and frustration. Unfortunately, both of these feelings are easy to come by in an office environment. Accordingly, it's a good idea to understand how your coworkers can become apathetic and frustrated. This way, you can get a better idea of what might help motivate them out of their situation.

Overview

When you look at this scenario, it's easy to immediately assume that your coworker simply didn't want to deal with the difficult task of addressing the issues with the computers and instead chose to be lazy and prioritized another project. However, you have to take into account one important thing: you were not present for the entirety of his workday.

As you attain more experience, you'll find that it's tempting to judge people for their actions. If Jimmy or Suzie didn't complete their project on time, it isn't because another higher-priority item came up; it's just because they're lazy. The boss isn't going out to a meeting; he's going golfing. As someone who's been there, I know the feeling. Seeing tasks not get done can really grate on your nerves and it's easy to fall into this trap. This is why it's important to define exactly what a lazy worker is. Consider the section that follows, where you'll find a detailed description of some of the more common "lazy" traits a person can have.

Key Concepts

The leading causes of apathy and frustration are feeling unimportant, disrespecting management, and feeling underpaid.

Feelings of Unimportance

The worst feeling in the world is to feel unappreciated. Chances are, you've probably experienced this at least one time in your life. In fact, you might even be experiencing it now in your present work situation. It's easy to fall into a pattern of feeling unimportant.

While this pattern is fairly difficult to break out of and generally requires psychological counseling, it can help you a great deal to understand why someone may be feeling negatively. Furthermore, it helps you think of some things you could say that would motivate someone out of feeling unimportant.

Disrespect for Management

Have you ever really not liked a boss? I have. It's not a fun situation to be in. When you dislike someone a lot, it can really ruin your working environment and cause you to want to strike back at that person somehow. Because of this, it's a good idea to remember that although people may be appearing apathetic to a situation, they might be feeling much the opposite of that emotion. They could care so much that they're striking out. This again gives you a lot of metaphorical ammunition with which to motivate someone.

Lack of Monetary Compensation

Money talks. If an employee is underpaid, they're generally not going to like working in that environment. No one wants to feel overworked and underpaid. Unfortunately, this is the trickiest of all forms of laziness. You can't really motivate someone who feels underpaid, because feeling underpaid incorporates both feelings of unimportance and a latent disrespect for management. However, there is a technique that you can use, which is described in the section that follows.

Resolution

Motivation

Nothing cures laziness like motivation. If you make someone believe that they can do something, you'd better believe that they're going to do it. It is a difficult technique to master, but motivation can be achieved in several ways, such as through encouragement. In this situation, you could tell your coworker how much you value their input and would appreciate their assistance. You could also tell them how good you think their work is when it is done. Or, on the other hand, you could talk about how good it is going to feel when the task at hand is complete. There are many things you could say, but the key is to be positive and motivational, not negative. It's a bit of a cheesy expression, but negativity only begets negativity.

Explanation

Have you ever heard the expression "only doing the bare minimum"? That expression very much applies to lazy people. It's difficult to work in an office environment with someone who isn't involved with the work they are doing and who doesn't want to do anything more than what is absolutely necessary. However, there is a simple way that you can use this to your advantage. You just have to explain the situation and the accompanying consequences if a task isn't completed.

Now, this by no means indicates that you should threaten a coworker with consequences. However, it does help to subtly say things such as, "You know that <Boss X> has said she wants this done by <Time Y>, right? I think she's going to be mad if we don't finish it." Or you could take a more indirect approach and say something like "Have you finished your portion of the project? I think <Boss X> said she'd like it done by <Time Y>."

Consultation

Leveling with people goes a long way. If you come to someone in confidence and tell them what you think might be a problem and are sincere in your delivery, people will usually respond in a positive manner. In this situation, you could easily approach your coworker and say, "Jason, I really think we should talk. I noticed that you haven't started on this project yet and I know that our boss would really like to have it complete. Is there anything I can do to help you out?"

This not only reminds your coworker that he needs to complete the project, but also indicates that you care and are willing to help. It also has the added benefit of creating a small amount of guilt in the coworker, which might also assist in motivating him into action.

People can be really strange when it comes to their money. If someone believes that they aren't compensated enough for the duties they perform, it's likely that they will react negatively to any sort of motivational technique intended to remedy laziness. In this case, it's a good idea to approach someone using the consultation method.

Skills for the A+ Exam

Here is an example of a question on motivating a coworker that's similar to something you might see on the A+ exam:

3. What should you say to a coworker who is running late on a priority project?

- **A.** Is there a way I can give you a hand? I'd like to help.
- **B.** You do realize that there will be consequences if you don't complete this project?
- **C.** If you don't complete this soon, I'll be forced to complete it myself.
- **D.** Report it directly to your supervisor.

Answer A: Correct. This will most likely motivate the employee into action and possibly result in an early completion date.

Answer B: Incorrect. You should never hand someone veiled threats in the workplace. They will only result in negative attention and resentment.

Answer C: Incorrect. This sort of a comment creates a great deal of tension in a work environment and makes a coworker view you as someone who is set against them.

Answer D: Incorrect. Remember that the first step in any process is never to report it to your supervisor. Instead, you should do your best to resolve it yourself before you involve any authority. It's better to step up than to step out.

An Issue of Trust

Choosing who to trust and who not to trust in an office environment is a difficult decision. With so many people in a standard office, it's hard to tell who is your friend and who, well … isn't. On top of that, one of the most difficult things about human interaction in an office environment is that people who may not necessarily be your friends, or even like you, may be much more trustworthy than people you have known your entire life.

Scenario

Fred is running late for work and it's the second time this month. Recently, Fred's company enacted a policy that penalizes someone a full day's worth of leave if they are late to work by more than five minutes twice in that pay period. Thinking of this, Fred realizes that his boss may not find out about him being late if he takes the time to call a coworker at the help desk and gets them to go ahead and start running his first job ticket as a favor.

Without further thought, Fred calls the help desk and Joann, an associate of his for more than three months, answers the phone. Joann says that she'd be more than willing to help Fred out and starts the ticket for Fred. Later that day, Fred arrives at work and finds a pink slip waiting on his computer, notifying him that he has been penalized a day's leave for his second late arrival this month. Within the note, his boss noted that Joann brought this to his attention.

Background

As you begin your career in the IT workforce, you're going to hear a lot of cliché phrases thrown around. People are going to pitch you expressions like "Think outside the box!" or "Let's get motivated!" daily. I may sound like a bit of a downer when I tell you that you're going to get tired of hearing them pretty darn quickly, but it's the truth. However, it doesn't mean that some of the cliché phrases that you will hear aren't true. There's one I'd like to bring to your attention in this case: "Be a team player."

Being a team player is important in an office, retail, or any business environment. People need to know that they can rely on you and trust you to be a loyal coworker. If you aren't, it can lead to many bad things, such as rivalries, mistrust, and animosity. In fact, this concept is so important that I'm going to bring it up again in Chapter 6, "Leadership." For the moment, what this means to you as an employee is that you should always be honest and up front with the people you work with. Although sometimes people may make hostile actions against you, it doesn't mean you should do the same to them. Remember the Golden Rule: "Do unto others as you would have others do unto you."

Overview

A few things to remember when it comes to choosing who to trust in your work environment:

Choose your friends wisely.   People can often surprise you.

Guard your personal information.   You should only tell people what they need to know.

Trust people slowly.   Always be the first one to welcome and befriend someone, but be one of the last to truly trust them.

Key Concepts

In this case, someone obviously misused your trust. Although Fred's decision to try to cover up his lack of performance may have been unethical, the situation still stands that someone Fred works with took the opportunity to cause him to appear incompetent in front of his superior. The reason behind this incident is that this person was untrustworthy. As an IT professional, you need to be aware of the characteristics of someone who may be untrustworthy or worthy of caution.

Untrustworthy Archetypes

Normally, untrustworthy people fall into one of the following categories. It's important for you to realize what these characteristics are and to avoid the types of people who engage in these activities as much as possible.

Lying   This is the single most common characteristic of an untrustworthy person. Just about anyone who lies, deceives, or makes up half-truths is someone who should never be trusted in an office environment. In fact, it's best to just generally avoid them in the first place.

Undependability   A good way to check as to whether someone is trustworthy is to look at how they conduct themselves at their job. If they commonly do what they say and go above and beyond the necessary requirements, there's a good chance that they're an honest person. However, be cautious. Sometimes the hardest workers are the most eager, and the most eager workers can also be the most vicious. Be careful of anyone who seems just a bit too earnest.

Boasting   In generally, the people who are most full of themselves are the most full of something else entirely. If someone in the office is always talking about how great they are, how much they know, or how much they make in any given day, take a simple step and avoid them. Or, if you hear them boasting, never make a comment. Boastful people will take offense easily to someone who catches their boasting and exposes them.

Excessive Silence   This is a really unnerving characteristic. Usually, quiet people are not bad. In fact, earlier in this book I went so far as to point out that quiet people can be full of good intentions but make few comments. However, you should make certain that you are highly aware of individuals who remain quiet purely so they won't say anything that can be used against them and instead wait for those around them to say something incriminating. Anyone who thinks like that is bound to be up to no good.

Brown-nosing   Of all these characteristics, this is perhaps the worst. A brown-noser is just about the most disliked person in the entire office, except by the people who matter the most— your superiors. A brown-noser is never to be trusted, because someone who is that interested in appealing to the good side of a boss is bound to be willing to do just about anything to make sure their stock remains high in their eyes. If you're a gambler, it's a pretty safe bet to say that Joann was probably a brown-noser.

Resolution

The saying "keep your friends close and your enemies closer" does not apply in an office environment. Instead, you should do your best to associate the most with people of upstanding character and keep a watchful eye on those of whom you are suspicious. You will find that you not only raise your own standing by associating with the good crowd, but you can easily find yourself surrounded by trustworthy people who will inform you of who is not to be trusted.

Skills for the A+ Exam

Here is an example of a question on trust issues involving workplace security that's similar to something you might see on the A+ exam:

4. What should you do if a coworker asks for your password and says he needs it for an action approved by your supervisor?

    A. Ask to receive the request in writing.

    B. Provide the password and make a note of it in your log.

    C. Inform him that this violates policy.

    D. Report it directly to your supervisor.

Answer A: Incorrect. This can not only be forged, but it is unnecessary. And, if it turned out to be an actual request, you very well may upset your superior.

Answer B: Incorrect. You should never hand someone your password for any reason.

Answer C: Correct. Additionally, it might be a good idea to show him where the policy is physically located.

Answer D: Incorrect. Although this may seem like a good choice, it is not. Before you approach a superior about anything, you should try to handle the situation at ground zero. In this case, you should inform him of the policy first.

This question involves a concept known as "social engineering" that will be discussed later in this book (Chapter 4). Although you should be able to answer it from the information supplied, don't be alarmed if you're unfamiliar with the concept; it will be explained in more detail later.

Working with Your Manager

Dealing with management is not always easy. Some people spend their whole life trying to learn to deal with a boss and still never manage to completely understand how to do it. Sometimes you may be working with a superior and believe you totally understand them, only to find out that you haven't been doing things the way they wanted since your first day on the job. In this section, we're going to take a look at some of the best ways to deal with management and examine some best practices for dealing with your superior on a day-to-day basis.

Scenario

After struggling with a project for over six months, you have devised a way to simplify the process in the future and eliminate overhead wasted time by over 150 percent. Excited with your newfound discovery, you quickly write a report for your superior, detailing the intricacies of your ideas and how they could enhance the capability of your entire department. Once you've completed your report, you leave it on her desk and wait for her to review it the next morning.

One week later, your report still has not been read and your boss is continuing to ask you if you have any ideas for efficiency maximization. After repeating to her for the ninth time that you wrote a report on the subject, you walk into your boss's office with her, open the report, and point out to her where in the report the things she has requested are located.

Background

Here are a couple of important points that you should remember when you're dealing with any superior.

They Got There for a Reason

Chances are, the person who is in a leadership position in your organization has a certain skill set, ability, or special talent that places them in their role. Because of this, it's a good practice to show your manager a lot of respect. Not everyone can be a manager, and thus they deserve your admiration. Granted, this doesn't mean you should worship the ground they walk on, but it does mean that you should recognize them as an authority figure.

They Are Experienced in Their Field

Hand in hand with the fact that they've been placed into their position for a reason, your superior is undoubtedly experienced in their field. Coincidentally, they've probably had experience in other fields that either are or aren't related to IT. This means that the person you're dealing with not only has a reason for being there, but also has an officially endorsed record of achievement and, if you think about it, that's a comforting thing to realize when you're dealing with a manager.

Overview

There are two clear issues presented in this scenario that involve communication. First, there is the communication from employee to employer, and second there is the communication from employer to employee. In this case, it appears that both are lacking.

First, while you worked hard on your report, it hasn't been brought directly to the attention of your employer. Second, part of the fault lies with your superior because she didn't take the report seriously. As you'll see in the following section, these sorts of experiences are quite common. Fortunately, they're not that difficult to deal with when they occur.

Key Concepts

Situations like this one happen. Whether we like it or not, sometimes people just don't communicate in the same manner. Thankfully, there are several strategies to ensure someone is receiving the message you are trying to send. However, you need to be aware of the following facts before I can begin to discuss how to put those strategies into practice.

You'll get mad.   Sooner or later, you're going to have a situation where your boss drives you nuts. It's human nature. It's tough to do something that people view as absolutely perfect. Invariably, either you or your boss is going to do something that offends one or the other and causes a rift between the two of you. The trick is to remember that things happen and to treat each day the same—as if the situation never happened in the first place.

You'll be confused.   Delegation is a tricky business. Your boss may want something out of you that she doesn't make clear. The unfortunate part is that it is your responsibility to make sure that you understand what your boss wants, not the other way around. If you do not understand something, you must make it clear in your mind or do your very best to interpret what you think she wants. Don't be afraid to ask questions, but be wary of asking too many.

You'll want to be the boss.   The most unpleasant fact about dealing with a superior is that one day you'll feel as if you should be the superior. Experience shows us our mistakes and inevitably shows us the mistakes of others. This will eventually cause you to think that you should be the one in charge and that your boss doesn't know what she's talking about. The truth is, you may one day be right. Unfortunately, for now you have to learn to deal with it.

Resolution

To succeed in IT, you have to learn how to communicate with management. Let's take a look at some of the best practices that you can put into use in an office environment that will make sure your points are clear, understood, and respected.

Inform in More Than One Way

Rather than just putting something in a report, it's a good idea to always back up a report with another form of communication. Send the report, but also send an e-mail, or accompany that e-mail with a phone call. If you let people know something is coming in more than one way, they're most likely going to pay more attention to it.

Repeat, Repeat, Repeat

If your supervisor hasn't noticed something, you can always repeat it in passing. It's important that you don't go out of your way to remind your manager of something that is of low importance to them, but occasionally mentioning it in team meetings or over the watercooler is a surefire way to bring it to her attention.

Reference

You can create a lot of interest in someone by referencing work that you have done. In this case, you could say, "You'll notice that in my <Report X>, I mention the following." Or you could say, "<Boss X>, what did you think of my idea on <Subject Y>?" Nobody likes to feel uninformed, so chances are she'll do what she can to see what you're talking about.

To understand and deal with your superior, communication is key. You must ensure that the two of you are on the same page and want the same outcome. If you fail to make sure that you are at least close to being on track for every single activity you are working on, you are almost certainly doomed to failure.

Skills for the A+ Exam

Here is an example of a question on dealing with management that's similar to something you might see on the A+ exam:

5. Early in the morning, a manager asks you to set up an Active Directory server on a Windows XP Home system. Being familiar with the platform, you know that this is impossible. How should you inform your supervisor?

A. Ask a coworker to inform her.

B. Schedule a meeting next week.

C. Tell her over several different mediums (phone, e-mail reminders, etc.).

D. Simply send an e-mail to save her time.

Answer A: Incorrect. You should never ask a coworker to inform someone of a duty for which you are responsible.

Answer B: Incorrect. Scheduling a meeting next week would take too long and show that you don't have any priority scheduling capabilities.

Answer C: Correct. Sending her the information over e-mail, by phone, and even in person are excellent suggestions. By sending information in more than one way, you ensure that it has been received.

Answer D: Incorrect. E-mails are often overlooked and should not be utilized as a primary form of communication.

The Technical Professional

One aspect of IT that you need to get used to is that there are going to be a lot of people who know more than you do about your field. Because IT is so broad a field, there are people who dedicate their entire lives to one small aspect of the industry and who specialize in it to a degree that is truly unrivaled. Moreover, people in IT have a tendency to become so detailed in their degree of specialization that they sometimes lose track of other areas of interest, such as social skills. As a professional, you have to learn to deal with this unique aspect of the industry and adapt accordingly.

Scenario

In the early morning, you receive a call at your local store from a person with an unusually gruff voice. After you greet him, the customer tells you that he is sick of a certain brand of CD-R that you keep at your store and that it has a consistent yield of only 94 percent. He then tells you that he has confirmed this yield by producing more than two test runs and allowing for a standard deviation of 2 percent.

Not understanding exactly what the customer wants, you ask him to clarify his request. The customer responds by telling you that he wishes you to fix the yield problem and improve your ordering system. Still not entirely understanding the customer's wishes, you calmly ask him to repeat himself. Instantly, the customer becomes extremely irate and demands to speak with a manager. When you ask if you can be made aware of the problem, the customer responds by saying, "I shouldn't have to tell you that, you idiot! Now go get someone who knows what they are talking about!"

Background

Believe it or not, the days of the "closet '80s geek" are not entirely gone. The truth is—I sort of am one, in a way. Chances are many of you are, too. Most technical professionals have some part of them that wants to descend to that level of über-tech where we have absolutely no contact with anyone whatsoever and are very unusual. Passion can create the desire to work on one thing and one thing only.

Fortunately, if you're reading this book, you're deciding to move beyond that stage (or already are beyond that stage) and are looking to hone your skills in professional communication. But it's important to realize that, while you may have made this decision, a large share of technical people have not. Therefore, you need to understand some of the best strategies to use when you're dealing with technical people.

Overview

Although this issue may seem silly to us, it is for darn sure not silly to the person calling in about it! In fact, this case is about a problem with yields from a CD company. Truth be told, from a business perspective, that really is a huge problem. If you have a loss of over 1 percent yield, someone at the company needs to be made aware of the problem.

We human beings tend to try to ignore minor squeaking wheels. We sometimes just wish that they'd resolve themselves and move along. Unfortunately, they won't. What makes this problem worse is that when we don't understand the mechanics behind the squeaking wheel (in this case, the customer), we tend to ignore it even further. Thinking hurts sometimes. But, at the end of the day, we get paid to think! So, whenever you have a problem like this, keep the concepts that follow in mind.

Key Concepts

A technical customer who calls or walks in with a problem is going to start out in a nasty mood. Chances are that if they're coming to you with the problem, they've been diagnosing and debugging it for quite a long time. Furthermore, it happens to be an extremely important issue to them. Knowing this, you should keep a few simple points in mind:

- Stay calm.
- Be extremely understanding.
- Offer alternatives.

Stay Calm

With a technical customer, almost anything you say that is negative or alarming can set them off. Since they're already frustrated, you have to be especially placid. You can almost appear nonchalant, saying encouraging things like "Oh, OK, I get it" or "Wow, that's pretty intense. Do you think you could explain it to me a bit further? It looks like this is a pretty involved problem." These leading questions, combined with a calm attitude, are a sure start to a successful interaction.

Be Extremely Understanding

You have to realize that whatever this problem is, no matter how minute or unusual, it is extremely important to this person. Some IT people spend their entire lives around a computer, network, or storage array. If there is the smallest thing wrong with it, they will likely report it. Therefore, if you aren't sympathetic to their situation, you will likely frustrate both yourself and them.

Offer Alternatives

Once you have calmed down your customer and you understand their situation, it's usually best to offer alternatives. All too often, a highly technical person has tried many more ideas than you will normally suggest, and it's highly unlikely that you will be able to debug a situation that they have spent so much time on. Remember, your job is only to solve the problem, not solve their entire situation. An alternative can usually work around a problem just as well.

Resolution

The key to success with an IT professional is to essentially be their friend. You have to understand their problem, be empathetic, and calmly help them resolve it. Always remember that when someone is coming to you for help, they are pointing out their own fallibility. They have come to you because they have found something that they cannot figure out how to fix. For highly technical professionals, that's a lot of pride to swallow. Once you understand that, you'll be in the right mind-set to assist this particular type of customer. And even if the situation is so complicated you won't be able to resolve it, you'll be providing excellent customer service.

Skills for the A+ Exam

Here is an example of a question involving the selection of a clear and concise response to a technical individual, which is similar to something you might see on the A+ exam:

6. An engineer has come to your store and asked if you can help her with a piece of software that is causing unusual errors in her system. Using clear, concise, and direct statements, inform her that you will be unable to assist her.

    A. I'm sorry, ma'am. I will not be able to assist you with that. However, you can call another company and they'll be glad to help.

    B. Ma'am, I'm afraid I can't assist with that problem.

    C. You should always try your best to help a customer, regardless of the issue.

    D. I'm sorry, ma'am. I'm afraid I can't help with this particular problem, but I think I might know a way to help with a product we sell.

    Answer A: Incorrect. You should never reference another company in any type of business.

    Answer B: Incorrect. While you did inform the customer that you can't assist with the problem, you failed to provide an alternative with this answer. It is important to help as much as you can.

Answer C: Incorrect. This is true, but you have to inform your customer that you are unable to solve this particular issue without an alternative.

Answer D: Correct. This suggestion not only helps resolve the problem, but also may generate revenue for your company. Alternatives are not necessarily a bad thing.

The Business Professional

People who really like business are truly a breed of their own. They speak, eat, and even breathe business. As an A+ Certified IT professional, you're going to deal with them on a daily basis. The truth is that nobody uses computers quite as much as businesspeople. But they don't use them in the same way as your average home computer user. Businesspeople are far more interested in using machines than in playing with and understanding them. Furthermore, their personalities couldn't be any different than the personality of your average IT junkie.

Scenario

You've been at your job a long time, and you've seen just about every single type of error that there could ever be. When something comes along that someone hasn't seen before, you are the one they call. You've finally managed to become the true IT professional that you've always wanted to become.

One day, an individual in a black suit comes into your retail chain store, speaking on a cell phone. He sets the briefcase on the desk and then immediately tells someone on the phone that "There is no way that I'm going to pay that much." After talking for another 30 seconds, he casually looks at you while still talking on the phone and says, "You can fix this, right?" He then reaches into his pocket, revealing a business card that indicates that this person is the vice president of your entire company.

Thinking it'd be a good idea to open the briefcase, you look inside and there's a laptop sitting there, with a large blinking blue screen. Fortunately, you know what the problem is and the diagnosis isn't good. Last week a malicious virus was sent out across the country and it's been wiping the hard drives and boot loaders of computers everywhere. It's been almost a national phenomenon, and this person has been a victim.

Before you even begin to further diagnose the issue, you realize that it's going to take quite a long time and this person seems to be in a hurry. Sighing slightly to yourself, you close the briefcase and begin to inform the customer of the problems. Surprisingly, before you even get finished, your vice president looks up from your desk and says, "Well, duh, I figured that was the case. I don't really care. I just want you to fix it."

Background

There's a huge amount of separation in the thought processes of the average IT person versus the average executive. Granted, occasionally you'll see a Bill Gates or a Steve Jobs come around, but

Bill and Steve are pretty far from the average tech geek. Normally, the fields don't mix that well. Because of this, it's sometimes hard for us as IT professionals to interact with bigwigs like this and make ourselves understood.

In the real world, you'll come across these sorts of issues a lot as you progress in your career. You'll find that the more experienced you become, the more you'll deal with influential people. It's almost a status symbol in IT—you're only as high up as the people you assist. Granted, that's sort of a callous way to look at things, but it is kind of neat to look toward the future and see who you could hope to be working with. Maybe even Steve Jobs!

Regardless of where you end up, the fact remains that businesspeople can be difficult to interact with. As you'll see in this section, there are a couple of concepts that you'll need to remember regarding them and some good practices you can begin to implement as you see them.

Overview

Sometimes the behavior you see in businesspeople may come off as rude, but it isn't intended that way. Businesspeople are simply extremely busy. In reality, they may be easy to deal with. You simply have to remember that they're educated, occupied, and complicated. When you adopt this attitude, you'll find such people more approachable.

In this situation, our businessman is probably having a pretty rough day. His computer isn't working, he's negotiating a deal on the phone, and he's having to deal with one of his local stores instead of the corporate environment he is most likely used to. Consequently, he has the right to be a bit frustrated and annoyed. Because of this, in addition to the practices I'll describe next, it's a good idea to put into practice some of the customer service skills I've talked about in the previous sections regarding frustration and anger in customers. Remember to be calm and understanding, and then follow the practices in the next section.

Key Concepts

As I said earlier, the most difficult part about dealing with businesspeople is understanding them. It's easy in IT to fall into what's called the "Tech Superiority Syndrome." It basically means that sometimes people think that because you understand technology you suddenly understand everything about the world and the people in it. In case you suffer from that yourself, let me be the first to tell you that people are smarter sometimes than you give them credit for and that no one understands everything. To further emphasize that, in this section let's talk a bit about the background and demeanor of the average businessperson. It may prove enlightening. But, if you're not interested, you can skip to the "Resolution" section for the straight truth on how to deal with them.

Educated

Someone in business is going to be extremely educated. Being successful in business is not easy, and you have to have a well-rounded education. You have to understand finance, the art of management, the balancing of accounts, and a myriad of other concepts. Usually, this means that their technical experience is slightly lacking. So it's important to remember that the person is in no way slow or mentally disabled. They are simply focused on another area.

Occupied

Once you jump into the world of IT business, you'll begin to understand exactly what the word busy means, if you don't already have a fairly strong grasp of it. Businesspeople understand this too, but it exists to an even larger degree. As busy as you may become in the entry levels of IT help desk work, there is a strong possibility that they may be even more overwhelmed than you are. In fact, in our scenario chances are that for every second you are disturbing this businessman with your time, he has five other things that have to be done at that moment. He's going to want his problem solved—and solved fast.

Complicated

Businesspeople work in many different fields, so they are going to display many different forms of communication. You need to understand that they may use:

Physical Signs   These can include gestures, facial expressions, and sign language.

Double Entendres   While they're speaking with you, businesspeople's words may have multiple meanings. It's important to try to understand not only what they're saying, but also what they really mean.

Multifaceted Speech   Businesspeople may be used to dealing with different types of people. They may come at you with one type of communication and then quickly switch to another type if they believe that you may be better suited to it.

Resolution

When dealing with a businessperson, remember that this person is important, hurried, and informed. As an IT professional in the workplace, your entire livelihood is going to depend on making the business people in your office satisfied with your performance. Sometimes it can be a tough skill to master, but some things only come with time and experience. In the meantime, I'd like to point out two guidelines:

Be respectful.   It always pays to be as respectful as possible to higher-ups in a company or executives who deal with your organization. The world is a pretty small place and the more respect you show, the more respect will be shown to you. It's a good practice and it will serve you well.

Be up front.   If you ever hear an average businessperson speak, they don't really dance around the point too much. They're up front, honest, and direct. They also respond well to people who are both polite and direct with them in turn. In this case, a good idea is to just tell your customer (technically, coworker) that you think it will be difficult to solve the problem quickly but that you will do your best and find a way to notify them when it's done. This way, you haven't overpromised but you've certainly overdelivered. That's always the best position to be in.

Skills for the A+ Exam

Here is a question to familiarize yourself with the type of professional-interaction questions you will see on the A+ exam:

7. While at your help desk, you receive a call from the CEO of your company. She claims that she needs you to drop what you're doing immediately and help her. What should you respond with?

   A. Sorry, ma'am, but I am currently full. But I can place you in the work queue.

   B. Yes, ma'am. How can I help you?

   C. Hello, ma'am. I'm currently assisting another customer, but I can transfer you to Sarah, if you like. She is not currently assisting anyone.

   D. Agree to help your CEO and then tell your customer that you are going to need to transfer them to another agent.

Answer A: Incorrect. Placing a CEO in a queue is not a good idea.

Answer B: Incorrect. This is always a good thing to say, but you need to handle your current situation first.

Answer C: Correct. This is by far the best way to handle the situation. It will show your CEO that you care about her problem and are willing to help, but that you won't sacrifice your level of service.

Answer D: Incorrect. You should never let a customer transfer to another agent unless you are unable to help them.

Summary

Although it's true that communication with customers is the way to make and maintain a successful company, the surest way to succeed at a company is to interact in a professional way with your fellow coworkers and business associates. A friend of mine once told me, "People who are well liked don't get fired." And although that's not an absolute truth, it's certainly pretty accurate. The better you can communicate with your coworkers, the better your working environment is going to be.

So when you get into the working world and you find yourself in a difficult situation, try to remember that although every person is a unique individual, people in the business world can usually be classified into groups. After all, it's why we have departments! Whenever you interact with a certain type of person, ask yourself, "What do I think this person is like?" Or, better yet, ask yourself, "What do I think this person would like to hear?" You'll find that your inner voice will usually lead you in the right direction.

Chapter

3

Using Proper Phone Techniques

With the advent of the new four-exam, three-track system for the 2006 CompTIA A+ certification, CompTIA has added an entire path that is specifically dedicated to remotely supporting users. By passing both the A+ 220-601 Essentials Exam and the A+ 220-603 Exam, a technician will be certified as an A+ Remote Support Technician.

This exam track differs greatly from the standard A+ IT Technician path in that the Remote Support Technician path concentrates heavily on both the use of soft skills and the types of situations that technicians will encounter in a remote support environment. In this chapter, I'll introduce several scenarios that will indicate some of the best practices to use when dealing with users through a remote, phone-based support system. Keep in mind as you look through these scenarios that over 20 percent of your exam will be based on communication and professionalism, so it's a good idea to take notes and remember some of the best practices shown here. This chapter is divided into seven different scenarios, which are titled as follows:

- Scenario 1: Focusing Distraction
- Scenario 2: Comforting a Crier
- Scenario 3: Handling Offense
- Scenario 4: Soothing Frustration
- Scenario 5: Creating Satisfaction
- Scenario 6: Callers with Accents
- Scenario 7: Interoffice Phone Conversations

Focusing Distraction

Maintaining a caller's attention is vital in a remote support environment. When most people prioritize their schedules, dealing with a remote technician on a troublesome computer issue does not get factored into the equation, so it's easy to understand that people may feel inclined to work on several other tasks during their computer repair time. As a technician, you need to understand some of the ways that you can maintain a user's attention and convince them to concentrate on the problem at hand. If you don't, the situation is ultimately doomed to failure. People who don't pay attention usually fail to solve the problem.

Scenario

You receive a call from your support center and immediately hear the sounds of heavy machinery being operated in the background. Then, after barking an order near the top of his lungs, a man speaks into the phone and demands, "Yeah, is this support?"

Before you can answer, he turns back to the person he was talking to and screams something about how they're "using the wrong part in that location" and "if you break that, you're going to buy it." Shortly thereafter, the man returns to the phone and says that he has a problem with his computer's screen turning blue and saying something about a physical dump.

You respond courteously by first asking when this problem began to emerge and gathering some background information about the problem. However, as you start to take notes and begin to diagnose the problem, the customer addresses another individual and begins to speak in a completely different tone. With a kind voice, he says, "No, that will be fine. Just make sure that you put it on my desk first thing in the morning and we'll call it even."

He then turns his attention to you. "So what was that? Background? The screen is just blue!"

Background

In case you hadn't noticed, the world is a pretty darn busy place! People use computers for just about every line of business, and so much information is exchanged per day that it absolutely boggles the mind. Billions of e-mails, untold amounts of text messages, and a myriad of phone calls are made every day. Most of them, not surprisingly, are powered by computers. Because of this, it's important to point out that a lot of very busy people simply don't feel they have the time to work on their computers.

People can, and do, call you from the absolutely strangest locations. From the field office to the bathroom, people use whatever time they have available to sort of "squeeze in" computer work. Logically, it behooves you to find a way to turn computer work and repair from a background issue to a primary purpose.

Overview

Before you begin to diagnose this scenario, there are several obvious points that need to be noted:

- The person is an individual with authority.
- It is an extremely busy time at the office.
- You do not have this person's complete attention.
- The problem may be highly complex.

Because of these issues, you're going to need to find a way to remove this person from a mind-set where he's just trying to get something done as quickly as possible to a mind-set where he wants to get something done as well as possible. Next, I'll discuss how to put someone into that frame of mind.

Key Concepts

One point in particular stands out: getting the person's attention. Unfortunately, it's not easy to do. Let's take a look at some of the basics before moving on to the rest of the issue.

Asking

It shouldn't be surprising that the single best way to get someone's attention is to simply ask. Unfortunately, it's difficult to consider doing this because it generally doesn't come naturally to us. Our society is based on a culture that values people's opinions, and interrupting someone for any reason is considered rude. However, certain situations can arise where there is no other option. In this case, you can easily establish your point by asking a positively reinforced request. Let's look at some examples:

"Excuse me, sir. I'd like to help you fix your problem. Can you spare a few moments so I can assist?"

Notice there is no lecture involved here. You are staying positive the entire time and not saying anything that could frustrate him or cause him to be negatively inclined toward you.

"Sir, can you hear me? I hear a lot going on in the background and I'd like to make sure that you can hear me so I can help you with your problem."

This serves as a gentle reminder to the customer that not only are you staying on the phone, but he has to concentrate on you to get his situation resolved. Always remember that you're trying to help, and remind the customer of that in a positive manner.

Selling

The old adage "You can't sell ice to an Eskimo" isn't really true. It just depends on how you spin it. In terms of support, it's not difficult to get someone to be inclined to listen to what you're selling (which is support). After all, it's the only way that they can get what they want—a working machine. Consider the following phrase and the impact it would have on the conversation:

"Sir, could I have your attention for a moment? I think the sooner I understand the problem, the sooner I can have you back in action."

It doesn't sound like a sales statement, but it is. You're using coercion by reminding him that you can help fix his problem. Coercion can go a long way toward getting people to see your point of view.

Lecturing

Note that this portion is for instructional purposes only. For the A+ exam, I *highly* recommend that you stick to the traditional polite customer interaction when answering the questions.

However, in real life, if all else fails and you've been as patient as possible, you can resort to a moderate form of lecture. You should be *very* cautious when you do this. It's normally not going to earn you any friends, but it can sometimes be the only thing that customers will respond to. Here is an example of a moderate lecture:

"Sir, in order to help you with your problem I have to make sure that you are listening to me. Could I please have your attention for a brief moment?"

Resolution

Once you have someone's complete attention, it becomes easy to resolve a problem. By using coercion, positive reinforcement, sales tactics, and polite requests, you can normally get the attention of most of your callers. In the rare case that these techniques don't work, it helps to have a backup plan. You can always ask someone to call back at a time that is more convenient for them, or you could offer to use an alternative form of communication, such as e-mail. But normally, this won't be necessary. They usually just want the problem fixed!

Skills for the A+ Exam

Here is an example of a question you might see on the A+ exam regarding focusing on a user and taking control of a phone call:

1. A customer calls into your center on a Monday morning and is currently speaking to another person at her desk who is not on the phone with you. After two minutes, she still has not addressed you. What action should you take?

    A. Say, "Ma'am, I need to speak with you."

    B. Politely wait until she is done speaking to the other person.

    C. Interrupt her conversation and ask what her problem is.

    D. Introduce yourself again and ask if you can help in any way.

    Answer A: Incorrect. Although this would be convenient, your needs do not come before the customer's. In fact, as a technician you're better off not using the word "need" at all. Normally, there are better words you can use that don't concentrate on you and that use passive voice. (I'll discuss this more in Chapter 5.)

    Answer B: Incorrect. The situation could take all day and you need to resolve the call as soon as possible.

    Answer C: Incorrect. You should never obviously interrupt a customer.

    Answer D: Correct. This is a nice tactic to use with distracted callers. It not only alerts them again of your presence, but also reminds them that they have an issue they need to address.

Comforting a Crier

In any sort of customer service, you deal with a wide range of emotions. From excitement to absolutely fuming rage, people run the gamut in how they deal with their troubles throughout the day. However, in computer support, we seem destined to only deal with the negative aspects of customers' demeanors. Therefore, it becomes necessary to understand how to deal with a customer when they break down emotionally and arrive at a point where you can no longer assist them. In this section, we're going to be analyzing a customer who calls in to a phone center and becomes so upset that it's difficult to deal with them.

Scenario

After coming back from your second afternoon break to the local bakery on the corner of your company's campus, you sit down at your desk expecting to calmly wind down toward the end of the day. As soon as that thought crosses your mind, the phone rings and you pick up to hear the quiet sound of a customer breathing heavily.

You ask, "Excuse me, can I help you?" You then hear silence on the other end of the line.

Remembering your basic customer support training, you patiently wait for 20 to 30 seconds and then ask, "Sir? Ma'am? Is anyone there? I'm unable to hear anything from this end of the line." You again are confronted with static.

Just at the moment you are about to release the call and continue about your day, you hear a sound from the other end of the line as a woman with a strained voice whispers, "Yes … I have a problem."

Cheerfully, you respond with "Of course, ma'am. Could I please have your first and last names so that we can begin to diagnose your problem?"

Instantly, the customer breaks down and begins to sob uncontrollably. In a fit of passionate rage, she starts screaming into the line and telling you that her computer will not work and that she is going to throw it out the window and break the keyboard over the table. Shocked, you remain silent.

Background

Computer problems can be very upsetting. I remember when I first got into computers I had a problem with a video game that drove me into such an emotional stir that I slammed my hands against my desk, called up the support company, and just started screaming. Turns out, it wasn't even their fault. In the old days, you had to deal with something called conventional memory, and I simply didn't have enough free.

Times have changed since then, but issues with computers haven't. You still have problems and they can still be extremely upsetting if you can't figure out how to fix them. This leads back to another one of the old adages of computer support: you're not just fixing a computer problem—you're fixing a person's problem. This means that you should take every problem and every situation seriously. The person isn't just having an issue. They're having an issue so personal or serious to them that they're taking time out of their day to call you about it. Therefore, we as professionals need to have a lot of sympathy or, if not sympathy, a lot of empathy for people in this situation. Furthermore, we need to figure out how to improve their demeanor.

Overview

You immediately know a few things before you begin to diagnose the situation:

- The person is emotional.
- There is a problem that's very important to her.
- This call is going to be time intensive, due to the emotional state of the caller.

The first thing you have to do as a support representative is get the phone call under control by apologizing, using active listening, and asking pertinent questions

Key Concepts

There are a few "standard" ways to bring someone in a bad mood back to a good mood again. In no particular order, they are:

- Apologizing
- Listening actively
- Asking pertinent and caring questions

Let's take a look at each of those in a bit more detail.

Apologizing

If you've heard the phrase "It doesn't matter if you were right or wrong, just apologize," you are going to understand the world of IT communication very well. The first thing you should do in *any* customer service situation that involves a problem is apologize. In particular, you must let people know how sorry you are that they are upset as soon as you detect any sort of discomfort whatsoever.

"I'm so sorry that you are having this trouble. Can I try to help?"

"You sound extremely upset. I really apologize that you've been put through so much with this issue."

What you're doing with this apology is not necessarily admitting to any wrong—you're simply admitting to something right. You don't like the fact that they're so upset. You're sorry that they have to call in to your help center, and you also don't want them to have the trouble again. Simply apologizing can make all of that abundantly clear and get you on the right track to solving their problem.

Actively Listening

The art of actively listening is something that a lot of people try to explain in a complex manner, but it is actually exceedingly simple. Active listening is the act of earnestly and accurately responding to cues that the customer gives you as you progress through an interaction. Some examples of this include verifying information, asking probing questions, and validating statements.

For instance, if someone were actively listening to a person who just told them, "My car broke down," they could respond in several ways to let the person know they were paying attention. They could:

Respond Physically   Show shock by placing a hand in front of their mouth or wringing their hands in alarm.

Respond Empathetically   "No! That's terrible!"

Respond by Asking Questions   "Oh heavens, were you able to fix the situation?"

When you boil it down to a science, active listening is just the process of receiving information and communicating back to a person in a way that shows that you are not only listening, but also hearing everything they say and inquiring further. It shows that you are interested and care about their situation. In this example, you could actively listen to the woman's distress and respond verbally.

"Ma'am, I can tell that you are very upset. Let me see what I can do to fix things and make it better; I'm here to help."

Asking Pertinent Questions

When you are dealing with someone who is upset, it's best to ask questions that are not only on topic but also extremely broad. This way, they'll give you as much information as they have available to them.

"So, it seems like there's a pretty big problem here. Can you give me a little history?"

"Could you start by telling me where this problem began?"

"Now what exactly is the symptom you are seeing constantly repeated?"

Resolution

After you have apologized, listened to their problem actively, and asked the questions you need to ask to help yourself understand the exact problem, you can begin to resolve the person's issue. Once this point has arrived, people will universally be much calmer and willing to begin to actually resolve their problem. You can bet that once you've figured out what the problem is they're not going to be quite as emotional. Remember, your goals (in order) are to:

1. Calm the customer.
2. Improve their mood.
3. Fix their situation.
4. Make them feel better for having called.

Skills for the A+ Exam

Here's an example of the type of question you may see on the A+ exam about emotional customers:

2. As soon as you tell a customer that his computer has a virus, he immediately begins to sob and tell you that it isn't fair, his grandkids' pictures were on that computer. What is the *first* thing you should do?

    A.   Remain silent and let him emotionally vent.

    B.   Ask him if there is a chance the data can be recovered.

    C.   Remind him that the virus may not have infected some of his files.

    D.   Apologize and say that you might be able to help.

    Answer A: Incorrect. If you allow someone to go through the stages of acceptance and then tell him that what you've suggested isn't really the case, he might very well become extremely angry with you for leading him on.

Answer B: Incorrect. The customer probably wouldn't know, and it's not a good idea to ask the customer anything like that at this point.

Answer C: Incorrect. Although you may want to shine a little hope on his situation, it's not the best thing to do at this point. You should remember that he is emotional and wants to be calmed down before anything else.

Answer D: Correct. Before you begin to diagnose any problem, you should apologize. It helps the customer feel cared for and lets him work through the situation more easily.

Handling Offense

When you're working in a call center, keep in mind that people come from all walks of life. More importantly, computer users come from different cultures, ethnic backgrounds, geographic areas, and business environments. It is therefore natural that occasionally a user will say something that will offend you in some way or another. This unfortunate fact of life comes coupled with the fact that there is no one single element to your performance that is more evaluated than your interaction with customers who are either very offensive or very angry. More often than not, promotions are based entirely on this simple fact: if you lose control of the situation, you lose the chance for promotion.

Scenario

A customer has called in with a minor consumer issue and has been extremely offensive throughout the duration of your customer support. Up until recently, the call has been at least tolerable. The person has only casually cursed and has just been slightly grumpy. However, the conversation has begun to take a turn for the worse.

Now, in addition to making the casual remarks, the person has begun to hurl personal insults toward you and is making extremely offensive racial remarks. Furthermore, you can barely get a word in before the person begins to loudly scream into the phone and say that you obviously don't know what you're talking about and that he'd like to speak to a manager immediately.

As it stands right now, the problem is only halfway diagnosed, and it looks like it's going to take at least another hour to fully diagnose the problem and implement a solution. After heaving a sigh, you begin to debate the proper action.

Background

There will be times in your career in support that you think you couldn't possibly meet a ruder person in the world than the one that you're dealing with at that moment … until you meet the next person. Don't let anybody fool you—people can just be *nasty* on the phone. Without having to look at someone, it's easy to yell, scream, get angry, or just channel the emotion that you're feeling at that moment at someone who you can't see at that moment and probably never will see in your life.

For us as support personnel, this means that a large portion of our job is going to be dealing with hostile people. Now, most professionals won't tell you this, but I think I should. If you have a problem dealing with angry or rude people, I have one piece of advice for you: you need to get used to it. Your job in IT is almost entirely centered around this concept and it's something you're not going to be able to escape. However, don't be discouraged. As you'll see next, it's not that bad if you know how to deal with it.

Overview

One important context clue that is given in this scenario is that the person you're speaking with has casually cursed throughout most of the phone call. For some people, this is just a way to communicate. In the real world, people living in certain areas just tend to swear a lot more than others. If you were to listen to stereotypes, most people will tell you that New Yorkers will swear more than Georgians but not as much as Texans. While this is in no way actually *true*, it does point out that "bad words" are entirely cultural in nature. Some people just don't view bad words as bad words. They could simply just be words to them.

However, this doesn't mean that you have to tolerate words or statements that you find to be offensive. There is a definite point at which you can transition from toleration to intolerance, but it takes a little bit of getting used to. In the section that follows, I'll begin to explore that.

Key Concepts

Just like in the background section, the first thing to remember is that as a professional, you're going to have to learn to deal with being offended on a daily basis. People in business can have a nasty habit of causing grief and agony over the slightest things, and it can pile up over time. Before I begin to diagnose ways to combat it, you just have to accept that this will be difficult at first.

Develop Thick Skin

IT is hard, and people can be very hurtful. Before you get into the industry, you need to stiffen your backbone and thicken your skin, because if you don't, things are going to be extremely difficult for you. The old saying, "Sticks and stones may break my bones, but words can never hurt me" isn't really true. Words can hurt. But we can always take comfort that there is at least one old saying that's true: "What doesn't kill you only makes you stronger."

Learn to Hear Meaning, Not Words

Words are a really funny thing. It's amazing how much impact we place on them. Whether someone says hello, thank you, or goodbye, or pays a compliment to a particular aspect of your life, it can completely change a friend into an enemy, a business associate into a competitor, or a content

IT worker into a raging behemoth. Of course, the last of these is just a joke (I can only hope), but there is a lot of truth to the fact that people place an extreme amount of value on a person's words.

As a businessperson, it's important to understand that in a remote environment, words are nowhere near as important as *intent* and *meaning*. Although someone may say something that is incredibly offensive, rude, or just not well received by you, it may be the normal method of communication in their area. Someone may *say* something laced with curse words, offensive terms, and demeaning language, but their intent may be purely innocent.

> It's important to remember that intent is a luxury that *customers* have, but it is not something that businesspeople can afford to rely on. Choose your words in an office environment extremely carefully.

The best way to break down intent in a conversation is to ask yourself what the person *really* wants. It's normally not too difficult to do if you allow yourself to remove the items you find offensive from a request or statement. As an example, let's take a look at a very offensive statement:

"You don't know what you're talking about. Fix the damn computer free of charge, and then apologize for taking up my time."

Step 1: Remove the expletives.   "You don't know what you're talking about. Fix the computer free of charge, and then apologize for taking up my time." Already, the statement is a lot less offensive, but let's take it a step further.

Step 2: Remove the insults.   "Fix the computer free of charge, and then apologize for taking up my time." The statement now comes down to one sentence that has two points. We're getting very close to the true meaning.

Step 3: Pay no attention to unnecessary information.   Since the first thing we do in customer service when there's a problem is apologize, we can remove the second portion of this statement. What's left is a very simple request: "Fix the computer free of charge." The customer doesn't feel as if he should have to pay for the repairs. Although this may or may not be able to be done, you can see how something that was once very offensive is now entirely innocent when viewed from the correct perspective. You'll find that in IT this is almost always the case.

Resolution

The proper way of dealing with an angry customer breaks down into three traditional methods that should be followed in order:

- Ignoring
- Requesting
- Demanding

Ignoring

This should always be your first reaction. If something offends you, try to ignore it. Count to 10. Remember a funny joke you heard on the radio and keep it to yourself. Do your absolute best to ensure that the user can feel as if they can speak in an environment that is best suited to them. If you can facilitate that need by staying silent, you should do so. Otherwise, you can proceed to the next step: requesting.

Requesting

Requesting that a customer change their behavior is a difficult process, but one that is attainable by using *indirect language*. Observe the effect *direct language* would have on a user:

Direct
Professional: "Could you please stop saying that word?"
User: "I can say anything I want!"

Indirect
Professional: "Do you think there is a way we could call that term *<x>* instead?"
User: "Yeah, I suppose so."

Granted, there will always be the odd person who insists on doing it their way, or worse, makes fun of you for your request. But at this point most people will do what is right in order to save face and make themselves appear more mature.

Demanding

If all else fails, there are ways that you can demand that someone change their behavior. However, it goes without saying that this should be done with caution and *only* if it is considered acceptable policy by your training department. Also, note that this policy may very well be a distracter on the A+ exam, so choose this option with caution.

In the rare case that a customer becomes so offensive that you cannot accomplish your goal of debugging the situation, you should draw attention to the communication *issue*, not the communicator. Here are some examples of ways you can divorce the individual from the issue:

"Sir/Ma'am, I can handle your problem, but I unfortunately can't handle your language. Could you please refrain from using that tone?"

"Sir/Ma'am, I am going to have to ask you to explain the issue to me in a more controlled manner. I am more than willing to help with your situation."

Helping someone once you have diffused a situation is easy. It's the actual diffusing that's the difficult part. By learning to listen to intent more than words, hardening your resolve, and using the three-phased approach of ignoring, requesting, and then demanding, you will go a long way toward conducting a calm and peaceful transaction. Or if not calm and peaceful, it will at least be highly professional, and your company will notice this. The more professionally you can behave in an environment with strict behavioral rules, the more positive attention you will draw from your superiors. It's easy to lose your temper. It's not easy to always be in control of a situation.

Skills for the A+ Exam

Here's an example of the type of question you may be asked on the A+ exam regarding customers who make offensive remarks:

3. What is the *best* way to speak to a customer who is making offensive remarks?

   A. Remind the customer of your company policy to hang up after three remarks.

   B. Inform the customer of the problem after first attempting to ignore it.

   C. Use the same types of terms in exchange, showing familiarity.

   D. Report to your supervisor that you will need assistance immediately.

   Answer A: Incorrect. Threatening a customer is never a good idea, and should be the last option on your list. However, it is a good idea to inform them indirectly that you would like them to adjust their tone.

   Answer B: Correct. After first trying to ignore the problem, you can always inform the customer of your preference and then move on.

   Answer C: Incorrect. You should never lower your professional standards for any reason.

   Answer D: Incorrect. Remember that you should only report to your supervisor as a last resort. You don't want to be viewed as someone who can't be independent.

Soothing Frustration

As you progress further in your technical career, you're going to come across problems that are consistently more complex. The paradox throughout IT is that the more you know, the more difficult your position will ultimately become. What's ironic is that although your situations and positions will grow in complexity, the people you assist will stay relatively the same. Therefore, it's safe to say that as the problems you encounter in IT become increasingly difficult, your users become even more frustrated than they once were. In this section, I'm going to take a look at some ways in which you can deal with a frustrated caller or coworker and some tips for avoiding customer frustration in the first place.

Scenario

After working with a customer over the phone for over two hours on a single issue, you are at your wit's end. Not only is the problem extremely complex, but the user's technical level is extremely low, which is requiring you to explain every single step of the process exhaustively.

To make matters worse, the customer has become extremely irritated at both the situation and you. Although the customer hasn't said anything, you think that he is also embarrassed by the fact that he knows almost nothing about computers and is constantly having to repeat questions about certain procedures for lack of understanding.

Just at the moment you are about to lose your cool and get very frustrated yourself, the customer sighs into the phone and says, "I don't even care anymore. Forget it."

Background

It may sound a bit repetitious at this point, but you have to understand that situations like this happen a lot. When people have technical problems, it doesn't necessarily mean that they are technically knowledgeable. In fact, most people who you will deal with in your office or retail environment are decidedly *not* technical. Because of this, it takes a great deal of patience on your part to be willing to cope with these situations and simply learn not to give up and say, "OK, I give up." But that's simply what's required.

Overview

In this scenario, you can immediately see a few obvious points:

- The customer is new to computers.
- The customer wants the situation to be over.
- The customer is humiliated by the situation.

This is a really terrible spot in which to start off a conversation of any type. However, as you'll see next, there are a couple of tactics that you can use to escape from a rough start like this.

Key Concepts

Whenever a user gets to the point of utter frustration, it's the job of an IT professional to get them out of that mood and help them see the light at the end of the tunnel. From a business perspective, it doesn't really matter how much you are frustrated with the situation or, for that matter, how you feel about it at all. What matters is that the customer's mood needs to be improved. There are several ways to do this, but the most common method by far is positive reinforcement, which consists of the three Ps: promising, praising, and promoting.

The best way to think of positive reinforcement is to remember what it was like to deal with your parents or someone who was a huge inspiration in your life. Whenever you felt challenged, overwhelmed, or just simply confused, they were there. As a positive reinforcer, your job is going to be to create this sort of trust and inspiration among the people you interact with.

Promising

Promising is a concept that many people understand but don't use very heavily. Effectively, promising is the fine art of telling someone that things are going to get better. It's a useful tool in any remote environment and is almost a surefire way to get someone out of a blue funk. Consider the effect of words like these:

"I know this is hard, but we're almost done and then you'll be able to <x>."

"Can you imagine how great it's going to be when we get this fixed?"

"You know, you may not believe this, but the worst is over. I promise you things are going to get easier now."

These types of words not only uplift someone but also inspire hope. Hope is a powerful thing. Taking advantage of it can soothe even the angriest beast.

Praising

Along with promising, praising can go a long way toward rejuvenating someone's attention in a subject. Can you remember that feeling you had when you were in school and the teacher told you that you had made such terrific progress? If you do, you'll remember that it felt really good, and you carried a sense of accomplishment with you for the rest of the day. The same thing applies to customer service in a remote environment. If you tell someone that they have done well, it just makes them feel *good*. Most people don't receive compliments all that often, and if they're stated with genuine intent it doesn't matter what the compliment is about—it's still a compliment.

Promoting

Unlike praising and promising, promoting is a tactic that is fairly difficult to use, and it can't be used separately from the other two. Simply put, promoting is the idea of making someone extremely interested in the subject by listening for oral clues. In this particular case, the person might be extremely interested in a subject that relates in some way to computers or technology. For example, if the customer says he likes football, you could tell him about how his computer can visit *Sports Illustrated*'s website once he gets it working, and how he can learn to play fantasy football with a group of his online friends. Finding a common interest with someone can bolster their morale and help them focus on what you're saying.

Resolution

It's easy to forget how fragile our resolves can become, more so in the field of IT than many others. There's a stiff learning curve, the results of our labor are difficult to understand, and a large part of the time the people who have problems and frustrations become extremely irritated because the issue as a whole is nowhere near important enough in their mind to warrant so much effort. Keeping this in mind, you still have to try to inspire as much as possible. By praising their effort, promising improvement, and promoting the field, you can go a long way toward not only resolving the user's issue but also making them so enthused that they become completely familiar with the subject on their own and feel confident solving problems.

Skills for the A+ Exam

Here's an example of the type of question you may encounter on the A+ exam regarding dealing with extremely frustrated customers:

4. What should you say to a user who has become extremely frustrated at a problem and has requested to give up the issue?

   A. Tell her that if she gives up now then all her work will be for nothing.

   B. Remind the customer that if she understands now, she won't have a problem later.

   C. Explain that you think there may be further problems and that you'll need to help her now for her benefit.

   D. Comfort her by telling her how much she's accomplished so far and indicate that you're getting close to a solution.

   Answer A: Incorrect. You should never guilt someone into doing something for you. It's not very nice and it can upset people.

   Answer B: Incorrect. This isn't necessarily true. She may very well have another problem the next day.

   Answer C: Incorrect. Although this may be true, telling a customer that you think there may be more problems when you still have an immediate issue can create a lot of anxiety.

   Answer D: Correct. Encouragement always goes a long way. When you combine that with a hidden promise of success, it will certainly help get you toward a resolution.

Creating Satisfaction

Ask any successful businessperson what the single greatest factor is in creating and retaining repeat customers and they will answer the same thing every time: customer satisfaction. At the end of the day, it is what makes or breaks business. You can have the most solid products, provide the greatest service in the world, and completely blow the competition out of the water in terms of quality, but if you don't keep your customers satisfied, your business is likely going to close and your position disappear along with it.

The real challenge in IT is to create a sense of complete fulfillment. From the beginning to the end of any interaction, you have to make the customer have the utmost confidence in you, your products, your service, and anything associated with you. This is a difficult thing to accomplish when you're dealing with an industry that is prone to problems and rarely creates a 100 percent satisfaction rate. Let's take a look at a scenario that gives an example of a typical case where it would normally be difficult to provide customer satisfaction and see if there are some tactics you can use to improve your chances.

Scenario

While attending your fourth service ticket of the day in the CompuComs Level 3 Technician center, you hear the sound of a newly arrived support e-mail question, and open your inbox to see what it's about. Inside your company's secure support inbox, you find an e-mail from a customer that reads as follows:

Dear CompuComs:

Today I purchased one of your machines, and I have never been so upset in all of my life. I plugged the machine into the wall and turned it on and it did nothing but make noise and didn't display. I then called your company for support and was placed on hold for 20 minutes. After being on hold for that long, the person I spoke to could barely speak English and I couldn't make heads or tails of what he was saying.

Afterwards, they transferred me to another person who had me do at least a dozen different things, none of which worked. I unplugged the monitor and plugged it back in, I installed something called drivers at least four times, I messed with all kinds of wires, and then they made me do something really strange inside the computer.

Once they'd put me through the wringer, they finally told me that I'd have to send the machine back and I could return it to your local store. When I got to the store, the employee started testing the same procedures I had already done and told me that the machine was broken.

Then, out of the blue, a young teenager walked over to the counter and said, "This model tends to do this, I did this to fix it." He then popped open the hood, pulled something out from inside of it, put it back in, and then turned it on and the machine worked.

I've now taken the machine home and it is making an unusual clicking noise. I'm tired, frustrated, and just extremely disappointed with the entire process. Please help me figure out how to make the machine I paid good money for work.

Angela Ashley

Background

I know what you might be thinking. This isn't a phone conversation! And that's the truth, it isn't. However, part of good phone techniques or, more appropriately said, good remote support communication techniques, is knowing that the same tactics you use on a phone when you try to create customer satisfaction can be applied to an e-mail as well. If you thank someone for their time on the phone, it has the same effect as thanking them in person. This frame of mind helps when you consider that almost everything you've learned to this point applies in more than one way.

Overview

Our customer is obviously very upset in this situation. Surprisingly, the e-mail is well worded. Typically complaint e-mails are filled with expletives, angry sentiments, and just a lot of negative emotions. Regardless, the overarching theme (as you've probably seen by now) is that you have to find a way to change the person from being dissatisfied to being glad to be a customer. Let's look at some of the ways you can accomplish this.

Key Concepts

The first thing you have to realize in a situation like this is that it's going to be almost impossible to provide 100 percent customer satisfaction. But as I pointed out earlier, that's fairly normal for this business. However, there are ample opportunities to exercise some great customer service skills and create a satisfied customer: you can practice the arts of resolving, amending, and suggesting.

Resolving

Obviously, in order to guarantee a satisfied customer you must resolve whatever the issue is in the first place. However, it bears mentioning that at the end of the day you have to make sure that the issue gets resolved. Even if you think achieving customer satisfaction is completely hopeless, you should try your best to make certain that the situation is fixed at its root. This way, it won't resurface again.

Additionally, it's important to note that a majority of customer satisfaction comes from simply doing the job that the customer asked you to do. If you think about it, you do that daily. Suppose the first time you order at a local fast-food restaurant they get the order just right, so you decide that you'll order there again and trust them. If they mess up your order, however, you probably decide right then and there to try your best to avoid that restaurant; if you ever have to eat there again, you'll probably scrutinize every aspect of your order.

Amending

Has someone in a business ever done something that just made your day? I once saw someone take a ride at an exciting dogfight reenactment program in Houston, Texas, called the Texas Air Aces. Not only was it incredibly neat, but it came with a free video of your flight from the view of the cockpit. Unfortunately, on this person's particular flight the video equipment failed and the record of the event was lost.

However, as soon as he discovered the problem, the head pilot for the organization said that they were ashamed that this had happened and offered to let the person do the entire experience again for free. Keep in mind, this was not a cheap ordeal. But because they had made a mistake, they made *amends*. This process of amendment, or simply making up for something they did wrong, created a customer for life—and the story of it actually made its way into a book on professional communication and customer service.

Suggesting

Sometimes a customer could have done something better. Actually, that's not true. There is almost always something a customer could have done in a superior way. Because of this, it's easy in terms of customer service to show off some of the assets that you and your company have available and make them aware of a service of which they may have been ignorant. Let's say in this case that there was a press release that noted a particular problem with her machine. One of the ways you could suggest to let you improve her service is by returning an e-mail with a line similar to:

> That is most unfortunate. From what I hear, it sounds like this was an issue with
> *a known problem*. I'm sorry that your first technician did not know this, but in the
> future if you should have any problems with your CompuCom computer, I recom-
> mend reviewing our "Getting Started" manual that accompanies each computer.
> This document not only instructs you on how to set up your machine, but also comes
> with additional information available on your specific model and any known issues
> associated with it.

This succeeds in both apologizing for the situation and suggesting a manner in which she can receive an additional benefit for being your customer. You may not realize it, but every feature and bit of service makes a difference in someone's attitude and opinion.

Resolution

In this case, it would be best to use a combination of all the tactics I've listed here. You could begin by first resolving the issue with the knowledge you have at your disposal, and you could then make amends by doing several things, such as apologizing, sending her to someone specifically in customer service to provide her with a benefit your company approves, telling her that if she ever has a problem she can connect directly with you at your number, or anything that your company allows in its policy. This last point not only makes amends but also suggests a way that she can capitalize on your company or, in this case, capitalize on your being an employee of that company. It's always nice to have a friend in the right place.

Skills for the A+ Exam

Here's an example of the type of question you may find on the A+ exam about creating customer satisfaction:

5. When trying to create customer satisfaction in an unsatisfied customer, which factors are the most important? (Choose two.)

    A. The customer's issue

    B. Apologizing for the issue and offering to make amends

C. What you believe the customer's wishes are

D. The marketing cost of implementing a satisfactory solution

E. What it will take to fix the situation

Answer A: Incorrect. The actual issue isn't important. What is important is what it will take to create customer satisfaction.

Answer B: Correct. Apologizing and making amends are an extremely important part of customer service, and should always be done when someone is unsatisfied.

Answer C: Incorrect. Although you'd like to make all of a customer's wishes come true, it probably won't happen. You have to consider what will benefit the company the most and then act accordingly. Usually, this involves doing what will make the customer happy.

Answer D: Incorrect. Thankfully, IT technicians rarely care about marketing, especially when there's nothing to market.

Answer E: Correct. Fixing the solution is always the number one priority. If you maintain excellent service, achieve a wonderful relationship with your customer, and then don't deliver, you will end up generating a negative reaction.

Callers with Accents

As an IT remote support technician, chances are that your calls are not going to be isolated to people from only one culture. In fact, if you work in a medium to large call center, there is a distinct possibility that you may receive calls from all over the world. Some call centers support numerous nations, including the United States, countries throughout Europe, and a good share of the continent of Asia. Naturally, this means that you're going to encounter a lot of different people who speak in a lot of different ways. And some of those ways can actually prove to be fairly challenging communication problems, just as in the scenario you'll see next.

Scenario

You've just gotten off the phone with a very rude customer and you're now really looking forward to 5 o'clock in the evening, when you can go home. At 3:30 P.M., you receive a phone call from a person identifying himself as Igor Rovanya. Igor politely introduces himself, but it's difficult for you to understand him. The rest of the conversation goes like this:

You: "So how can I help you, Mr. Rovanya?"
Igor: "Des. I am having da problem with dee farwar."
You: "Excuse me, sir?"
Igor: "Des. Des. You see I am sorry for having accent, but I is the from having a problem because I am from Ukraine."
You: "OK, sir. No problem. Could you tell me what the problem is?"
Igor: "Des, de farwar."
You: "The farwar?"

Igor: "Des. Des. Farwar. Ya?"

Having no idea what "farwar" could possibly be, you freeze for a moment and then dare to ask again.

You: "Could you try that again."

Igor: "Bah. Is da Farwar, for dee printer."

Background

Often in a remote environment you'll run across someone who is difficult to understand, whether or not they come from a foreign background. Because of this, you're going to have to truly work on your listening skills in IT. Imagine, for a moment, dealing with someone who not only has an accent but also a speech impediment. Or worse, an accent, a speech impediment, and poor speech patterns. These situations can and do happen.

Overview

A couple of important points to remember when you're dealing with people with an accent are:

They're not stupid.   Just because someone speaks differently than you, it doesn't mean that they're unintelligent. It just means they're from another part of the world.

They have a legitimate problem.   Another thing you need to keep in mind when you deal with people from foreign locations is that, although you may be inclined to ignore their problem because of the communication difficulty, their problem is legitimate and worthy of attention.

Key Concepts

Along with keeping in mind that your customer has a legitimate problem and understanding that your customer is probably pretty intelligent, there are a few tactics that you have at your disposal as a call center representative for when you're faced with a difficult situation like this one.

Look for Patterns

A useful strategy when you can't understand someone is to look for patterns in their speech. If the person tends to use sounds like the letter "b" in the space where the "wh" as in "whale" would occur, you can remember to insert that in other locations. So if someone were to say "bi-fi," for example, you could interpret that they are trying to say the term "wi-fi." This can really help you from having to ask someone to repeat themselves a lot and can also help you file it away for other people from that area, just in case you meet someone like that again.

Take Notes

It never hurts to take notes when you don't completely understand someone. Write down ideas like "Did he says 802.11b or g?" or "Think he's talking about USB." This allows you to keep up with the person at their normal pace, without having to ask them to continually repeat themselves. This way, as they're speaking and you're writing down notes about what you think they might be trying to say, you can keep track easily of three to four questions at a time. This not only helps you understand but also saves the customer a lot of grief in repeating themselves.

Be Direct

When you're dealing with a communication barrier, it's sort of understood that you don't need to be quite as formal or hold quite the standard of kid gloves you would need to hold with either a fluent or familiar speaker. Granted, this doesn't mean you can be rude, but it does mean that it's OK to speak more directly. You don't have to sandwich your comments with niceties. Instead, you can just say:

"Take the cover off your computer."
instead of:
"Excuse me, sir/ma'am, could you please take the cover off your computer?"

Be careful when you're doing this to watch your tone, however. You're not giving orders; you're simply truncating statements down to their simplest form. By speaking a bit more slowly, softly emphasizing words, and helping someone through clarification, you will truly prove yourself useful to your customer.

Resolution

There are two key tactics that can be used in a situation like this to help you better understand your customer. Those two tactics are things you've already learned in previous lessons, but you haven't seen a real application of them: active listening and repetition.

Active Listening   Don't be afraid to ask questions! Clarify what you believe the customer said. Inquire about what it is that they believe you are telling them. Chances are the communication difficulty doesn't just go one way. You probably sound just as strange to them as they do to you.

Repetition   As I said earlier, repetition can be a useful trick to keep in your repertoire of communication skills, and it's something that you'll need to employ heavily when you have difficulty understanding someone. Be polite, but also don't be afraid to ask someone to repeat themselves if you have to. Furthermore, you should do your best to reinforce your comments with repetition. For example:

"Sir, I need you to remove your jump drive. This means I need you to take the jump drive out of the slot on the back of the machine, removing it completely."

Skills for the A+ Exam

Here's an example of the type of question you may encounter on the A+ exam regarding dealing with customers who have different types of accents:

6. You're on the line with a heavily accented customer who has repeated something to you four times in a row and you still don't completely understand what she's saying. What is the best tactic to take?

   A.   Apologize profusely, but inform her that you will have to terminate the call.

B. Politely ask if there is someone else available who has a less thick accent.

C. Rephrase what you think the customer is asking and ask if what you're thinking is correct.

D. Try to see if another associate speaks the customer's native language.

Answer A: Incorrect. It's never OK to terminate a call over a communication issue.

Answer B: Incorrect. This is very rude, and will probably greatly upset your customer.

Answer C: Correct. By repeating the customer's statement and using abstract thought, you will bring yourself very close to a conclusion.

Answer D: Incorrect. Chances are that there is no one in the office who does and, if there is, they may be occupied and this is your customer.

Interoffice Phone Conversations

There is no truer statement in all of remote business than this: you never know who is listening. Now, don't get the wrong impression. I'm not saying "Be afraid" or "Big Brother is watching you" but that you just need to be aware that you never know who you are speaking with on the phone. Therefore, you should do your best to stay in a professional mode at all times. Let's take a look at some of the consequences of what can happen if you *don't* do that.

Scenario

At four o'clock in the afternoon you receive a phone call from your friend Josh in the cubicle down the hall. Immediately, you greet him with an enthusiastic hello, followed by a "What's up?"

Josh then responds with, "Hi, do you have a minute?"

"Sure, what's going on?"

"Well, I think I have a problem with form A," he responds.

"Oh, that stupid thing?" you say. "That thing is absolutely worthless and I can't believe we have to do it. No one cares about it but Tritty."

After hearing you mention Mr. Tritty, your superior, Josh then says, "But Mr. Tritty wants it done and I think I need to take care of it."

You laugh. "OK, man. Let me tell the truth. Tritty doesn't care and wouldn't know the difference. Just don't even look at it, and then mark 'done' at the top."

There is silence on the other end. Still giggling, you probe for a response. "Josh, you there?"

Instantly your blood runs cold as the stiff and unyielding voice of your superior breaks through the other line. "Is that a fact, technician?"

Background

You wouldn't believe how often things like this happen. And they don't just happen in professional situations; even with family, friends, and associates you sometimes don't realize who is listening and you can say the wrong thing. The big difference is that a mistake like that in a social setting doesn't normally cost you your reputation. Just as I said at the beginning of this section, the best policy to adopt when it comes to remote support and phone center environments is to always assume that someone is listening. Phone calls are monitored, people report to others, and sometimes even users can be known to record phone conversations for legal or personal purposes.

Overview

What's obvious from this situation is that you and Josh have a friendly relationship. As I'm sure you're aware, casual relationships like this are easy to form and, in some cases, are beneficial to a corporate environment. However, there are cases where you can become *too* casual with someone and potentially expose yourself to saying the wrong thing, just like our make-believe "you" did in this scenario. Be sure to guard against this. Don't allow yourself to be exposed by saying the wrong thing at the wrong time on the phone or in person. To practice guarding against this, let's take a look at some procedures to use when you're dealing with interoffice communication that involves the phone.

Key Concepts

The following are several procedures that you will probably do several times a day in a call center environment. Don't be fooled by some of the titles, because some of the activities may contain different information than you might think. Just like the nature of IT support, complex issues can easily be mistaken for something unimportant.

Answering a Call

Whenever you answer a call, you must answer it in a professional manner. This seems obvious on the surface, but let's say something happens that you might not have planned for. For example, let's say that on your caller ID you see that your friend Josh is calling. You could pick up the phone and answer with something like "What's up?" However, it could just as easily be Josh's boss calling you to ask you a question. On the other hand, you could easily be expecting a phone call from a business associate and in fact be dealing with a friend with the same name. But here's the thing—you're not going to lose a friend because you were too professional on the phone. Always err on the side of caution.

Transferring a Call

While transferring a call seems pretty easy on the surface, remember to make sure you adhere to the following two rules before you do it:

Rule 1: Identify Yourself and Your Company When Calling Out You simply have to do this. If you have to call someone within a call center and don't immediately identify yourself and those with you (as Josh did not do), you open yourself up to communicative liability. The person you're talking to could say something damaging, unprofessional, or otherwise inappropriate. Instead, try transferring a call to someone like this:

"Hi, Josh. I have Daniel on the line. Daniel is having trouble with his mouse and keyboard. May I transfer him to you? Thanks!"

Rule 2: Always Assume There Is Someone on the Line   Whenever you receive a phone call, you should first assume that it is a transfer call until they make it explicitly clear that it is not. For example, you could easily have picked up the phone with Josh and said, "Hi, Josh. Is there something you need?" Then, after a little bit more patience, you could have concluded that Josh was indeed with someone else and then appeared completely professional.

Hanging Up

You should always make sure that you know when and where you can hang up a phone call. It's a fairly basic concept, but you want to do three things before you terminate any phone call:

Ask if there's anything else they need.   You should always close a phone call by asking if there's anything else you can do to help. You never know what someone might also need in addition to your first issue.

Make sure they've said everything they need to say.   Before you hang up, wait a few moments to be sure you've heard everything they have to say. You never know when something might come to them at the last moment.

Ensure they're off the line.   My advice is to wait for the dial tone or for the light on the phone's base to shut off. People can be *very* strange about ending phone calls. Some people might want you to say a certain phrase or make a certain statement.

Resolution

Once you've made a mistake such as insulting a manager, the only thing you can do is apologize. It's not much of a resolution, but it's the truth. However, the important thing to learn from this scenario is to not let yourself be exposed to make the mistake in the first place! You should remember that the phone is the most important communicative tool in the world—even above e-mail. It can help people figure out what kind of person you are and how much attention they should pay you, and it can change their feelings toward you in the span of a few seconds. The best advice on the subject is to remember that you are a professional every second that you are on the phone and to act accordingly. You'll find that it's the safest way to operate, as well as the most rewarding.

Skills for the A+ Exam

Here's an example of the type of question you may see on the A+ exam about proper phone etiquette in a call center environment:

7.   What is the first thing you should do when you're transferring a call to another associate of your company?

   A.   Give a rough diagnosis of the problem.

B. Explain the methods you've tried so far.

C. Introduce yourself and those on the line.

D. Ask for permission to diagnose the issue further.

Answer A: Incorrect. This process comes immediately after you've introduced yourself and the person on the line.

Answer B: Incorrect. Although this in an important step, it comes after you've explained the diagnosis.

Answer C: Correct. You should first introduce yourself, and then those you have on the line with you. Not doing so can create an awkward situation.

Answer D: Incorrect. This really isn't something you need to do at this point.

Summary

Just in case it's not clear by now, the point you need to take away from all of these exercises is that supporting someone over the phone takes two characteristics above all others: understanding and patience (and patience much more than understanding). In even the calmest call centers, professionals are going to deal with some very trying calls just about every hour of every day that they're working. If it ever gets to be difficult, don't be afraid to sit back, calm yourself down, and remember that at the end of the day the person on the other end of the line is there to get help from you and you're there to help them.

Also remember that on your A+ exam you are going to face some challenging questions involving phone procedures and the proper way to handle a customer in a difficult situation. If you need a refresher, look over these scenarios again and consider acting out a similar situation with a friend. You'll find that acting out, or role-playing, can benefit you with a lot of practice. After all, practice makes perfect!

Chapter 4

Security in Communication

Security is one of the key focuses of the new CompTIA A+ exams. From a communication perspective, this creates an interesting dynamic because so much of security is based on communication and interaction within and outside a company. In this chapter, I'll review some of the concepts of the CIA security triad (confidentiality, integrity, and availability), social engineering, and other general security practices that need to be used in an office environment. At the end of this chapter, you should be familiar with some of the primary concepts of communication security and how it plays a role in the ethics of business and the ethics of security as a whole.

Chapter 4 contains the following seven scenarios:

- Scenario 1: Ethics in Security
- Scenario 2: What Can I Throw Away?
- Scenario 3: Confiding in Your Superiors
- Scenario 4: Caution with Coworkers
- Scenario 5: What If It Isn't My Customer's Computer?
- Scenario 6: Phone and E-mail Security
- Scenario 7: Social Engineering

Ethics in Security

There are some times in your life when it pays to open your mouth and say something, but there are far more times when it's a good idea to say nothing at all. Our lives as professionals can be either made or broken by this concept. It's not easy to know when you should behave a certain way and when you shouldn't. However, there are a certain set of situations that you should know to look out for and be prepared to deal with. In this scenario, I'm going to jump into one of these situations and expand on the effect it would have if you didn't observe these precautions.

Scenario

As a technician for an Internet service provider, you've been onsite at a customer's home for over three hours and it looks like the situation has almost been resolved. In a way, you are almost sad, because you haven't had this much fun with a computer or a person at work in your entire career. As soon as you came in, the customer greeted you with a cold beverage, asked you if there's anything you'd like to eat, and showed you the problem.

While you diagnosed and began to fix the problem, the customer was very polite and hardly interrupted, except to occasionally ask if you needed any help or inquire if anything could be done to avoid this sort of problem in the future.

As you are about to leave, the customer thanks you one last time and then asks if you wouldn't mind one more question. The customer then tells you that he's just recently decided to switch to another service provider, but the change won't happen for several days. Because of this, the customer would like to know if you'd mind disconnecting the service on paper but leaving it attached for just a few days so that he can have access to his e-mail.

Background

If you ask any serious IT security professional what the most difficult part of their job is, you will most likely get one single answer: ethics. Ethics in security is serious business, and there are an absolutely unlimited number of ways in which ethical situations could be interpreted and viewed according to each person. In fact, there are actually real-world positions where individuals forensically investigate decisions that were made in security and determine whether they were legal or ethical. But while you have the option to make this a career goal, for the moment I am only going to concentrate on some of the more basic ethical issues in this scenario. The rest of this knowledge will come with time and experience.

Overview

There are legal, ethical, and moral reasons to not be involved with a number of different issues. In this particular scenario, all three of these concepts rear their head. But the trick is that they're not easily defined. An often-repeated saying about ethics is that you either have them or you don't. This is partially true in that a large portion of being ethical is just using good judgment, but it's not hard to see when something would be ethically wrong and not a wise path to pursue. The trouble is, although it is easy to say that you know you "should" take the high ground in situations like this, it's tough to know how to do it. Next, I'm going to take a look at how to get out of situations like this and why it's wise to avoid them in the first place.

Key Concepts

As a trained professional, you're going to have access to a lot of power and authority. Something like this is bound to come up in the course of your career, and it's within your capabilities to do it. However, there are several reasons that you should *never* do something like this and should instead refuse to comply.

Professional Ethics

It's important to remember that as a professional there are certain limitations that you have to abide by in order to maintain ethical behavior. In case it's unclear, the definition of "ethics" in *Merriam-Webster's* dictionary is "a set of morals or principles." This means that actions that you know are morally wrong, such as stealing or deceiving, should not be utilized in your place of work. In this case, it would be professionally unethical to take cable from your ISP and give it to someone for no charge.

Legalities

You may not realize it, but there are a *lot* of laws in information technology. I won't pretend that I entirely understand them or that I could sit here and tell you the ins and out of the statutes as they pertain to computing. However, I *can* tell you that there are some pretty cut-and-dried laws, and taking free Internet service breaks one of them. It's even worse if you're taking it from someone who is employing you! It's just not a good idea to capitalize on anything that you didn't earn yourself. You may be tempted at times, but it's best not to give in for any reason.

Liabilities

Another important reason for not taking part in any inappropriate activities while on the job (or away from it, for that matter) is the issue of liability. In everything you do professionally, there's always a piper that will need to be paid. If you do something that violates a policy or law, you're exposing yourself to a lot of liability that can't go away. In this case, if you gave this customer free Internet access, there's no telling what the person might do without leaving a trace. What would happen if the person turned out to be a terrorist? You would be the single person responsible for giving him an open channel to the World Wide Web that he could use without any worry.

Reputation

It goes without saying by now that the way you conduct yourself both inside and outside the office when you are a certified technician will be remembered. The IT industry isn't that big, and when you do something that is viewed negatively by the industry, a large portion of the industry will remember it. It wouldn't be fun to be known as "the person who allowed someone free access to the Internet" in your company or in the industry. This is another reason why it's important to guard your name and your actions well—you never know what consequences they may have.

Resolution

The first thing to remember before you're confronted with a situation that you find to be unethical is to try to find a way to avoid the circumstance if at all possible. However, in situations where the circumstance can't be avoided, as is the case here, you should do your very best to make sure that your stance on the situation is perfectly clear, and refuse to participate.

Ethical Refusal

In my opinion, there's no easier way to refuse to do something than refusing to do it based on ethics. The reason this is so effective is because it is so simple. All you have to do is add, "because I don't believe it's ethical" to the end of a refusing statement, or simply say that it isn't ethical and don't refuse to do it at all. Here are a few examples:

"I don't believe I should do that because I don't believe it is ethical."

"I don't believe that would be ethical."

You'd be amazed at how fast this can stop disruptive behavior. People will realize that you have a strong moral fiber and they will stop trying to bend the rules. This is because the more they try to make you become less of a person, the less of a person they become themselves.

Informational Refusal

Another easy way to get out of a complicated situation is to refuse with cause. This basically means that you are refusing to take an action based on a reason or principle. In this case, you could say something along the lines of:

"Unfortunately, hooking up your Internet in that fashion violates the law."

"Unfortunately, SuperInternetCom has a way of tracking all active accounts and it would ultimately be discovered."

The one flaw with this method is that it exposes your answer to debate. Someone could counter with an equally valid point or claim that your logic is irrational. So I highly recommend that when using this method, you couple it with some ethical ground. It will ensure your success when dealing with a situation that you find to be questionable. Two methods are almost always better than one.

Outright Refusal

Although it's not the most elegant way to fix a problem, there is a lot of merit to simply refusing to do something. Some people may not understand your motives, but it's hard to combat someone who comes at any given point with an absolutely unmoving point of view. For instance, in this situation you could simply say, "Sorry, I can't do that."

This method can, of course, lead to a series of questions from the other party. Among the most popular are questions about the reasoning behind your decision: "Why can't you do that?" or "Could you tell me the reason?" However, when you are presented with these types of statements you can easily dodge them by refusing to give your motives. Nothing silences people like the words "I'd rather not discuss it."

Skills for the A+ Exam

Here is a good example of a question you might be asked on the A+ exam regarding ethics:

1.   Which of the following is an unethical practice?

    A.   Maintaining password histories

    B.   Questioning unusual procedures

    C.   Memorizing users' passwords

    D.   Documenting situations

Answer A: Incorrect. There's nothing wrong with maintaining password history policies on your server. However, it should be noted that it's not a good idea to physically write down passwords that you have used in the past.

Answer B: Incorrect. This is completely ethical. In fact, it is even encouraged.

Answer C: Correct. You should never try to memorize a user's password. In fact, you should do everything you can to not remember it in the first place.

Answer D: Incorrect. Documentation is almost always ethical and almost always a good idea.

What Can I Throw Away?

Business has a bad habit of creating a lot of paperwork. The reason for it is obvious: it's difficult to keep track of so much information, and people need a way to monitor it. However, some information is extremely confidential and should be treated with the utmost respect and care. As an IT professional, your career will often focus on the documentation and storage of personal and highly confidential material. In this scenario, I'm going to explore the concept of confidential material and see how it pertains to communication as a whole.

Scenario

You've been working in the IT department of a large computer business for over five years now, and you couldn't be happier. Productivity is up, sales are doing great, and your personal support rating is at an all-time high. Today, however, a new problem has begun to emerge.

Due to the large number of customers your business interacts with, your company decided during your second month of employment that IT personnel would be required to collect personal information from all customers in order to ensure their identity and their hardware, and to keep them up-to-date with any updates they may not be aware of.

Although this concept was extremely good in its intent, the practical implementation of it has become a real hassle. In the past five years, you've dealt with thousands of customers, and the files you and your team have collected have risen in size such that your personal computer has run out of space and you can't see any new customers.

Looking back, you notice that some of these files were from the period when the policy first started and aren't even up-to-date with the current documentation standards. Thinking very little of it, you decide to delete the old files and create more space on your computer for future customers. However, in order to make sure that you have the customer data in case an emergency should arise, you decide to back the data up onto your own personal laptop if it's needed.

Background

As mentioned earlier, when CompTIA decided to revise the exam objectives for the 2006 A+ exam, the association noted that one of the most important, yet neglected, aspects of help desk support was security. Therefore, all new CompTIA A+ exams contain a section on security and will question candidates on the correct procedures for dealing with common security problems in an advanced environment.

In particular, the A+ exam wants to make sure that you as an A+ Certified Technician are equipped with the knowledge to not expose a large or small company to a major security risk. Therefore, the exam will most likely ask questions that involve preventive measures and use of confidential information, purely because of the liability you can become if you are unfamiliar with basic security practice and unknowingly expose your network. Because of this, it's a good idea to pay particularly close attention to this scenario. Some issues in it might pop up when you least expect them.

Overview

Security, as a whole, breaks down into three sections: confidentiality, integrity, and availability. Together, they form what is known as the CIA triad. You can find a picture of the CIA triad in Figure 4.1.

This particular scenario pertains to confidentiality and how confidentiality affects the world of IT. Let's examine this section in some detail and see if we can understand how this concept is vital for the success of any support business or business in general.

FIGURE 4.1   The CIA triad

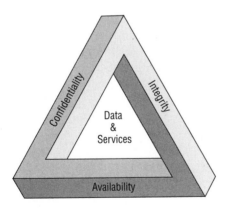

Key Concepts

Confidentiality in the technology business has two distinct meanings: confidentiality in terms of data (technological confidentiality) and confidentiality in terms of entrusted information (business confidentiality).

Technological Confidentiality

In terms of technology, confidentiality means allowing the proper people to access the correct data and restricting data from those who should not have access to it—in other words, making sure that people only have access to the material that they should. This integral part of security is the foundational reason that we actually have a need for security. If it didn't matter who had access to what, the world would have no need for security in the first place.

Business Confidentiality

In business, confidentiality means that certain data has been entrusted to certain people and should not be disclosed to anyone who isn't trusted. While this isn't necessarily that much different from how you handle standard data, the point to take away from it is that data that is entrusted to a business should be highly guarded and taken with the utmost seriousness. Many businesses will risk their entire reputation on the custodianship of data, and it's important for us as professionals to realize this and take the necessary steps to guard that trust.

What Can Be Considered Confidential?

The quick answer is: anything. Let me go ahead and repeat that: *any piece of data can be considered confidential.* However, there are some ways to categorize who has access to data. These categorizations and groups are referred to as "policy."

Most businesses will have a defined security policy that dictates what data can be viewed by whom and what data can be destroyed or discarded in some fashion. A good practice to start whenever you join a new company is to ask whether they have a clearly defined security policy. If they do, it makes it easier for you to understand what you can consider important information. If they do not, you should take care to consider all information that you receive as confidential and treat it accordingly.

How Is This Policy Violated?

In this scenario, you violated the security policy by disregarding the company's note that data should be maintained and instead deleted it. In addition, you violated the confidentiality of both your business and your customer by taking the information you were given and copying it to a personal computer. This not only is unethical but also could be viewed as identity theft or theft of information and could result in more severe consequences.

Alternatives to the Presented Scenario

There will ultimately come a time when you are confused about what to do with a certain piece of information. You may not know where something is filed, whether you need to keep something on file, or who needs to see what at any given point. While this is a given, what is also a given is the fact that it never hurts to ask. Furthermore, it behooves you to suggest alternative solutions.

For instance, you could go to your supervisor and say:

"I've noticed that I've acquired a lot of customer tickets in my time here and it's actually gotten to the point that I've run out of space on my computer. Can you think of a way I could store them?"

Or better yet, you could notify her of the situation and suggest a solution:

"Today I noticed that I've accrued so many tickets that my computer has actually begun to run out of space and I don't have any place to put the customer's information. I think that it might be a good idea for us to invest in a database where we could place all customer information, so we don't run into a situation of people deleting files in order to function."

Resolution

Whenever you're faced with a situation that you don't know how to handle concerning sensitive information, the best solution is to play the "I don't know" card and ask someone. You may not realize it at the time, but decisions that you make without consulting someone could cause serious security risks for your business and could also violate company policy. While it may save you some time in the short run, taking shortcuts with information can ultimately cost you a lot of long-term effort.

Skills for the A+ Exam

Here is a good example of a type of question you might see on the A+ exam regarding file security:

2. Which of these pieces of information can be disposed of frequently without consideration?

    A. Customer records

    B. Official company documents

    C. Federal tax information

    D. None of these

    Answer A: Incorrect. Customer records are extremely important pieces of information and should not be discarded.

    Answer B: Incorrect. Official company documents should always be treated as confidential and sensitive data.

    Answer C: Incorrect. The federal government actually requires tax documents to be kept on record for a number of years.

    Answer D: Correct. All of the above information is extremely important and should not be lightly discarded.

Confiding in Your Superiors

When you work in close proximity to someone for several years, it's inevitable that some sort of bond is formed. In some cases, this bond goes as far as close friendship, whereas in others it's a sort of mutual dislike in which people tolerate each other in order to accomplish a certain goal. In the case of superiors, the bond that's created can begin to make the relationship a bit fuzzy, and can actually be confused with a casual relationship. In the case of management, this can extend to the point that the person of authority is not simply viewed as someone in authority but almost in a parental fashion. As problems happen in the workplace, we have a tendency to want to inform our superiors. If something isn't working right, we tell them. If there's a problem that we need assistance with, we tell them.

Eventually, this sort of relationship can escalate to the point where the supervisor is contacted on almost every single matter and turns from being a supervisor into almost a sort of employee-afflicted micromanager. As IT professionals, we need to understand when it's appropriate to consult with management and when we should handle situations ourselves. This further has an impact when you consider that there can be security situations that management should be aware of and some that they need not be. Next, I'll look at a case of two coworkers who are put into a scenario where they are not certain management should be contacted, and then discuss the best solution to their predicament.

Scenario

Early this workday morning you received a phone call in your support office regarding a high-profile contract whose systemwide network had been afflicted with a virus. Due to the severity and nature of the phone call, you called in a third-party support consultant from another department to more expediently process and diagnose the situation.

Halfway through your diagnosis, you and your partner decide that it would be best to sample some of the files from the infected network in a contained area and see if you could further classify the type of virus or security breach to experiment with ways to contain it. After making this decision, the two of you set up a makeshift research lab in your cubicles and load some of the infected software onto the test computer. Almost immediately, the system goes down.

Less than two minutes later, you are beginning to reboot the test machine again when your main system suddenly crashes. You then notice that your coworker's mobile laptop is beginning to behave erratically and starts accessing random files. Suddenly, you realize that you forgot to disconnect your test computer from your local four-port switch and it could communicate to your main computer. Thinking that the virus may have leaked onto your network, you immediately disconnect the hub from the wall and power down the computers. After listening for a few seconds, you don't hear anything from users in other cubicles.

Your coworker then turns to you and says, "I bet you we got it. That was a close one. Should we continue?"

Background

It probably wouldn't do any good to scream at you and say, "Trust your superiors!" but I think I'm going to anyway. Trust your superiors! There will be thousands of times in IT when you will be confused, concerned, or otherwise in a "not so good feeling" mood and need to check on something with someone and confide that you've made a mistake. In the real world, this happens all the time. Shipping plants, oil rigs, and many other highly profitable businesses simply would not be profitable if people did not confide in their leadership and then capitalize on it by learning from a mistake. Remember, making a mistake is not necessarily a bad thing the first time. It can often be a learning experience. If anything, management would actually *prefer* you to make a mistake and then realize it, instead of never making a mistake and not learning a valuable lesson.

Overview

This scenario is particularly concerning to you as an IT professional for several reasons; among them are the facts that:

- Data may have been compromised.
- There could be more potential fallout from the action.
- If left alone, the problem could worsen.

In the next section, I'll discuss how this situation should have been handled in the first place and what you can do in your own experimentation in the workplace to avoid such a potentially dangerous situation.

Key Concepts

In a situation like this, there are a lot of factors to consider, not the least of which is the possible infection of the network and the fact that some of your business data might have been compromised. Because of this, I'll break this scenario into phases and discuss the different parts of this process when it would have been wise to consult management, and the decisions that were made incorrectly.

Phase 1: Problem Assessment

From the very first moment of this situation, a manager should have been involved. If you're in a situation where you are the final stop in terms of technical support and can handle all different levels of problems, it's important for you to be aware that you are going to need to inform your supervisor whenever you will be utilizing extra resources. The reason for this is twofold: First, the manager could very well have already allocated those resources (personnel in this case). Second, unless you are a supervisor you simply do not yet have the authority to make the call of how severe a problem is and whether or not it is a priority.

In this case, it's probably pretty clear that the problem would have been escalated to the next level. However, it's important to realize that the person who should have made this decision is the supervisor, who wasn't consulted. She may have even felt so strongly about it that she could have assigned an entire team to the case, which certainly could have been more useful than just two people.

Phase 2: Data Collection

It breaks almost all IT personnel's hearts when they hear the words "Never make a lab without permission." When you know a lot about technology, it is so very tempting to use your knowledge base and begin to tackle a problem head on. Unfortunately, this tactic doesn't normally work well in a business environment. Without a lot of careful planning, the lab or setup environment/solution you create could compromise your workplace.

In 1999 a common problem that occurred in early large-scale networks in universities across North America was that students liked to use their own routers so that they could have access to multiple computers from within their dorm room. While this was fine in theory, the problem was that many students would accidentally plug their routers in reversed. This caused the main router on the network to hear the request from the student's router and made the main router believe that the *student's* router was the primary router responsible for the network! It was an innocent mistake, but setting up a small lab within a real-time business environment (the university network) brought down the entire network, and issues of that nature can still happen to this very day.

Now, this isn't to say that setting up a lab is always a bad idea. It isn't. The rule of thumb for this situation is simple: whenever you think you need to see a symptom in person, you should always ask your supervisor. Not only does this give you the authority to put your ideas in practice, but it also gives you a way to be almost blame free if you make a mistake. After all, you warned them!

Phase 3: Security Breach

If you are in a situation where there is a possible security breach, you had better make *certain* that you inform your supervisor. Better yet, in a situation like this it is actually a better idea to take an authoritative approach and notify the IT security personnel directly. Despite the recommendations of Chapter 2 on always following the chain of command, the urgency of security situations makes it important to go directly to the security department. Although it's also a good idea to tell your supervisor, the supervisor is ultimately going to have to inform the security team, and the time that she spends evaluating your security situation with her limited knowledge base can prove to be valuable time that could have been used by the security department. However, it should be noted that the idea of taking a problem to a security team directly can begin to form a sort of slippery slope. No one likes someone who cries wolf, so you should only notify your security personnel if there is an actual emergency, which a malicious and obviously spreading virus certainly qualifies as.

Phase 4: Further Steps

The best next step to take in a situation like this obviously is to inform your supervisor. But it's fair to say that, while this situation is extreme, points will arise in your working career when you will be in a situation where you've messed up and you will need to inform your supervisor after the fact. In this case, your best friend is documentation.

Document everything you have done, down to the letter. You'll find that putting your actions down on paper will not have the result of getting you in trouble, but will actually look good for you as people can see all the work you tried to do to correct the problem and can see where the mistake was made. By using documentation, you create a trail that others can use to make headway on the problem through data you have already collected.

Resolution

The best policy when dealing with a complex situation that involves several factors that management might need to approve is to ask yourself one question: "Which of these decisions would require authority?" Once you've determined how many, if any, of the questions that you are thinking about require authority, you'll be able to determine whether you should bring them to the notice of your supervisor. Consider the case earlier. The situations in phases 1, 2, and 3 required managerial approval in order to proceed. If those factors had been considered, management would have been involved from the very first point and a lot of the complications could have been avoided. Remember, you should never be afraid to ask about decisions that you don't have the authority or expertise to make.

Skills for the A+ Exam

Here is an example of one of the types of questions you might see on the A+ exam concerning managerial relationships and security:

3. When should you *not* inform your supervisor?

   A. When accessing information that you don't have permission to access

   B. When dealing with an angry customer

   C. If you have potentially exposed the company network

   D. If a customer requests to speak with the supervisor

   Answer A: Incorrect. If you need to access sensitive data, you should always ask permission. It's generally a good idea to make sure your supervisor is aware of what you are doing.

   Answer B: Correct. Angry customers may be intimidating, but it's ultimately up to you to make certain they are taken care of.

   Answer C: Incorrect. You should always inform your supervisor if you believe there is a serious security risk.

   Answer D: Incorrect. If a customer requests to speak with a supervisor, you should immediately connect them with one.

Caution with Coworkers

In Chapter 1, I explained that it's a good idea to not inform coworkers of every detail of your daily routine or your assignments. In this section, I'm going to further expand on that concept and explore some more of the information that you should and should not communicate to coworkers, particularly as it pertains to security. I'll explore the concepts of trusted information, security protocols, and the impact of secure information in the workplace.

Scenario

Dan Davidson has been in his new small office for a little more than six months and his boss has begun to show a lot of faith in him. Now that he's passed the initial trial phase, he's been entrusted with the key to the office and granted the administrator password for the network. With this information, he has the power to do virtually anything the business needs.

While entering the office and opening up for the first time, Dan notices several security issues. First, the door to the server room doesn't actually require a key. Although the lock still works, it is assembled in such a way that the bolt doesn't completely close and you can just push the door open. Furthermore, the administrator password is highly insecure and is just "password."

Thinking it's a bit humorous, Dan chuckles to himself as he logs in to his machine. A nearby coworker asks him what is so funny. Still laughing, he responds "Oh, just the lack of security around here."

Remember that you should never give any clues regarding your company's security layout to anyone! As a professional, you should know that this information is completely confidential.

Background

I've mentioned once or twice in this book that it's a good idea to keep your personal life personal and your secrets secret when they concern your coworkers. In this section, I'm going to get into a bit more detail of why this is a good idea. However, before I look at that, I'd like to emphasize just how big of an impact this factor can have on your life in the working world. In the real world, jobs are literally gained, lost, and found based on this subject. People who tend to divulge information freely don't tend to be trusted as much, and people who are known to have loose lips, well, they tend to sink ships. Consider your average "special agent." Do they speak out a lot about what it is that they do? They don't. The reason is because if they did, they wouldn't have the job they do. The same concept applies to IT, except for IT professionals the subject they're guarding is security information and passwords.

Overview

This scenario is primarily concerned with three concepts:

- Information and the protection thereof
- What you should/should not say in front of a coworker
- The implications your knowledge and information can have

By the end of this scenario, you should thoroughly understand some of the policies you should adopt toward your coworkers and how to guard yourself appropriately, yet at the same time be somewhat approachable.

Key Concepts

The unfortunate truth is that you never know who may mean a company harm. Workers who feel frustrated, underappreciated, or abused can react surprisingly when they are granted information that may provide them with a way to hurt a company they feel has treated them wrongly. This truth gets even darker when you consider the fact that you may never know who in a company might mean it harm for even darker purposes, such as illegal activities or even cyberterrorism.

Exposing Security Flaws

One of the first duties of IT personnel is to be aware that all information regarding company security is to be kept secret at all times. Whenever a person is given secure information, it is considered *trusted information*, which basically means that it is given to an employee with the expectation that they will not disclose it to anyone else. In business, trusted information almost always directly equates to salary. The more trusted you are, the more money you are worth to the company.

In terms of security, this means that it is your duty to never reveal any hints regarding the structure of your company. In this particular scenario, the small hint that was given to the coworker could cause that employee to become curious about the layout of the company's security structure. These can then turn into thoughts like "What is the problem?" or "Could I solve that puzzle?" and can ultimately lead to a complete security violation and a serious problem.

It is therefore vital that you should never hint to anyone for any reason that your company may have a security hole. Not only is it unethical, it is also potentially a serious problem. Instead, you should do your best to notify your supervisor of the problem or simply fix the problem yourself if you have the authority.

Security Liability

If you've ever heard the statement "Knowledge is power," you've probably also heard the statement "With great knowledge comes great responsibility." These statements are both very true and extremely accurate in the world of IT. With your knowledge as a professional, you have the potential to perform some damaging actions against your company. Because of this, you have to maintain a vigilantly protective standard regarding your security measures and understand that if you do not there will be consequences.

In the case above, let's say a third coworker overheard the conversation between Dan and his nearby coworker. If there was a violation of the company network the next week, there's a fair chance that the person who overheard the conversation might comment and mention that he had heard Dan telling person X that there were serious problems with company security.

If that should happen, Dan might be held liable for hinting that the company could be easily hacked. This could not only mean Dan's job, but also mean potential civil suits and, in extremely serious cases, criminal suits. This is why you have to be aware of the power of your knowledge base and carefully guard it, or else you might find yourself in a situation similar to this.

Remember that you can always suggest ways to fix a security problem. If you notice it, you should quickly and discreetly notify your supervisor of the issue and make a note of when you did in your personal records.

Resolution

If you see a problem, fix it. Notify the right people or take the corrective action needed to make a security hole become a security fix. And if you can't find a fix for it, you should never make someone even casually aware that there may be a problem. As an IT professional or IT security professional, you need to make absolutely certain that you keep the trusted information that is granted to you strictly for your eyes and ears only. If you tell someone another person's secret, you have violated their trust.

Skills for the A+ Exam

Here is an example of a security question that deals with both interoffice communication and social engineering:

4. What information should you *never* give a non-IT coworker?

   A. Your home address

   B. The company security policy

   C. Your username

   D. Power user access

   E. Network administrator access

   Answer A: Incorrect. This is up to you. If you have become friends with someone, you can trust them with your address. Just be careful of the types of people you associate with.

   Answer B: Incorrect. This document should be given to every employee on their first workday.

Answer C: Incorrect. While this might present a very small security risk, most companies usually use a particular scheme for usernames, such as first initial, then last name.

Answer D: Incorrect. Power user access allows someone to install files on their computer and can ease your workload.

Answer E: Correct. Providing network administrator access to non-IT personnel can cause serious security risks.

What If It Isn't My Customer's Computer?

If you work in an office or support environment, there will inevitably come a time when you are asked to work on a machine that doesn't belong to a customer of yours. As an A+ Certified Technician, your skills are going to be highly in demand. If you think about it, this situation is not any different from any other specialist's. If you know a doctor, you might ask him about medical questions. If you know a lawyer, you may want to ask her legal questions about your will or estate. As a "computer person," you are going to get asked tons of questions about computers. Because of this, it's important to know when you can and cannot give assistance.

Scenario

Two hours ago you were sent out on an onsite call to oversee the repair and defragmentation of a nonfunctioning hard drive of a customer's computer. While there, you notice that in addition to the hard drive function, the customer's computer is full of adware and a large number of potential viruses. To make the issue more complicated, the customer is an avid computer game player and has set up a home network for not only his computers but his friends' computers as well.

When you point out that there seems to be an infection on his computer, the user asks you if you would mind cleaning out the computer. In addition, he'd like for you to check over the rest of the computers on the network to see if there are other infected computers.

In total, six computers are connected to the network, of which four belong to friends and two belong to your customer. You suspect that in order to diagnose the entire network you would need at least four hours of review and then another two to three hours to eliminate the problem. What should you do?

Background

Have you ever been to the doctor's office for one symptom and then questioned him about two or three more health issues, just because you happen to be there? It's a pretty common habit that people tend to use with any sort of professional. If you have a friend who's a lawyer, chances are that you might ask her an interesting legal question or two. Or, if you are in the presence of a computer person, you might very well ask him about something odd a computer does occasionally and then ask if he'd mind just stopping by sometime and taking a look at your machine.

The reason this occurs is that people who are professionals in a subject are fairly rare. Despite the fact that there are millions of cars, there aren't that many mechanics. In our field, the technician-to-machine ratio is even worse. Most families have one to four computers (and sometimes many more) in their household, and chances are that none of them know more about the computer than you do. Because of this, you're going to get asked to do a lot more than you're assigned to do on a frequent basis, and it's good to know your limiting factors.

Overview

There are many more reasons *not* to work on a computer than there are reasons to work on a computer. Whenever you open a machine you inherit a lot of legal exposure and also expose your company to the potential of negative repercussions. In this section, I'm going to talk about why you should or should not work on a computer in any given circumstance and make you aware of what can occur if you aren't careful in both your time management and the advice you give.

Key Concepts

There comes a point where we as technicians must accept that we can't do everything. Problems can be so complex that they'll need to be itemized into symptoms that can and cannot be fixed by a desktop technician. In this particular case, there are so many problems that they *must* be itemized. The reason for this is threefold. First, as was just mentioned, a standard technician cannot fix some of these problems. Second, there are so many problems that they need to be written down in order to maintain a diagnostic trail. But the third, and main, reason for itemization is security, as you will see next.

Deniability

When you're working on a customer's computer, the customer documents the problem and has officially requested assistance. Usually, this assistance requires some type of waiver or warranty, which protects the desktop technician in the case of a disaster.

With a random person's computer, however, there is no paper trail and nothing to protect the technician from liability. If a technician operates on a machine that doesn't belong to a customer, it completely removes any protection that the technician may have had. This means there is nothing to prevent someone who has had work done by a technician from simply claiming that after a technician serviced their unit it began malfunctioning. They could simply say that the fault lies with the technician and that their company is responsible. Therefore, you should never attempt to diagnose a computer that isn't properly recorded or in the system.

Complexity

One of the surest statements in the world of computers is that people can do some strange things to their computers. To boot (no pun intended), the computer could have a complex setup. In the previous example, a personal home computer could easily have a SCSI array installed in it, an overclocked processor, or other complex component configurations. And while you may have the best intentions at heart, there is a possibility that you will have no idea how the machine is configured. With a well-documented computer, you will know what type of machine it is and what exactly the problem is, and you'll be able to reference earlier diagnoses in order to expedite your service.

 Remember, being an A+ Certified Technician does not mean that you know "everything" about computers. Extremely complex situations can arise, and you'll need to be careful to ensure the security of your customer's setup before proceeding.

Time Constraints

You're going to be processing a lot of service requests as an A+ Certified Technician. What makes these requests more difficult is that performance is usually evaluated based on how many tickets you can service in a single day, and situations such as this one can eat into your time. Therefore, it's a good idea to ask the customer in a situation like this to submit a general ticket for each machine. That way, you wouldn't be dealing with just a side issue, but 10 or 20 service requests that would justify a day's work.

If you don't prioritize your time like this, you can bet that your supervisor or manager is probably going to be pretty upset with you. After all, if you did help this customer and took over four hours out of your day, you'd basically end up having to do all of your normal work and then working four hours of unpaid overtime. That isn't really a fun way to start or end the workweek!

Resolution

If you can keep it to yourself, I'll tell you a little secret: at the end of the day, your job is not really to fix computers—it is to fix people. When someone has a complicated issue, you need to treat it like a complicated medical, mechanical, or legal problem. You should gather all the facts, see if it's in your realm of expertise, and then capitalize on a way to fit it into your work schedule. Although you may want to be the hero technician and always be there for your customers, reality dictates that you have to treat each situation you become involved with as a distinctly individual case and make every effort to treat each case in the order in which it was received.

Skills for the A+ Exam

Here is an example of a question you might see on the A+ exam involving computer service policies:

5. Which of the following is a good practice when dealing with a computer that doesn't belong to your user?

    A. Ignore the computer except to suggest minor maintenance concepts.

    B. Diagnose the situation in order to show your level of service.

    C. Ask if there's a time when you could come back to fix it.

    D. Recommend the customer file a request and that you will return once it is filed.

    Answer A: Incorrect. If a computer isn't documented, it's best not to present any ideas whatsoever.

    Answer B: Incorrect. If a computer has not been properly logged in to the system, it is best not to diagnose the situation.

    Answer C: Incorrect. This is somewhat correct in that you will want to return, but not without suggesting that the proper channels be followed.

    Answer D: Correct. If the customer files the request, it will assist you because the situation will be documented, and will assist them in that their computer will ultimately be serviced.

Phone and E-mail Security

It's unbelievable how much security goes into communication over an electronic medium. In the first days of the telegraph, the possible security holes in long-distance communications were probably the least of the inventors' worries. However, in today's world, millions of e-mails, instant messages, and telephone calls are made every single day, and a large majority of these calls have to do with sensitive financial and personal information. Moreover, each electronic medium presents its own security concerns. As an IT professional, it's important to understand when it's appropriate to use the phone, to send an e-mail, or to deliver something in person.

In this section, the scenario format is going to be slightly changed. I will present a short scenario, which will be followed by a section describing the appropriate medium that should be chosen and the reasons behind it. After reading through the situations, you should be able to easily identify the reasons why that medium was recommended and why other mediums would not work as nicely.

Mini-Scenario 1

You have just finished working with a customer on a support ticket. While working on this ticket, you defragmented a hard drive, cleaned the computer of viruses, updated Windows, reinstalled a broken driver, and installed a new graphics card. As is standard policy, you need to inform the customer of the procedures that you have completed and you are ready to do so. What method would be the best way to inform the customer?

Medium 1

This is a classic case where an e-mail would be an excellent choice. E-mails not only succeed in providing a documented trail of events, but also can be easily stored and filed so that they can be referenced in the future. If the customer should have any questions about future problems, a technician will be able to reference earlier e-mails and then see what procedures have been completed on the computer before they begin more work.

Mini-Scenario 2

After at least ten hours of effort over the course of three days, you have finally determined that a customer's computer is completely dead. The hard drive is corrupted, the motherboard is unpredictably erratic, the CD-ROM randomly ejects, and the fans are all grinding. You believe the only possible way to fix the situation is with a total replacement. What would be the best method to use to inform your customer?

Medium 2

This is a tough situation to be in, and no one wants to give a customer such bad news. Because of that, it's best to do it in person and to show them how genuinely sorry or sympathetic you are to their situation. While the news has to be bad, it doesn't have to be delivered in such a manner that there is no human element to it. Remember your customer's feelings and strive to make them as comfortable as possible in a difficult time.

Mini-Scenario 3

The system that your company uses to look up parts is an old point-of-sale system that keeps track of inventory, and must be at least 15 years old. The keyboard on it is so worn out that you can't even read the letters, and it looks like the orange and black monitor has begun to fade out. Realizing that the current system simply won't do anymore, you decide to inform your manager that it may be time for an upgrade. How should you inform him?

Medium 3

In this situation the best medium to use is a report, specifically, a printed document. As of yet, no innovation can replace the outright quality and official nature of a printed report. It succeeds in both presenting the information in a formal manner and indicating that the matter is of a serious nature. You'll find that using printed reports to your advantage not only will display your material better, but will actually cause people to pay closer attention to it.

Mini-Scenario 4

Your supervisor recently requested that you perform a light system audit on your company's network. This light audit involves checking the password history, reviewing requests to log in as root on the Unix server, and checking to see if any accounts have more than 100 access denials. As you conduct this audit, you find that the root password has been changed more than 10 times in the past day and that it has over 2,000 denials from a user "fthompson." You know this user and you *must* report this to your supervisor. What would be the best method?

Medium 4

This mini-scenario is different in that it's actually going to involve multiple forms of business communication: e-mail, print, and phone conversations. In a case where something is this important, the first thing that you should do is make a phone call. During this phone call, you should state the reason why you are making it and inform your supervisor of the security breach. Once you've done this, it's important to follow up immediately with an e-mail and point out the date and time that you made your supervisor aware of the issue. Finally, you should also begin documenting the situation and everything you have observed. This way, when your supervisor arrives or decides to discuss it in a meeting, you'll be prepared to present them with some printed material that will indicate the status of the situation.

Resolution

Almost every method of communication has its benefits and its hindrances. What's important is to have a general sense of when it is generally appropriate to use each. For a trail of documentation, remember to use e-mail. To personalize a message, deliver it in person. When you need to present something in an official manner, printing a report out on paper is still the preferred method. There are, of course, exceptions to all of these rules, but following these general practices is a sure foundation for the rest of your IT career.

Skills for the A+ Exam

Here is an example of a method of communication question you might see on the A+ exam:

6. How should you notify your customer that you have closed a service ticket if she is not physically present?

   A. By phone

   B. By e-mail

   C. By letter

   D. By report

   Answer A: Incorrect. You shouldn't take too much time out of a customer's day just to let them know that you're closing a ticket.

Answer B: Correct. After a problem has been diagnosed, the ticket can be closed by sending off a completed e-mail alert.

Answer C: Incorrect. Letters take far too long to reach a customer and could arrive long after the fact.

Answer D: Incorrect. A customer will not want to read a report on what they just experienced.

Social Engineering

Ask any security professional what the single greatest bane to a business environment's security is and they will all answer with one response: employees. This is because employees can be compromised in manners both intentional and unintentional, and malicious hackers have gotten to the point where they try to capitalize on this using what's known as *social engineering*.

Social engineering is the process of manipulating the general good nature of people in order to gain an informational advantage over a secure architecture. Examples of social engineering include manipulating, lying, deceiving, and befriending in order to gain a specific piece of information that otherwise would not have been given. In this scenario, I'm going to take a look at one of the tactics that malicious hackers can use to gain access to secure information and then review some of the methods you can use to prevent them from gaining said information.

Scenario

While working at a help desk in your corporate office you receive a call around lunchtime from a user. At first the user is silent when you greet them, but after you again introduce yourself the person introduces herself as Dana Porchan, the vice president of your company. You've met Dana on one occasion, and this person sounds somewhat similar, so you are fairly certain that this is her.

Dana then tells you that she's managed to lock herself out of her account and would like for you to reset her password and to change her security code for future lockouts. When you ask to verify Dana's information, she becomes extremely annoyed and says, "Look, I'm an executive and your boss. Just change the account immediately and don't make a big deal out of this."

Background

Social engineering is a concept that's been around since before the time of computers. As you'll see in this section, social engineering could more aptly be simply called "manipulation." People have always been trying to take advantage of the information and authority of individuals for their own benefit, and this hasn't changed as of late. Computers have simply made the problem worse.

In your job as a computer support technician, you will be constantly plagued with this issue. Identity theft, fraud, and other nefarious activities are at an all-time high. Therefore, it's your responsibility as a professional and as a good citizen to make yourself aware of these activities and do everything you can to guard yourself and your customers against it. Make no mistake—it is a real problem.

Overview

This has to be a little awkward. Imagine yourself on the phone, speaking to someone you think is your boss, and then demanding that they verify their information. If you were a less informed individual, you might think you could get fired for something like this. The truth is, however, that you probably won't get fired for this. In fact, your boss should be thanking you for it. This can be a bit difficult to understand, but once you can clearly identify to both your superior and yourself how necessary it is, you will find that almost everyone in your organization will thank you for your thoroughness. It's just like the person who IDs your credit card when you make a purchase. It's a bit annoying, but you're thankful that they care about your security.

Key Concepts

Scenarios like this can and do happen daily. You would be amazed at how many people desperately want to have access to something immediately and don't want to wait for the proper chain of events. However, as a professional, it's actually your duty to make sure that those events are followed to the letter and that information is given only to trusted parties. There are a few ways that you could do this, namely by:

- Verifying information
- Probing for specifics
- Avoiding vulnerable changes

Verifying Information

You should always, always, always verify your user's information. It doesn't matter if you work in a small office or in a large company; as an IT professional, you have to make sure that the person you are talking to has access to only the information to which they are entitled. By verifying a customer's name and username and any security-specific information required by your company, you not only ensure their safety but also prevent someone from socially engineering a situation by posing as a user and compromising data. In the previous situation, by not verifying the user's information you could face a situation in which someone improperly has access to executive-level authority, and that is *not* a good thing.

If you have trouble demanding this information, try saying something along the lines of:

"Ms. User, we follow this procedure to make certain that no one has access to your account but you. I'm going to have to ask you to verify your information before I can continue."

The truth is they may not like it at the time, but you can take it to the bank that they'll be even less happy if someone has unauthorized access to their account!

Probing for Specifics

If you're ever curious about someone's identity even after they've verified their information, you can always satisfy your concerns by asking questions that only that person would know, such as where she might like to store files on the server or what the last file she was working on was. By collecting pieces of information like this on the phone, you enable yourself to be more certain of the actions you are taking.

The only drawback to this approach is that people may not remember all of the information. In truth, I don't remember the last file I was working with. However, most of the time there will be something there that you can verify. And if you can't, it may be a good idea to ask for another level of security that may be defined in your company's policy. Some policies even go as far as requiring employees to verify their mother's maiden name and blood type!

Avoiding Vulnerable Changes

The surefire way to avoid compromising someone's data is to not make any changes that could permanently affect a user. There are many ways to fix a security issue. In the previous example, you could accomplish your goal by simply changing the user's password and then requesting that the vice president log in again with her old e-mail account before you make another change. Afterward, you could then change the security code.

This avoids a situation in which every level of security is changed in such a way that the original user could not access it if this was a socially engineered situation. If you only change one piece at a time or structure your procedure in such a way that one part depends on another, you can easily avoid being scammed and ruin a malicious hacker's perfectly good day, making your business very happy.

Resolution

The best tactic for dealing with social engineering is to be aware that it exists. Not all people are honest! There are literally thousands of hackers in the United States alone who would love nothing more than to pretend to be an executive and suddenly have access to an entire department or organization's phone list, financial data, and possibly even more sensitive data, such as human resources' identity files. By verifying information, probing for specific data, and avoiding possibly vulnerable changes, you can almost always avoid this. If you combine these tips with a lot of common sense and security awareness, you're almost certain to succeed.

Skills for the A+ Exam

Here is an example of a general security question you might see on the A+ exam:

7. Which of the following could describe social engineering?

   A. The art of being well liked at the office

   B. A form of security auditing

   C. Creating excellent customer service

   D. Taking advantage of trust in business

   Answer A: Incorrect. This would be more appropriately named "the art of schmoozing."

   Answer B: Incorrect. Security audits are designed to test vulnerabilities in a network, not to capitalize on social structures.

   Answer C: Incorrect. This is simply a good practice.

   Answer D: Correct. Part of social engineering involves taking advantage of trust in a business environment in order to be granted restricted information.

Summary

Keep in mind as you reflect on this chapter that a large portion of your exam is going to consist of questions concentrating on security. Specifically, a large portion of the exam is going to test you on your ability to apply security in a retail, remote, or depot. Because of this, it's a good idea to make sure that you're intimately familiar with concepts such as the CIA triad, social engineering, and information security. That way, you'll be well prepared for any questions that come your way on the subject, and also be of great value to your organization when you enter the business world. Companies adore people who can keep secrets.

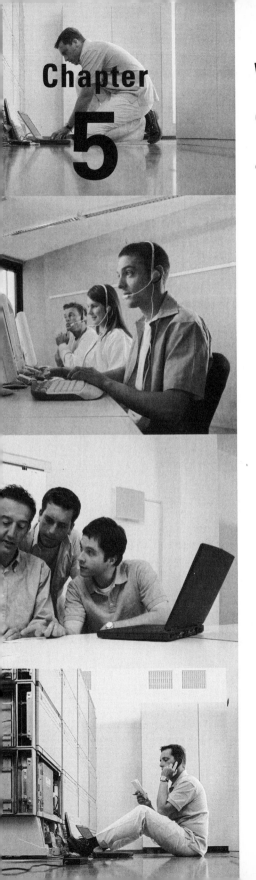

Chapter

5

Workplace Communication and Practices

While it may surprise you, the most important thing that you are going to need to know as a new IT professional is not technical information or even business practices. The most important piece of information you are going to need to know in an office environment is how to properly communicate with your peers and affect a positive environment. This is crucial because it both demonstrates that you are familiar with how to interact with your peers and shows that you care about the working conditions you create in your place of work. In this chapter, I'm going to explore seven different scenarios involving work practices concerning communication and how they play a role in your A+ exam. They break down as follows:

Scenario 1: Slang and Vernacular
Scenario 2: Gender Barriers
Scenario 3: Conflicts
Scenario 4: Tone and Mood
Scenario 5: Teamwork
Scenario 6: Staying Appropriate
Scenario 7: Apologizing

Slang and Vernacular

Slang is an unusual subject because it is something that is used quite often in the real world. Most people use slang almost every day when communicating with their peers, friends, and even with professionals. Nowadays, it's just considered to be the proper way to speak. However, in a business environment, slang can have a negative impact on your workplace. The reasons for this are fairly complex, but I will explore some of these reasons in this scenario and determine how we as professionals can avoid using slang and yet at the same time maintain an approachable demeanor. Consider the following scenario.

Scenario

David Thompson has just started as a new employee with Tech-U-Comm Industrial as a new bench technician and is beginning to learn the ins and outs of the company. Because David is a recently certified A+ technician, he has been placed in a special entry-level class that is designed to teach all new associates at Tech-U-Comm some of the basics of their duties as employees and encourage them to stay with Tech-U-Comm as a long-term career.

During the first few days of this class, David is surprised to see that most of the class and the instructor have taken an affinity to swearing on a casual basis. The instructor often refers to the customers of Tech-U-Comm in a very demeaning manner, calling them names like "stupid" and "idiot" frequently. David grew up in a conservative family, and not only does this sort of talk make him feel uncomfortable, but he doesn't feel that this sort of attitude suits the organization as a whole.

However, because David is a new employee and truly desires to have a positive impact on the company, he begins to take up the new pattern of behavior and emulate his associates. From now on, David begins to casually throw around abusive language and throw around derogatory terms at every corner.

At one point, David is walking around some of the cubicles and talking with his friend Gregory. As is their norm, David and Gregory are throwing back and forth casual vernacular between the two of them. However, unbeknownst to the two of them, they have been overheard by Sarah, another new associate, who takes extreme offense to one of the terms they just used.

Furthermore, as David begins his position as a Level 1 Technician with Tech-U-Comm, he makes the mistake of addressing a customer in a similar manner. Just like Sarah, the customer takes offense at the term and reports David to his supervisor. Consequently, David is forced to repeat his introductory course and formally apologize to both Sarah and the customer on behalf of the company.

Background

Some companies in the United States and abroad have a relaxed corporate environment that allows many styles of speech, such as vernacular slang and even a light tolerance of abusive language. However, by far the large majority of companies firmly do not tolerate any abusive language and only lightly accept slang and vernacular when used with customers.

By and large, most companies and organizations view speech that isn't "proper" business speech as having a negative effect on the company, and there is a reason behind this view. Consider the following as we begin to explore this situation and break down the effects that speech and vernacular can have on an individual or a customer.

Overview

This scenario breaks down into two distinct parts. First, there is the subject of slang in general. While it's the least detrimental of all the concepts presented, it is certainly the most common form of informal language used in the workplace. Second, there is abusive language. Although this isn't as common, it is by far the most troubling and serious of the topics that will be discussed.

Regarding slang, I will break down the use of slang and jargon in the modern workplace and what its effect can be on both a working environment and customers. As far as abusive language, I'll concentrate mostly on the emotional effect it can have on customers and coworkers, but I will also briefly look into some of the more serious ramifications it can have for your company.

Key Concepts

Vernacular is usually divided into three categories in workplace communication: slang, jargon, and abusive language. The three are extremely different in nature and have dramatically different purposes.

Jargon

As I discussed very briefly in Chapter 1, jargon is defined as language used exclusively in a trade or field of technical expertise. In IT, we professionals tend to use jargon a lot. Complicated terms such as Small Computer Systems Interface get truncated into just "SCSI." Specifically in the IT field, some jargon has become so common that it is simply associated with the standard way of identifying an item.

For example, in truth, a computer's "memory" is divided into three distinct portions: the memory available to the CPU (central processing unit) in cache, system memory, and memory dedicated in the form of a hard drive. However, in the traditional field, the only memory referred to as "memory" or "RAM" is system memory. We completely ignore the other two types because we so commonly deal with diagnostic issues concerning system memory. This shortening creates an interesting paradox that breaks down into two portions:

Positive Benefits   Jargon is short, easy, and casually familiar to us as professionals. Therefore, it's a lot less difficult to try to remember a few acronyms than it is to say the entire given name of the component. In the workplace, it allows us to quickly communicate back and forth between other professionals, without wasting time having to excessively define very long terms.

Negative Aspects   When dealing with customers, jargon should be used as infrequently as possible. It creates a confusing and unapproachable atmosphere for a customer if people are trading acronyms and terms back and forth that they, as someone who isn't a professional in the field, are completely unfamiliar with. On the A+ exam, you will probably see some questions on workplace jargon. Remember that for this exam (particularly the A+ 220-603 exam) you should always answer that jargon should never be used when dealing with customers.

Slang

Unlike jargon, slang has a much less elegant purpose. The true origins of slang in language are unknown, but almost every language and dialect around the earth evolved it at one point or another. The idea of slang is to break complicated words or excessively long terms into short phrases or expressions. Instead of saying that you could "haphazardly operate on a device until you produce success," you could just say "jimmy it."

In IT, this sort of slang is tempting to use. There are a lot of reasons behind it, but the driving one is that it's a bit annoying to waste a lot of words in using long explanations. In fact, it can even get to the point where it gets a little frustrating and sounds a little snobbish to use every technical term.

However, while this may seem like a good excuse on the surface, slang has the effect of creating two side products: confusion and unprofessionalism.

Confusion   If you use slang that someone is unfamiliar with, it's going to be very difficult for them to comprehend. The term "jimmy" isn't at all similar to the complete definition. If someone isn't familiar with your slang, there's no possible way that they could be expected to understand it or even figure it out on their own.

Unprofessionalism   By using slang, you place yourself on a lower technical professional level. People who call in for technical support are expecting you to be honest, upright, and extremely well put together. If you start throwing around casual expressions, you will undoubtedly lower their impressions of you and create doubt in the mind of the customer, which isn't a good thing if you want them to have faith in your capabilities.

Abusive Language

Abusive language is any language that is designed to insult, cause harm, or demean another person. Although I won't go into excessive detail on this subject, it is important to say that in the workplace, abusive language should never be used at all. Not only can it harm the feelings of coworkers, but it can also dramatically affect your interaction with customers.

In addition, by using this sort of language you expose yourself to liability. Not only can you guarantee that a large portion of your customers will be unhappy with your service, but it's also possible that they may become so unhappy that they decide to become legally involved—and that becomes very messy.

Resolution

It may seem overly simple, but the resolution for this scenario within the workplace is very simple. The rule of thumb is to always behave in the most professional and upright manner possible. At all times, guard your language in the workplace and avoid any term that would be listed in the dictionary as slang. Furthermore, you should make certain that you never insult, demean, or ridicule anyone involved with your company. It decreases your reputation with the company and reduces the hard-earned reputation of the company as a whole.

Skills for the A+ Exam

Here is an example of a question you might find on the A+ exam regarding slang and jargon in the workplace:

1. What is wrong with the following statement? "Don't try to stick the IDE cable in the SATA slot; you may cause a short circuit."

    A. It uses jargon.

    B. It uses slang.

    C. It uses abusive language.

    D. It is unprofessional.

Answer A: Correct. Both of the terms "IDE" and "SATA" are jargon terms that are used in the IT industry exclusively. Instead, you could say something equivalent to the "wide interface cable" and the "thin interface cable."

Answer B: Incorrect. Both IDE and SATA are jargon terms. Using slang would involve the use of a completely unrelated word.

Answer C: Incorrect. There is nothing rude or harsh about this statement.

Answer D: Incorrect. You could partially argue that this statement could be rephrased more elegantly, but it is not unprofessional. Remember that to be unprofessional you have to do something that is out of line with what a technical professional would normally be involved with.

Gender Barriers

It's no great secret that men and women are very different creatures. Despite the fact that they're the same species, they are physically, mentally, and emotionally composed in an almost completely different manner. This is so much the case that until fairly recently our entire society operated within very distinct gender-based roles. Up until the past few decades, for example, you didn't see many female military officers or male nurses. It simply wasn't socially acceptable.

However, times have changed and we are beginning to see more and more men fill traditionally female roles and more women fill traditionally male roles. Unfortunately, IT is one of the more slowly changing fields, and to this point males are still in the majority, but there are thoughts that this may one day change. Regardless, as an IT professional you are going to need to understand what you should and should not say in the workplace in order to maintain a very gender-neutral environment. In this scenario, I'll take a look at some examples of detrimental gender communication and explain why these aren't good ideas in the workplace. After that, you'll see a "Resolution" section that recommends some tactics for achieving an environment that is suitable to both men and women.

Scenario

Samuel Grayson and Cherri Smith are two employees of the large technology corporation known as International Grading Machines and have been employed with IGM for over three years. Just recently, both Sam and Cherri were informed that they'd been transferred from the customer desktop support branch of IGM to the machine assembly division.

Thankfully, both Sam and Cherri are very happy that they've had this change. Neither of them fancies dealing with people all day long as a full-time career, and the machine assembly area gives them the opportunity to just relax and have a good time with the technology at work. The only problem with the transition is that the two of them are both going to have to spend a great deal of time in training in order to learn the ins and outs of the new division's policies and procedures.

As the training has gone on, Sam and Cherri have begun to take lunches together. Since only a few people go to lunch at roughly the same time, it works out well for both of them, even if they don't know each other all that well. While they're at lunch in the company cafe–teria, they have the following casual conversation that, unbeknownst to them, is overheard by their manager.

Sam: "So what do you think of this new training class?"

Cherri: "Eh, it's OK. I'm not really a huge fan of our teacher, Ms. Heinz."

Sam: "Oh yeah? Why not? She seems like a pretty cool chick."

Cherri: "Um … I suppose. She just seems a bit dictatorial, almost like a guy."

Sam: "Right. I kind of like that about her. She gives it to you straight."

Cherri: "Well, maybe. What do you think about the color of the walls in the room?"

Sam: "The wall colors? I hadn't noticed. Aren't they red?"

Cherri: "Yeah, they're red. I think they seem really angry."

Sam: "I guess. Did you get a load of Ms. Heinz's supervisor, Dan? He is so flaming."

Cherri: "Oh, yeah, totally. I thought he was going to hit on you."

Sam: "Yep. What a sissy."

Background

Gender-based communication has become an area of concern only recently, but it's been a prev–alent issue for nearly a century. Without giving a long history lesson, until the late 1800s the United States was a very male-dominated society. In that era, women were expected to be seen and not heard, to care for children, and not to concern themselves about political and financial issues. However, in the early 1900s, women decided they were sick and tired of that sort of treat–ment and led a protest to be allowed the right to vote. In 1920, the U.S. Congress passed into law the 19th amendment to the constitution, granting the right to vote regardless of sex.

While this was a radical first step, it was by no means a complete fix-all to the current polit–ical and business situation. Afterward came the civil rights movement and the feminist move–ment, urging that women should be treated completely equally to men. Nowadays, society has evolved to a point that most people would consider gender roles to be fairly equal, but there is still a lot of tension. In the workplace, casually derogatory terms are tossed back and forth frequently. Without thought, many people still fall into the habit of using sexually harassing terms. And while the blame lies mostly upon men, the roles have recently begun reversing as women have started to become more authoritative.

Overview

On the surface, some might say that the conversation between Cherri and Sam is relatively harmless. While it's certainly casual, there were no real insults hurled between them, except to pick on their teacher. In fact, if you were to sit "most" people down and ask them if it would bother them to hear that sort of talk, chances are that they would say no.

However, the workplace is not in any way concerned with "most people." In fact, office environments are very concerned about special cases. One special case can actually cause a large amount of legal liability. If someone is offended by this conversation because of its usage of offensive gender-based terms, it could cause a great deal of trouble for the company. Next, I'll discuss some of the biggest mistakes made in this conversation and highlight some of the most important aspects to remember about what you should and should not say in the office.

Key Concepts

This scenario is primarily concerned with what was said in this particular office environment and, more important, what the effect of those words could be on the workplace. In total, three "no-nos" were committed in this situation:

1. Gender-based slang is used.

2. Many degrading statements are exchanged back and forth.

3. Both individuals make derogatory comments alluding to sexual preference.

Let's take a look at each of those mistakes and see why you should avoid making them in the office.

Gender Slang

The first mistake in this situation was made by Sam. In his second line of dialogue, he made the critical mistake of including a piece of gender slang. Gender slang is any term, slur, or expression used to identify someone by their sex or orientation. It includes, but is in no way limited to, words such as "chick," "dude," "guy," "babe," "fella," "toots," and a hundred other euphemisms.

While you're in the office, you should try your best to stay away from any gender-related word that is not "man," "woman," "male," or "female." This way, you can be assured that no one is going to be offended. Almost every term other than these few carries with it a potential for stigma that people might find offensive. This is important to note because, as was mentioned previously, the important thing about harassment (especially sexual harassment) is that it does not matter what is intended by the comment—the only thing that matters is what the individual hearing it feels.

Degrading Statements

Although Sam did make the mistake of throwing the first metaphorical stone, Cherri quickly followed it up with a statement that was equally damaging. And, from the way she said it, it's pretty likely that she didn't mean any offense by it. Consider the statement:

"Um … I suppose. She just seems a bit dictatorial, almost like a guy."

On the surface, you might again say that it is fairly harmless. But realize, some men might take great offense at being called dictatorial. One of the greatest misconceptions in the office is that the phenomenon of making degrading statements is mostly done by men. This is not in any way true. Both men and women can make equally insensitive remarks if they are not careful.

When you're in the office, it's a good idea to guard yourself against anything that might be a generalization to a specific group. Generalizations are never a good idea; they don't account for anything specific and can accompany unnecessarily derisive comments.

Gender-Based Sexual Comments

You probably didn't even need me to say it, but the next big "do not do" on this list of bad habits to keep out of the workplace is to make *any* insulting joke based on someone's sexual preference. In the first place, it isn't your concern. What someone chooses to do with their time in their way is their own business. Second, in most cases you have no idea what their practices are. Although you may see someone conduct themselves in a certain manner, it may not mean anything.

Consider, if you see a pair kiss each other on the cheek in the parking lot, you might assume that they are together in a relationship. However, many cultures around the world do this as a way of expressing platonic friendship. Furthermore, it's completely acceptable for members of the same sex, and in no way denotes a homosexual relationship.

When you consider opening your mouth and inserting your foot when it comes to someone's sexual preference, keep this in mind: business is business. Sex should not be a factor. While it's true that it's a fact of life, it's a fact that doesn't belong anywhere near the place where someone chooses to earn a living. By violating that rule with someone you work with, you are exposing yourself to punishment and exposing them to ridicule and judgment that they do not deserve. It's simply not fair.

Resolution

The best way to avoid any type of gender-based comments or harassment in the workplace is to use the following tactics:

Tactic 1: Keep Quiet.   If you can't say anything nice, don't say anything at all. It doesn't make you wrong if you object or think the way someone conducts themselves is inappropriate or interesting. It only makes you wrong if you make your opinions about their private life publicly known. Keep in mind that the best way to make yourself stay generally liked and to not offend most people is to just not give an opinion.

Tactic 2: Keep an Open Mind.   As a professional you are going to be exposed to hundreds or thousands of people who are going to work in your field who come from all walks of life. While some of them may seem strange or interesting, they're going to have different opinions on what is and is not appropriate to say about someone's sex (and sex life). In some cultures, words like "babe" or "dude" can be very friendly terms; in others, they can be extreme insults.

Because of this, it's best to keep an open mind and a bland and conservative policy when it comes to this subject. Don't let your opinion be known, but instead just be open to those of other people. You'll find that it both gives you an interesting insight into other people's psyche and keeps you from exposing yourself to unnecessary risk.

Tactic 3: Respect Your Peers.   If people know that you respect them, they're going to respect you in return. By not using any terms that someone could find offensive, you will be reinforcing this respect. It's important that you as a professional understand this because your career will succeed or fail based on how much people respect you. Nobody wants to work for someone that they don't think appreciates them. And you'd better believe that by making rude comments they will certainly believe you don't appreciate them!

Skills for the A+ Exam

Here is a good example of a type of question you would see on the A+ exam concerning gender-based language/sexual harassment:

2. The statement "Look, lady, I don't have time for this call" could be interpreted as which of the following types of harassment? (Choose all that apply.)

   A. Verbal

   B. Physical

   C. Sexual

   D. None of the above

   Answer A: Incorrect. Verbal harassment normally needs to involve name calling or threatening in some way. Being rude doesn't classify as verbal harassment unless it accompanies one of these.

   Answer B: Incorrect. Physical harassment involves actually touching someone or doing something to their body they do not wish.

   Answer C: Correct. Any other term besides something proper like "ma'am" can be considered sexual harassment. This includes "lady," "guy," "boy," and "girl."

   Answer D: Incorrect. The statement could be considered sexual harassment because of the manner in which the word "lady" is used.

Conflicts

Unless you are truly blessed in your work environment, chances are that you're going to get in at least one conflict with a coworker at some point in your career. This doesn't mean you'll get into a physical fight, but you may very well get into an argument or disagreement. For most people, this actually occurs early on, and it's usually something to learn from. Like most things, people generally take it is a right of passage that you have to undergo in order to understand more about yourself.

However, by the same token, most people find that after they have learned the lesson that involving yourself in a conflict is generally not a good idea, they wish that they could have just learned that in the first place. In this scenario, I'm going to explore a case of conflict and extrapolate what some of the long- and short-term consequences of this conflict could be. Ultimately, the goal of this scenario will be to show that if at all possible it is best to avoid conflicts in the office. Then I will explore some of the resolutions that will help keep you from being put into a similar situation.

Scenario

Jim Branson and Jay Berry have been working together all day on a broken computer system, and they are extremely frustrated. Even though each of them is a fully certified A+ technician, they cannot figure out what is wrong with the system and it's really puzzling them. The reasons behind this are twofold. First, the computer is an extremely complicated setup, and second, the actual problem is very complex.

Although Jim and Jay are used to working on a standard IDE/SATA interface, this computer uses SCSI. Additionally, the computer has a hardware RAID (Redundant Array of Inexpensive Disks) setup and it uses a custom boot loader native to the particular brand of the computer, making it extremely difficult to access necessary features for them to properly diagnose the machine. Instead, Jim and Jay have been arguing back and forth about what the next best step would be to take.

As soon as Jim has an idea and begins to attempt it, Jay comes up with his own idea and tries to push Jim out of the way. After Jim gives Jay a chance and sees that his idea isn't working either, Jim then tries to present his own new method and push Jay out of the way. Ultimately, they only succeed in making it difficult for each other to completely try anything. Eventually, Jay loses his temper.

"Look," he says, "if you're not going to let me try my ideas, then you should just work on this yourself."

"What?" Jim responds. "I've been letting you butt into my business for over two hours now and we haven't gotten anywhere. If you'd just leave me alone for ten minutes, I might be able to figure something out."

Jay blinks. "I leave *you* alone? You're crazy! I haven't been able to get a word in because you're so antsy. Calm down for a second and let me work."

"You're just trying anything you can think of off the top of your head," Jim accuses.

"And?" Jay retorts. "You aren't? It doesn't look to me like the computer is fixed. All I know is that I'm glad this isn't my ticket. The overtime on it is going to be extremely high."

Jim waves his hands furiously. "What do you mean it isn't your ticket! You're the one who picked it up!"

Jay chuckles. "Yeah, but you're the one who put your name on it when I was trying one of my ideas out. It belongs to you now."

"Look …" Jim says, sighing. "I put that on there because you were busy and I thought I could save us some time. Had I known your problem was going to escalate, I wouldn't have done it."

"Tough luck," Jay says. "It's yours now."

Background

Just as I said earlier, conflicts in the office happen a lot. They occur so often that most companies even have a predefined procedure to use in case there is a conflict. Some go so far as to have human resources act as an intermediary between personnel as these conflicts occur. The thought behind this approach is that if there is someone to stand between two people in conflict, it's pretty likely that the intermediary can convey the feelings of the individuals involved better than they could themselves in their angered conditions.

Not many companies have this level of commitment to conflict resolution, but it doesn't change the fact that even though events like the one I just described happen a lot, they are still very serious and can have dire consequences. Next, I'll begin by presenting an overview of the situation and making an initial diagnosis of how all the players involved are feeling before I point out some of the important aspects of conflict in the office.

Overview

The main problem in this situation is that both Jay and Jim are upset over two issues that occur frequently in the workplace: control and frustration. Each in his own mind believes that he can do the job better than the other. This is further complicated by the fact that the problem has become extremely complex and that neither of them is completely familiar with the technology.

On the A+ exam, you may be quizzed on soft skills regarding conflict in two ways—first, as they concern your customers and, second, as they concern your coworkers. Part of your duty as a certified technician is making sure that the environment that you work in is relatively conflict-free. Companies do not just want you to be a technical professional; they also want you to be a technical professional who plays well with others in a business environment. As I review the key concepts in the next section, keep in mind that you will not be tested on everything that is explained here. However, you will need to understand on your exam that your goal is to avoid conflict at all costs. If you are in a hurry, you can skip to the "Resolution" section and be prepared for your exam.

Key Concepts

This section of the scenario breaks down the reasons for, stages of, and results of conflict, and illustrates them in a fairly easy-to-understand manner. I'd like to note that a valuable resource for this section was provided by the people at `http://www.beyondintractability.org/ essay/conflict_stages/` and Eric Brahm in his paper "Development and Conflict Theory." Most of this section would not have been possible without their knowledge and assistance.

Reasons for Conflict

In most cases, there is no single reason why a conflict emerges. Normally, conflict is the result of a combination of several things that have been building over time that result in turmoil between two people. Granted, there are exceptions to this rule, but they're normally fairly rare. In fact, sometimes while we might even think that one single action caused a conflict, often an underlying reason exists for it that we are not aware of. For instance, some people are just naturally opposed to one another. No matter how much they may try, they will never get along.

That said, there are a few main causes that should be pointed out.

Blame

One of the oldest sayings in business, and life for that matter, is "It's not my fault!" Nobody likes to be blamed for anything. If someone makes a mistake, they don't want it to be known; they'd rather pretend that it never happened. Or, in other situations, the fault of the situation may not clearly lie on any single event or person, thus causing people to play "the blame game" as they toss their thoughts back and forth regarding who made the mistake in the first place.

Because of this, blame can be a huge source of conflict. When people are playing the blame game, it can become downright vicious. In business, blame can be a serious problem. The person who makes the huge mistake that costs the company millions of dollars is not normally promoted, and people will try their best to not be that person. However, a true professional realizes that making mistakes and blaming others is not a reasonable way to act. Instead, it is very good advice to be sure to own up to your mistakes early. Both people and business respect honesty when it has no underlying hope of reward. If you confess early, the punishment is almost always less. In fact, you might even get rewarded in the long term as your superiors remember your actions.

Ego

Ego is a word that has several different meanings, the most common of which is a sort of self-identification. This originates from psychology, where the ego is the part of the human psyche that differentiates between primal need and social demands. Plainly put, it means that you need to eat to survive, but you also need to be civil to impress your friends. Therefore, you eat civilly.

In conflict, ego plays a huge role because it is the key reason why an individual may have a personal problem with another. Their set of values or beliefs does not line up with someone else's. In another person's opinion, you may not be worthy of their respect or attention.

Because of this, it's a good idea to keep other people's beliefs and egos in mind as you go about your daily tasks. Although some may call it conceding, it's certainly a lot easier to let someone believe something that may not necessarily be true. For instance, just because you smile when you come into the office at six o'clock in the morning, it doesn't mean that you are happy to be there.

Stress

In a way, this seems almost too obvious to point out. When people are stressed, they make rash decisions and take reckless actions. No one likes to feel put under the gun or worked to the bone. When people are worn out, tired, or very stressed, they can easily snap at one another. Keep this in mind the next time you find yourself yelled at. The person you're talking to may just be upset.

Miscommunication

Miscommunication is the mother of all reasons for conflict. In fact, I'd wager that it's the reason behind *at least* 50 percent of all conflicts in the world (not that I can prove it). What is definitely true is that it is beyond easy to miscommunicate something. Some people spend their entire academic lives and careers dedicated to this subject, because it is so complex.

In fact, in our scenario there is miscommunication over who is responsible for the machine. Both Jay and Jim thought that they were being fairly clear in assigning who had ownership of it; however, they both appear to have interpreted what they said differently. Just like ego, this is something that you should keep in mind as you find yourself approaching conflict. Before you get angry, remember that you may just not be understanding what the other person's saying correctly.

Stages of Conflict

Eric Brahm, a professor at the University of Nevada at Las Vegas, wrote a paper that defines conflict as occurring in an eight-stage process:

- No conflict
- Latent conflict
- Emergence
- Escalation
- Stalemate
- De-escalation
- Settlement/resolution
- Postconflict peace-building

These stages can be visually represented, as you see in Figure 5.1.

As you can see, conflict in most people starts latently, as there is something that has the potential to become a conflict but isn't yet. The conflict then emerges and escalates to the actual argument (stalemate), and then de-escalates as people adjust to the situation and reach a settlement. Ultimately, a process afterward begins as people try to create peace once again.

Results of Conflict

Conflict at the office almost never results in something positive. Normally, after a conflict people will avoid one another in an office, only associating if it is absolutely necessary. This can cause long-term damage to a company because if a conflict emerges that results in employees not communicating, it also creates a situation where information may not be exchanged that should be. This can in turn have negative effects on productivity and your work environment.

FIGURE 5.1   The seven-stage conflict process. Source: Brahm, Eric. "Conflict Stages." Beyond Intractability. Eds. Guy Burgess and Heidi Burgess. Conflict Research Consortium, University of Colorado, Boulder. Posted: September 2003 http://www.beyondintractability .org/essay/conflict_stages/.

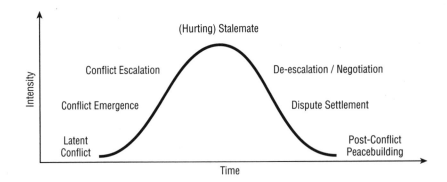

Resolution

The key to resolving conflict is to break it down into three philosophies (or attitudes): being agreeable, yielding when you can, and trying to understand someone else's perspective. As you'll see, following these philosophies can be quite easy and help a great deal with the conflicts you'll encounter in your career.

Be Agreeable

The best way to avoid getting into a conflict in the first place is to not give a reason to have a fight. In the scenario earlier, both Jim and Jay fail at the concept of being agreeable. If the two of them had started out beforehand by offering to work together on the problem, or perhaps brainstorming on possible causes for the situation, they could have saved themselves a lot of drama.

In IT, it pays to be agreeable, not just because it avoids conflict but because it saves you a lot of headaches. Almost every day at the office, there will be something that makes you a little upset. But if you take it all in stride, it simply won't bother you as much. A little serenity goes a long way.

Yield When You Can

Whenever you find yourself about to be in any conflict, just ask yourself one question: "Is this really worth it?" If you can't look at the situation and say that your point is unequivocally worth the frustration, annoyance, and heartache that you're going to go through in a conflict, it's best to just yield your point. However, you don't have to admit you are wrong. Check out some of the ways that you can yield a point without losing your own point of view:

- "I've never thought of it that way; interesting."
- "That could be. I'm not certain."
- "That may be a good idea. I think mine would be better, but I'd like to try yours first."

Notice that you never truly give ground, but you do yield to the other person's opinion or thought. It's a nice trick to use on someone who's very grumpy.

Try to Understand Someone Else's Perspective

Understanding is almost always the key to avoiding an argument. If most people would stop for a minute and try to understand what it is that someone believes or is trying to say, most of the trouble we have in the workplace could be avoided. Whenever you think someone is upset, try to understand *why* they're upset. Have you done something? Do you think you could apologize? Is there something you can do to help?

These thoughts start you on the path to healing whatever the situation is. Not many people want to argue with someone who cares about their beliefs or situation. It's just not smart, because you wouldn't want to fight with someone who you believe is on your side. In this situation, both Jay and Jim could have learned a lot from each other if they had stopped their bickering and just tried to see where the other was coming from. They could have shared the ticket, shared the problem, and then shared their knowledge and come up with a solution. Instead, they're just going to go to leave work angry. And that's no way to spend the rest of your day.

Skills for the A+ Exam

Here is a good example of a type of question you would see on the A+ exam concerning conflict resolution:

3. What should you do if an angry coworker screams at you, claiming that you have made a terrible mistake?

   A. Scream in return. Showing that you don't believe you have made a mistake will help your case with your superior.

   B. Ask if the person has some sort of problem and if he or she would like some help.

   C. Remain silent, but file a complaint with human resources.

   D. Try to understand what the problem is and see if you can find a reasonable solution.

   Answer A: Incorrect. Screaming in return will just promote a fight.

   Answer B: Incorrect. Comments like this (while they may be tempting sometimes) can actually do more damage than screaming back and can further infuriate people. Instead, you should just try to find a solution yourself.

   Answer C: Incorrect. While human resources can help with extreme cases, it's best to handle minor incidents like this in a more rational manner.

   Answer D: Correct. By trying to understand the person you're dealing with, you will work toward a better solution.

Tone and Mood

Have you ever noticed that people who are excessively negative are difficult to like? It's not really a surprise. Negativity is not one of those things that jumps out at you and says, "Hey! I'm negativity! It's nice to meet you!" If anything, it sort of meanders out of a dark dungeon and sighs at you before returning to the doldrums below.

In this scenario, I'm going to look at one single statement; however, the statement will be said in eight different ways. By reviewing each of these eight statements, you'll be able to see the effects that the tone, mood, and extra words of a person have on how a message is both delivered and received by a coworker.

Scenario

The following eight sentences will be reviewed individually in the section that follows:

- Statement 1: "How do I access system resources?"
- Statement 2: "Could you tell me how I can access the system resources?"
- Statement 3: "Hey buddy, how are ya? Could you do me a quick favor and tell me how I can access system resources?"
- Statement 4: "Tell me how to access system resources."

- Statement 5: *"Can't* you just tell me how to access system resources?"
- Statement 6: "How do I access the freakin' resources?"
- Statement 7: "How are the resources accessed?"
- Statement 8: "What would be required for me to access the system resources?"

Background

Tone and mood can change people's opinion about something in a heartbeat. As a customer support professional, much of your success in dealing with customers is going to be based on how well you can deliver information. In fact, CompTIA's A+ exam objectives for the 220-601, 602, and 603 exams contain an entire sub-objective on maintaining a positive attitude and tone of voice.

I can't recall how many times in my professional life that customer service and the tone I used came between me and a sale or a good review. Truth be told, I honestly believe that every time that I received a poor evaluation from a customer or didn't make a sale I should have it was because my tone wasn't properly presented.

In the real world, you're probably going to notice the same thing. People do respond better when you tell them bad news with a sympathetic smile. At the end of the day, how you present something to someone can make a difference.

Overview

The A+ exam requires that you understand how to present a good attitude and remain positive when you're interacting with customers. However, it's important that you realize that you need to maintain that sort of attitude with customers *and* with your coworkers because you will frequently encounter situations where people will not appreciate a negative attitude or tone of voice while at the office. It is therefore important that you know which types of speech can have a negative impact on your environment and which can have a positive one. Additionally, you need to become familiar with some of the key semantic elements of harmful speech. If you don't, you very well may catch yourself using them out of habit.

Key Concepts

Let's take a look at each of these statements one by one.

Statement 1: Straightforward

There's something to be said for being straightforward and dispassionate when you're asking someone a question. However, for the A+ exam you shouldn't choose this sort of answer when you're presented with your options. It is very useful, though, when you're interacting with someone and you'd like to maintain the utmost professionalism. By not adding any emotion, you succeed in divorcing yourself from any feeling for the person you're engaging with, positive or negative.

Statement 2: Engaging

Engaging is a positive reinforcement technique that reinforces and soothes another concept we spoke of earlier: the ego. By adding the word "you" to almost any statement, you are making the other person an active player in your game of communication. People love to be valued. Think about it: what makes you feel better? When someone says, "How do I get to the restaurant?" or "Could you tell me how I get to the restaurant?" The second not only involves the other person, but it makes the question very intimate and personal.

Statement 3: Schmoozing

Schmoozing is an unofficial, but still entirely real, communication concept that basically means that you are speaking to someone using excessive flattery. People who tend to be overly complimentary or use the words "my friend" or "buddy" excessively fall into this category. While schmoozing isn't exactly a negative influence on your tone (because most people can't detect it), it can have negative results if it is detected and unappreciated. Be cautious of this if you decide to use it.

Statement 4: Demanding

One of the stronger negative influences on your tone is the idea of phrasing questions as a demand. When most people think of demands, they tend to think of ordering someone to do something "right now" or "immediately." But that isn't really the case. Demanding can be something as simple as telling someone to do something without adding the word "please." Consider these two sentences:

- "Pass the salt."
- "Pass the salt, please."

One of them is a demand and the other merely a request. This ties directly into how you should approach customers and coworkers. Use common courtesy and phrase your statements in such a way that they are inquiries, not demands.

Statement 5: Mocking

Don't do this. Now that that's said, let's define what "mocking" is. Mocking is the belittlement of someone's talents, abilities, intelligence, demeanor, or capabilities in any way, shape, or form. This includes, but is in no way limited to, overemphasizing negative traits, teasing, and pointing out flaws. In this statement, emphasizing the "can't" increases the negativity of the statement, which is then reinforced by the belittlement of the task with "just." The person hearing this would think that you a) don't think much of their abilities, and b) don't think much of their position. By removing these words, you take away both of these features and come much closer to a more reasonable statement.

Statement 6: Attacking

This is another one of those communication methods that you shouldn't implement in your day-to-day communication at the office. Attacking is a communication method that is used to intentionally adversely affect the person you are speaking with and provoke them to conflict. Since your intention is to not cause conflict, it's just not smart to use this sort of derogatory language.

Statement 7: Passive Inquiry

Turning back to a positive communication technique, inquiring is a useful skill that takes advantage of the third-person voice. If you were to boil it down to one sentence, passive inquiry removes the individual from the equation and places the action onto an inanimate object or concept. Consider these two questions:

- "How do I kick the ball?"
- "How is the ball kicked?"

One of these questions directly involves "I," whereas the other merely implies it. This is useful when you're not trying to be personal. However, you should keep in mind that you should use this method only when you are attempting to be extremely professional. You should not implement this type of technique when you're trying to provide excellent customer service when the customer or coworker is without blame. It should only be used when you want to remove blame or responsibility from them.

Statement 8: Theoretical Questions

Theoretical questions aren't what you might think. They're not scientifically advanced questions. Instead, they're questions that show that you are trying to consider a subject and understand it. In this case, by asking what would be required to access the system resources, you are both showing that you don't understand what is needed and hinting that you may need to have access to them without actually saying it. Keep this in mind; it's a very powerful technique.

Resolution

As I've said already, maintaining a positive tone in the office is necessary in order to succeed, but it is also relatively easy to do. When you're faced with difficult situations where it's hard to remain positive, just remember to avoid these few things:

- Insults
- Attacks
- Demands
- Mocking comments

If you can manage to do that, you're almost there. But avoiding these things alone isn't enough—you have to try your best to consider the value and condition of the person you are dealing with at that time. Your goal as a technician is to make sure that all of your coworkers and customers are as happy as possible. As long as you remember that, you should do fine on the exam and in the real world.

Skills for the A+ Exam

Here is a good example of a question you would see on the A+ exam about maintaining a positive tone and attitude in the office:

4.   If you're dealing with a customer in a difficult situation, such as a hard drive failure, what is the MOST important thing you should do when informing her?

   A.   Keep the comments brief and lessen the blow.

   B.   Be understanding and compassionate.

   C.   Inform her in writing.

   D.   Deliver the information in a very professional manner, without emotion.

   Answer A: Incorrect. Sometimes people need a lot of explanation. If you hear that your year's work has been lost, you're going to want to know why.

   Answer B: Correct. The most important thing you can do in this situation is be understanding, compassionate, and helpful. She's in a difficult situation, and it's your job to help her through it.

   Answer C: Incorrect. Informing someone of this in writing would likely just enrage them. They would have a lot of questions that required explanation.

   Answer D: Incorrect. A little emotion is very important when someone's having a difficult time. If you speak with no compassion, you may very well upset someone even further than they already are.

Teamwork

If you've ever played a sport, been involved in a community project, or just done a lot of multi-person activities, you've probably heard the expression "being a team player." Being a team player, also known as teamwork, is difficult for a lot of people to master. It's hard for some people to understand that as a part of a team you are going to have to rely on team members for assistance and also provide team members with assistance and vital information in order to help them do their job as well as they can. In this scenario, I'm going to explore a situation involving teamwork and then explain why it is important to keep your commitments to a team and some of the benefits of working as a team.

Scenario

John, Billy, Catherine, and Alexandra have been working on a team project to create a document that more clearly outlines the procedures for long-term support issues that will require multiple personnel. While this project hasn't been officially condoned by management, all of the people involved with the project firmly believe that it's something that could advance all of their careers and impress upper management.

At their first meeting, John, Billy, Catherine, and Alexandra have all divided out their tasks equally and are anxious to get started. The team as a whole has decided that John will be responsible for the creation of the strategy, but Billy and Catherine will be the two individuals involved with bringing that strategy to life through written documents, illustrations, and charts. Lastly, Alexandra is the member of the team who is going to be responsible for presenting their new project to management when it is completed.

Since the project began two weeks ago, the original deadline has passed. At the first meeting, the team as a whole decided that they would have a five-stage deadline, each phase being done every two days. At first, John would brainstorm ideas, and then give them to Billy and Catherine, who would in turn prepare everything so that Alexandra could present them at the end of stage 5. Currently, the team is at this status:

- John has completed brainstorming.

- Billy and Catherine are 50 percent complete with their portion.

- Alexandra has arranged to meet with management this afternoon.

While Billy and Catherine are working as fast as they can to finish their material, Alexandra has received a call from their supervisor, who asks if they're still ready to have this meeting. Looking at her clock, Alexandra realizes that they won't be able to finish in time and then asks if there is a way they could extend it to next week. The supervisor agrees, but then says that he's rather busy next week and would appreciate more notice next time she has to move a meeting.

Background

You can safely say that at least 99 percent of all jobs in IT involve some sort of teamwork. It's very rare that you'll find the sort of "1980s" closet computer guy jobs that you heard of some 20 to 30 years ago. Now, IT has become a living and breathing part of the business environment. You're part of the team.

Therefore, it only makes sense that you need to know how to deal with the team that you are inevitably going to be a part of. If you're not willing to take my word for it, take a look at just about any job opening that you'll see on any of the major job or recruiting sites. On every one of them, you'll see two preferred qualifications: excellent communication skills and the ability to work well with a team. So, with this in mind, let's look at the explanation of this scenario with the mind-set that this is something that you truly have to understand to succeed in IT.

Overview

There are several very common issues presented here in this scenario. They are, in no particular order, as follows:

- Overambition

- Lack of coordination

- Procrastination

Each of the subjects is fairly complex, but they will be discussed in some detail in this section. Keep in mind that the goal of this scenario is to familiarize you with some of the issues that you'll encounter as a team in the real world. By familiarizing yourself with these concepts and seeing how they could be resolved, you will be more prepared for the challenges that await your future team in the office.

Key Concepts

In this section, I'm going to review the following three concepts and what they have to do with teamwork as a whole: goals, coordination, and scheduling. I'll return to the scenario by explaining how the problems experienced in this situation could have been avoided.

Goals

Every project has a goal. Some business managers and project managers go as far as to define goals, deliverables, and overarching hopes for development. The reason behind this is that projects, teamwork, and, for that matter, "work" in general aren't worth doing unless they produce results. In a business environment, our entire careers are based on this concept. It's what makes the world work. Unfortunately, many pitfalls can happen along the way when you're defining project goals. Some of these include:

- Unattainable goals
- Concentration on unimportant details
- Ineffective strategies

But problems with ambition are by no means limited to just these three concepts. When you find yourself involved with a brainstorming session, or a team that looks a bit overly ambitious, don't be afraid to put in your two cents. Honesty is always a good policy, but it's a good idea to frame your input. Don't be so honest that you're cruel, but don't be so overly positive that your point is convoluted.

Coordination

Every project needs to have a clearly defined structure that involves defining project leads, members, associates, and consultants. In this case, our team didn't define roles; instead, they simply assigned duties and hoped for the best. Whenever you're dealing with a competent team, be aware that individuals are going to have clearly defined goals and roles. Furthermore, there are going to be people who show how the roles interrelate. As far as teamwork is concerned, you should remember one thing before any other: Know your role and try not to go outside of it. Being a team player means you know how to play both for your team and in your team.

Scheduling

Scheduling is both the most important and most difficult part of dealing with team projects. Everyone wants to come in early and before a deadline, but often this isn't possible. As you begin your career in IT, you will find that the scheduling concerns you will have as a team member will mostly be demands. As you transition into management, you'll deal with this in a wholly different manner. What you once saw as demands will soon become goals. Regardless, scheduling is going to play an important role in your career.

Consequently, it's a good idea to take schedules and deadlines seriously. Don't put off until tomorrow what you can do today. If you do, you might place yourself into a situation where you could ultimately cost yourself a loss of reputation and possible advancement.

Resolution

This situation could have been easily avoided if John, Billy, Catherine, and Alexandra had remembered that the most important part of teamwork is communication and knowing that your team is going to follow through with what it said it would in the first place. If the four of them had sat down, decided who would lead the project, and had that person ensure that each stage of the project proceeded on time and uninterrupted, they could have avoided the embarrassment. Furthermore, the embarrassment could have been further avoided by determining early on that there was a problem with the project's deadline.

But, at the end of the day, the single greatest mistake that this team made was not communicating with one another. Projects cannot succeed without a team that communicates together well. Remember, when working as part of a team you should always keep your teammates aware of your status. Let people know if you're in trouble, let them know if you're doing well, but above all, just let them know that you're a part of the team.

Skills for the A+ Exam

Here is a good example of a type of question you would see on the A+ exam regarding assisting a coworker or teammate:

5. A coworker feels intimidated by the process of installing a new driver, but you know that it is the only way to fix his computer. What should you say to the coworker?

    A. It's OK, I know you don't understand. I'll talk you through it.

    B. If you would just listen, I could help you with this.

    C. Please pay close attention, because this will fix your computer easily.

    D. I know that this is a bit strange, but I also know you want to fix your computer. Would you like my help?

    Answer A: Incorrect. By saying, "I know you don't understand," you have succeeded in insulting your coworker.

    Answer B: Incorrect. Accusing someone is not a way to persuade them. Instead, you need to appeal to a concept someone would find to be positive.

    Answer C: Incorrect. This is close, but ultimately incorrect because you provided very little understanding for the coworker. You didn't take into account that he's intimidated by it and adjust accordingly.

    Answer D: Correct. By comforting the coworker and establishing trust, you could succeed in persuading him to let you help him.

Staying Appropriate

It's all too easy in the office to find yourself talking about things that you shouldn't. Most of the time, it simply happens out of boredom. You've been in your office for so long that you just feel like you are about to explode and you'd do anything to get away from the same old conversations about the same old work.

Naturally, this leads to topics that interest you. Something like football or baseball seems like a great choice when compared to status reports. Unfortunately, when we do this, some of the topics that we choose to speak of can be offensive to others. On top of that, there's no easy way to tell what might offend someone and what might not. In this scenario, I'm going to take a look at a conversation that starts off as a normal everyday conversation and then turns into an inappropriate topic. Then, I'll examine some of the fallout this conversation could have and discuss the reasons that you should guard against it in the first place.

Scenario

Martha and William are two employees in the desktop support department of a major oil company, and today has been a very dull day. Oddly enough, the reason for this has been that the rest of the company has been extraordinarily busy. Last week, a new superfield full of crude oil was discovered in some territory owned by their company, and the entire organization has been scrambling to get ready to capitalize on it. As a result, the standard users who would normally be doing their mundane tasks in Windows and Outlook have changed gears and have constantly been on the phone.

After about an hour of tedium, William finally leans back in his chair and says, "Man, what a dull day."

Martha smiles. "You're telling me; it's been hard to stay awake in the office. I kind of wish they'd just let us go home."

"Ha!" William laughs. "That would require them being reasonable. You better believe you can't count on that."

"Yeah, I suppose," she responds. "Did you do anything fun over the weekend?"

"Actually, I went to see the Bucs play and they won 10 to 0. It was pretty darn awesome. What made it even cooler is that the president was in the audience."

"Yuck, the president?" asks Martha.

"Yep, in the flesh. What's wrong with that?"

Martha smirks. "Other than the fact that he's a jerk? Nothing."

William stays quiet for a minute and then says, "Yeah, I know a lot of people think that. So did you have a good time over the weekend?"

"Eh," she shrugs, "I had a pretty good time. Some of my nephews came in for the weekend and we got to play with their new Xbox after church. Those things are so cool!"

"Boy, are they! I think I'm going to buy one myself. The trouble is they're so damn expensive. And you have to buy so many accessories just to enjoy the game. Microsoft makes such crappy products. What church do you go to?"

Background

You're bound to end up speaking about things other than work at the office. It's as common as paperwork, but it's potentially dangerous because people can be incredibly sensitive about a wide variety of topics. While something may just be a casual conversation to you, it could be deeply personal to another person.

Talking about topics unrelated to work is so prevalent in modern America that some companies simply do not allow anything that isn't directly work related to be discussed on campus. The thought behind this is that if nothing but work is discussed, the potential for conflicts and harassment suits is lowered. However, the percentage of companies implementing this policy is very low. Thus, it forces us to consider what can and cannot be said while we're working.

Overview

William and Martha have had the bad luck of picking the three most deadly topics in all casual conversation: sports, politics, and religion. Things are made even worse by the fact that a few casual opinions are thrown in there that could also be detrimental. In the next section, I'll discuss these "deadly three" and show why they can have such a negative impact on your work environment.

In the real world, most companies will have a short discussion with new employees about human resource policies as they concern interaction between employees. Some organizations will specify what topics are and are not appropriate in the office, but most will simply outline some general guidelines for not being offensive. But at the end of the day, it's up to you what you choose to discuss.

Key Concepts

To understand the impact that discussion can have on the workplace, I'll first discuss the deadly three: sports, politics, and religion. Afterward, I'll expand on this topic and you'll see how it's not just these three subjects that should be avoided. By the end of this section, you'll have a good idea of what to avoid.

Sports

Most people who are new to the working world are surprised when they see this topic flagged as a potentially dangerous discussion subject. After all, what could be more harmless than sports? However, before you begin to think that, let remind you of a situation I once was in the middle of with some average "extreme" football fans.

When I was visiting some relatives in Georgia, the air was thick with excitement as the battle of the century was going on in the realm of college sports. The undefeated Auburn Tigers from Alabama were set to prove their might against the home team, the Georgia Bulldogs. According to the announcers at the sports bar I was visiting, this was to be an extremely unfair match. The Auburn team was the strongest team they'd ever seen statistically and Georgia was having a record low year. Upon hearing this, the Auburn fans erupted with a cheer in the audience. Before

the game had even begun, the Georgia fans began to take offense at these cheers and started yelling expletives, urging the Auburn fans to be quiet.

The game turned out to be a marvel to watch, actually. In an upset that stunned the nation,
Georgia managed to defeat the incredible Auburn in a David-versus-Goliath sort of match.
While I'm not the biggest sports fan, I'm told it was quite a rare event. What I was keenly
aware of was how upset the Auburn fans became. They were screaming, crying, and angrily
hitting their tables, furious at their team for performing so poorly.

What this made me realize is that you shouldn't talk to someone about sports, because you
never know if they're a huge fan. Consider that saying something as harmless as "I like the Oilers"
may extremely anger someone who was a huge Oilers fan and was devastated when they moved
to Tennessee. If this doesn't make a lot of sense or seems irrational, I'm going to have to ask
you to take my word for it: Sports in the office is just not a good idea.

Politics

This one shouldn't be a huge surprise. Politics is the mother of a huge number of arguments. In fact,
it's something that is specifically designed to be argued about! Although, like everyone, I'm sure
you feel strongly about a lot of different political subjects, they should never, *ever* be discussed in
the office. The potential damage this can cause is just absolutely unimaginable, and in some cases,
it can even lead to termination if you are adamant enough. Be smart—avoid the topic.

Religion

Religion is a double-edged sword in the office. Many religions encourage their members to
spread the word of the religion. In fact, some denominations fund the spreading of their word
and arrange worldwide benefits to promote themselves. Unfortunately, this makes it the most
difficult of all subjects to discuss at the office. Although some religions may believe certain
ideas should be expressed, people may not want to hear those ideas.

Spiritual beliefs do not go over well in an office environment. People have different opinions on a lot of subjects, and while you may feel the need to discuss religion, some people will
be offended. I could go into exhaustive detail for you, outlining some of the world's religions
and then showing how much they contradict each other, but I encourage you to once again
take my word for it. As much as you may feel led to, do yourself a favor and save religion for
a time when you are not in service to someone else.

Other Dangerous Subjects

Unfortunately, the "deadly three" are not the only topics that should be avoided. A short, but
in no way complete, list of other dangerous topics includes:

- Jokes
- Sexuality
- Drinking
- Narcotics
- Crime

- Smoking
- Heritage

In total, there are hundreds of subjects that should be avoided at the office. What you should remember as an employee of an organization is that almost anything that isn't work related can potentially be interpreted incorrectly if you aren't careful. Guard your words wisely.

Resolution

The best way to avoid being exposed to any sort of potential for offense or misconduct in the office is to not discuss any non–work-related topics in the first place. What this means is that you shouldn't find yourself discussing any topic that you believe isn't 100 percent inoffensive. Unfortunately, other than work and weather, this is pretty hard to do. As a result, some of the best advice I can offer is a short statement that you can take to the bank: Business is business. Don't confuse your professional life with your personal one. If you guard yourself against exposure to these subjects in the first place, you'll be a lot better for it.

Skills for the A+ Exam

Here is a good example of a type of question you would see on interoffice communication on the A+ exam:

6. Identify THREE of the following SIX subjects as topics that are not appropriate for work:

   A. Politics

   B. NASCAR

   C. Tax information

   D. Harassment prevention

   E. Partying

   F. Promotion discussion

   Answer A: Correct. Politics are completely inappropriate for the office and can cause major damage to interoffice relationships.

   Answer B: Correct. NASCAR is a sport and is therefore not work appropriate.

   Answer C: Incorrect. Discussing tax information as it pertains to work is fine. However, discussing your wages and personal deductions should be avoided.

   Answer D: Incorrect. Harassment prevention is a good thing to discuss at the office and can lower the risk for exposure dramatically.

   Answer E: Correct. Your weekend activities should stay private and personal at all times in the office.

   Answer F: Incorrect. Promotions are a good thing to discuss at the office. However, they should be discussed in an appropriate manner. It's not a good idea to discuss who is and is not getting a promotion.

Apologizing

Even though it's something we learned to do at a very early age, apologizing is something that is difficult to learn to do in the workplace. In addition to being polite, we as professionals would like to appear to be genuinely professional and as free from flaws as possible. What makes this difficult is that the very nature of apologizing admits to fault. Therefore, it's important to understand when it is and is not appropriate to apologize at the office, as well as ways you can get around apologizing but still remain professional. In this scenario, you're going to read about Frank, who's an expert at apologies and knows how to handle both his customers and his coworkers expertly. While you read over the scenario, pay attention to some of the subtle things Frank says and does, because they will be expounded on later.

Scenario

Frank Thompson has been working as a security audit professional for a small natural gas company for over three years and he has just recently passed his A+ exam. Despite the fact that Frank was fairly familiar with security practices and procedures, he hasn't been the best at desktop support until recently. The reason behind this recently acquired knowledge is that the company is experiencing a difficult downtrend in available contracts and is looking to lay off several employees. Frank, understanding this, has decided to familiarize himself with the role of a support manager as well and has now begun taking phone calls for the support center in his office with the permission of the company.

Just as Frank is finishing up some of his reports on unauthorized attempts to access the "root" account on the Unix server from within the company, he receives a phone call from Steve, a coworker who is screaming mad that his computer doesn't seem to be sending or receiving e-mails. Immediately, Frank falls into line.

"OK, Steve. Wow, I'm sorry to hear that you're having so much trouble. Let me see what I can do to help. Could you please open up Outlook for me?"

"It's already open," says Steve, grumbling.

"OK, great," Frank responds. "Could you do me a favor and click the Send/Receive button at the top of Outlook? It should be on the second row by default."

After a couple seconds' hesitation, Steve sighs and says, "Well, there you go. That fixed it. What was wrong?"

Frank chuckles slightly and says, "Great! It looks like your computer isn't set to send or receive e-mails from the server automatically. To briefly explain it, your computer receives e-mails from another computer here in the office and has to be told to occasionally look for them on that other computer. If you'd like, I can help you set up your computer so you don't have to manually click that button."

"Wow, that'd be great," says Steve. "Let's do it."

Five to ten minutes later, after fixing Steve's computer to automatically receive e-mails, Frank receives a phone call from his boss, David. David says, "Frank, you forgot to run a ticket on that last call. Whenever you get done with a support question, you must document it. If you don't, we can't track what you've done."

Checking, Frank realizes that David is correct and he made a mistake. "Oh, OK," he says. "It looks like I did forget. I'll put a note on my desk so I don't forget from now on. OK?"

"Sure, that's fine," says David. "Good luck with the transition."

Background

What comes naturally to many people in the office is to simply apologize for everything. If you make a mistake, apologize. If you offend someone, apologize. However, this is not a good practice. If you are constantly apologizing, you seem to be constantly making mistakes. Furthermore, by apologizing you automatically place yourself in a lower position than the person you are apologizing to. In effect, it's basically saying that you have done something wrong that you need to make amends for and, consequently, you will need to go out of your way to do it.

This isn't a very good office practice, and in the real world you'll find that most people don't apologize overly much. If you're new to the workplace, don't be alarmed or discouraged, because it's perfectly normal. People are not trying to be rude; they are trying to protect themselves.

Overview

In this scenario, Frank is placed into two positions where he is given the opportunity to apologize. Notice, however, that he only takes advantage of one of these. Only in the case of the customer (coworker) with the problem does he actually make the effort to apologize. Although it might seem odd, the reasons he does this are actually very sound. First, the coworker is in a situation where he is upset and needs someone to blame. Therefore, apologizing that there's a problem doesn't really admit any fault with Frank; he just admits that there's a fault with the situation. Second, as callous as it may seem, Frank doesn't stand to lose anything by apologizing to the coworker. He did nothing wrong and, furthermore, he's trying to correct the situation.

However, in the case of the manager, Frank did not choose to apologize. Instead, he chose to show that he would correct his actions. In the section that follows, I'll diagnose his actions and then justify why they were the appropriate method to follow. By the end of this scenario, you should understand some of the basics of apologies at the office and when and when not to use them. As you begin your career, they will be useful in figuring out your role within your new company.

Key Concepts

Because it's important to understand the different roles that apologies can play within your organization, this section is divided into three parts: customers, coworkers, and managers. Each section contains a short description of things to consider about each of the roles. Finally, we'll analyze Frank's two decisions.

Customers

Never forget throughout the course of your entire career that customers are the backbone of your existence as an IT professional. If you don't have customers, you don't have a career. As a result, it's important to consider two things above anything else when it concerns them:

- The customer must be made to feel welcome.
- Your feelings are not as important as the customer's feelings.

This means that customers are basically given free rein and that you should make sure they have it. Normally, this means that you'll have a lot of apologizing to do for their situations. Not only does it make them happy, but it also keeps your ratings high and improves the look of the company.

Coworkers

Coworkers fall into two categories for IT professionals: customers and true coworkers. Remember, as an IT professional there is a strong chance that people who work for the same company as you are actually going to rely on you for service and evaluate your performance from a consumer's point of view. It's very important to make this distinction when you first start your position. If you do not make a distinction between the people you work *with* and the people you work *for*, you will have a hard time adjusting to the fact that people who you see as an equal are evaluating you.

In terms of the people you work for, you should treat them as customers and do whatever it takes to keep them happy—whether that means you apologize or not based on the situation is up to you, but I strongly urge you to always apologize for the situation they're in. Just like someone who you deal with in a call center or in a retail environment, they're going to be frustrated. An apology goes a long way.

However, concerning coworkers, it's about a 50-50 call. Remember, apologizing places you in an open position, so you need to weigh whether apologizing is worth it. If you've truly made an egregious mistake, apologize. If not, you'd be better off saying that you'll do better next time, or that you'll endeavor to change something they didn't like. It will guard you against reprimand and lecture, and it will also show them that you can learn to adapt.

Managers

If you can possibly avoid it, it's a good idea to never apologize to your manager. As I've already discussed, it makes you look like you truly made a mistake and it doesn't accomplish anything. In business, people don't care about feelings—they care about results. If you're sorry, that's great. If you can fix it, that's better. It sounds a little harsh, but it's true. Granted, there are many times when you'll make a mistake so large that you'll just *have* to apologize, but I'd advise only doing that if you strongly feel the need.

Remember this three-step path:

Admit to the fault.   "I can't believe I did that. What a silly mistake."

Say you will correct the mistake.   "Next time, I won't do that."

Follow through.   Don't make the mistake again.

Resolution

Frank's reactions to these situations are good to emulate. Frank did the following:

1. He made the customer feel better by apologizing.
2. He showed his boss that he would improve by not apologizing.

Unfortunately, the concept is easy, but the implementation is hard. As you progress in your career, you will encounter numerous situations where you'll feel awkward and wonder if you should apologize or not—and, truth be told, you'll probably make a couple of mistakes.

While we'd all like for everyone to just get along and understand that you're saying sorry for the sake of saying sorry, business makes life a little difficult for us. It's hard to balance being a successful businessperson with being a successful person as a whole. However, with a little practice you will catch onto it quickly. Good luck and, no pun intended, I'm sorry if it's a little hard at first.

Skills for the A+ Exam

Here is a good example of a type of question you would see on customer interaction on the A+ exam:

7. What is the FIRST thing you should do after a customer informs you of a support problem?

   A. Ask for a brief history of the changes she's made to her computer.

   B. Tell her that it will be OK.

   C. Apologize and ask if the problem has occurred before.

   D. Slightly chuckle and tell her you've seen this before.

   Answer A: Incorrect. This is a good question to ask, but not at the very beginning. This comes after you have apologized.

   Answer B: Incorrect. It's most likely that you don't know whether or not it is going to be OK.

   Answer C: Correct. Before you even begin to troubleshoot, you should apologize to her for the problem. It helps her demeanor and lets her know you care.

   Answer D: Incorrect. Chuckling or mocking a problem is not a good idea at all. It will most likely anger and upset the customer.

Summary

What you need to take away from this chapter is what I stated at the very beginning: Interoffice communication and communication between coworkers are the most important aspects of your career in business. Because of this, it's a good idea to look over these scenarios more than once. While some of it may seem fairly obvious to you, you can pick up a lot of intricacies. In fact, I suggest reading over one of these scenarios when you become a professional and try to put it into practice. Make a game out of it. Today could be your "slang" day, when you refused to use any unprofessional word. Or you could make it your gender-neutral language day, trying your best to avoid anything that could be misinterpreted. Granted, it's not as fun as playing Quake after hours in the computer lab, but unlike computer games, this can help your career!

Chapter 6

Leadership in IT

It is very likely that at some point in your career in information technology you will eventually be placed into a position of leadership where you are charged with the management of several of your peers and coworkers. This is one of the greatest benefits of belonging to an organization and will undoubtedly be the culmination of a lot of hard work and the potential for leadership. Therefore, it's important that you understand some of the fundamental principles of leadership and realize that it's not necessarily important for you to be "the boss," but it is important for you to be a leader. In this chapter, you will find seven scenarios demonstrating some of the most classic examples of good and bad leadership in a corporate environment and how certain behavior can permanently affect the opinion of personnel in the workplace. After studying this chapter, you should be able to understand and identify the following seven concepts listed in the scenarios and realize the result that each of the concepts will have on your work environment. While the situations covered in this chapter may not specifically be on the A+ exam, questions involving some of these concepts will come up, and these lessons will prove vital to your working career. Pay careful attention here, because you probably will see situations like these throughout your career.

Scenario 1: Authority
Scenario 2: Discipline
Scenario 3: Delegation
Scenario 4: Mentoring
Scenario 5: Fraternization
Scenario 6: Micromanagement
Scenario 7: Feedback

Authority

Theodore Roosevelt said it best when he was quoted in a speech in Binghamton, New York: "The leader holds his position purely because he is able to appeal to the conscience and to the reason of those who support him, and the boss holds his position because he appeals to fear of punishment and hope of reward. The leader works in the open, and the boss in covert. The leader leads, and the boss drives."

The point to take away from his wise words is that authority is not something that should be exercised because it is your right, but instead is something that should be utilized to instill a sense of purpose. In this scenario, we're going to look at a twofold situation where one person is leading first by threat of authority and then by creating purpose.

Method 1: Threat of Authority

Two new employees of a large organization, John and George, have quickly become fast friends and are enjoying their time in their new corporate environment. It is relaxed, friendly, and very well paid. In fact, they have begun to enjoy it so much that they have started to take excessively long lunches. While the company has no "official" lunch period, it is expected that someone should be able to comfortably eat a meal within the span of an hour. For the past week, John and George have been taking almost an hour and a half.

Today, John and George have come back from lunch after having been gone for over two hours. They were gone for so long that some of their coworkers actually began to express concern and commented that they feared there might be some sort of a problem or emergency.

Upon seeing them return to the office, John and George's boss Fred calls them into his office and asks them to shut the door. After asking them to take a seat, he calmly says the following:

"John, George, here at ComfyCorp we have a very clear policy when it concerns our lunch breaks. The common rule of thumb is that it is expected that employees take no more than an hour to leave, eat, and return. Today, you both have been gone over two hours and this is simply unacceptable. Because of this, I'm going to dock you one hour's pay, and if this happens again I am going to be forced to take more serious action. Do you understand?"

Key Concepts

By taking this approach, Fred will achieve his desired result in that John and George will most likely no longer take excessively long lunch breaks. However, this approach will also create two unfortunate side effects that Fred would not want if he knew that they were being created. These two side effects are resentment and negative aspiration.

Resentment

Resentment is one of those ugly words in society that implies multiple layers of discomfort, hatred, dissatisfaction, and an overwhelming desire to see a change from the norm. In this situation, Fred has created this in both of his employees and he may not even realize it. This is because every time an excessively harsh action or chastisement is made against an employee, the employee remembers it and adjusts their view of you as an employer accordingly.

If your employees believe that you are irrational or excessively harsh (as Fred was being in this situation), they won't like you as a person and probably won't work for you very long. This problem is best avoided by remembering that just because you have the capability to exercise your authority, it doesn't mean that you should. Instead, you should find a way to inform your employees of the wrong action that they have taken and then encourage them to take action to correct it.

Negative Aspiration

When people become resentful of a situation they're involved with, they usually try to find a way out of that situation. In professional environments, the process of people coming and going as they join and leave a company is referred to as *turnover*. Normally, a high turnover rate in a company indicates an unstable organization and can make the company look bad to people both internally and externally who are evaluating your business. Unfortunately, turnover is a slippery slope that tends to beget more turnover, creating an almost snowball-like effect.

If you were to sit down and ask a human resources specialist what they viewed as the primary cause of turnover you'd probably get several different answers, but a commonly recurring theme would involve people not being content with their position any longer and seeking greener pastures. This process is known as *negative aspiration.*

In management, not only are you challenged to lead the people who you are with, but you are also responsible for assuring that they are content with their position so that you can avoid such perils as turnover and negative aspiration in a corporate environment. There is no single way to ensure this, but a good practice is to check in on your employees and ask them to confide their feelings and beliefs to you, creating a sense of trust (which will be discussed more in the next scenario). This will not only let you know how they are feeling, but it will also make them aware that you are concerned about their situation and would like to see them prosper.

Method 2: Creating Purpose

In the same situation presented earlier in this scenario, our two employees (John and George) have come back from their lunch break excessively late and are assumed to be operating under the assumption that this sort of behavior is acceptable and normal. However, this time Fred takes a different approach.

After seeing John and George return, Fred stops by their cubicles and asks each of them if they have a few moments to talk. Casually, the three of them make their way into Fred's office, and Fred himself only partially closes the door and sits down on the front of his desk, remaining mostly standing. He then greets them with a smile and asks both of them how they're enjoying their time at the new company. Answering honestly, both John and George inform Fred that they're very happy with the new company and are looking forward to working with ComfyCorp over the next several years.

Once they've answered, Fred then says, "OK, that's fantastic. I just wanted to make sure that you guys were getting well adjusted. One of the things I try and do during people's first few months here is to make sure they have everything they need to succeed and understand some of the policies. The only one I think I should point out right now is that we like people to put in a full eight-hour day and so we allocate a lunch break of one hour. So it's really in your best interest to try and keep your lunches down to an hour. Once you've both started doing that, I think we'll start on a really good path toward advancing you into higher positions. Other than that, do you have any questions for me at this time?"

Key Concepts

By taking this approach, Fred both succeeds in his goals as an employer and creates two useful side effects in his employees: He informs the employees about the policy and layers a blanket of understanding on the situation.

Informs

Fred makes his employees aware of the situation and what is expected from them. Whenever you have to use your authority to let someone know that they are in violation of a policy, it's a good idea to make sure that they were aware of it in the first place. By creating purpose, you will succeed in letting your employees know what is expected of them. This way, they tend to correct the action themselves.

Understanding

No one should really be chastised for making a mistake once. The point to take away from this is that authority should be laced with a thin layer of understanding. You're not a total-itarian dictator; you're a manager. Furthermore, you're a manager who's probably been in their same situation before. By doing this, you'll make someone feel comforted that you aren't lecturing them—you're simply informing with a level of understanding that they wouldn't have expected.

Resolution

What you should take away from these two variations on the same scenario is a fairly simple concept. It boils down to the fact that you should try your best to not seem angry, judgmental, or something akin to a tyrant, simply because you aren't. As a supervisor, your authority is just the authority needed to keep the company running. Although that includes such privileges as hiring and firing, you should make sure that you don't view this as a license to loom over your employees, but instead, as a pass to be a reasonable manager.

Discipline

Depending on whom you ask, disciplining employees can be either your best asset or your worst enemy in a business environment. As was discussed earlier, discipline can build a great deal of resentment in employees, but in some cases discipline, or the fear thereof, can be the single driving force that holds an organization together.

In this section, you're going to examine a scenario in which a manager uses the author-itative power of discipline in several ways and then observe the effect that each of these actions had on the members of his team. You'll then take a look at some of the key tactics and rules for using discipline in a corporate environment and will be able to understand when discipline should and shouldn't be used, and the best way to enforce the rules that you create.

 Webster's dictionary defines discipline as training that corrects, molds, or perfects the mental faculties or moral character.

Scenario

At approximately six o'clock this morning, SolutiaCorp suffered from an attack by a malicious hacker. After browsing the internal contents of the website, the hacker gained access to the internal database and was able to retrieve extremely sensitive information, such as credit card numbers, customer social security information, and employee health benefits. Immediately after realizing that there had been a security breach, the IT department shut down the connection to the Internet and began a forensic investigation.

Later that morning, John Malcolm, the senior vice president in charge of personnel, came into the office and was made aware of the situation and given a formal report of the intrusion. The security team believes that the hacker was granted access to the network by negligence, either by someone from inside the company giving out a password or by an employee failing to realize they were with a packet sniffer that was able to evaluate encrypted messages sent outside of the company containing login information.

Concerned, John calls a meeting of his three top employees, James, Susan, and Sharon. James is responsible for the management of the help desk support team and has been with the company for only a few months. Susan, on the other hand, has been with the company for over 20 years and is in charge of quality assurance. Finally, Sharon is the head IT professional and the person primarily responsible for preventive maintenance to guard against the incident.

At this meeting, John declares that he expected higher audit performance out of his staff and expects them all to discipline their lower ranks accordingly for their lax security practices. He then leaves the room while making a call on his cell phone to the legal authorities to inform them of the situation. He is quickly followed by each of the three managers, who make their way back to their own departments.

Susan, the most senior employee, immediately makes her way to the watercooler in the center of her cubicle area and asks everyone to gather around. She then informs them of the situation and asks her team to remain calm but to be aware of some of the potential downfalls to insecure employee practices. To assure that her employees are made aware of the situation and all the factors involved, she orders each of them to draft a three- to four-page report on the subject, including a section on what they can do to improve security within the company.

Using a different method, James bursts into the help desk area and makes a furious hand gesture for everyone to place their phone calls on hold. After getting everyone's attention he then says that there has been a "serious screw-up" in security and that everyone needs to stay late today for an intensive meeting on the subject. He then turns and makes his way back to his office.

On the other side of the building, Sharon makes her way back to her office and thinks about the best way to inform her team. She decides that an e-mail would be a good idea and sends out a message saying that a security breach occurred and that all employees will now have to perform a series of security steps after each day's work before returning home; she will draft and deliver these steps tomorrow.

Background

Some of the important information to take from the background this scenario provides is who is involved and what level of competency they are expected to have. In this scenario, their qualifications breaks down into five parties (Table 6.1), each of whom has a different experience level and technical abilities.

TABLE 6.1   Employee Qualifications

Name	Rank	Experience	Technical Expertise
John	Senior vice president	Assumed to have the most	Unknown
James	Manager	Less than 6 months	High
Susan	Manager	Over 20 years	Low
Sharon	Manager	Unknown	High
Security Department	Employee	Unknown	Very High

Overview

In a situation like this, everyone is feeling pretty lousy. The company has been compromised, data have been lost, and there could be a lot of potential fallout from the incident. In the real world, Valve Software (the makers of the smash-hit video game "Half-Life") experienced an attack similar to this one and had their entire "Half-Life 2" video game's source code stolen before it was released. You can read about it here: http://news.com.com/2100-7349_3-5087698.html

When Gabe Newell, the managing director of Valve, reported on this incident to the world he noted that the event had crushed the morale at Valve, causing some to despair and fear that the company might be ultimately doomed to failure because of the incident. Fortunately for Valve, this did not turn out to be the case. However, there have been other cases in which companies have become so compromised that the name and reputation of the company were destroyed. So, with this in mind, let's assume the following temperaments are universal for the crew in this situation:

- Morale is low.
- The company is nervous as a whole.
- Individuals are afraid of further reprimand.

Key Concepts

Throughout this scenario different individuals used different leadership strategies to motivate and discipline their crew. Some of these tactics are highly effective, and some not so much. To understand the difference between the educated decisions and the uneducated ones, let's examine each employee's actions, in order, and determine the value of the decisions they made, not only as they pertain to discipline, but to leadership as a whole.

Security Team

The security team took one action in this scenario that concerns us:

Action 1: Informing Their Superiors

As was referenced in earlier chapters, this is a perfectly logical action to take. If you find yourself in a security position later in your career, you'll learn that each company maintains a security policy that dictates how security issues should be handled at the corporate level. Normally, a company's security policy will say what can and cannot be done, along with what should and should not be done, in a situation such as in this scenario. Chances are that these employees didn't take any further action, so they have at this point ceased to be players in the scenario.

John

John took two actions that concern us in this scenario: he met with the managers and then disciplined them, as you will see below.

Action 1: Meeting with the Managers

John started off on the right foot here. The chain of command flows in both directions, and it's a good idea when you're in a leadership position within a corporate environment to inform those who directly report to you. This way, you can entrust those who are closest to you with maintaining the discipline and structure of the organization, areas with which you are not normally involved. If John didn't utilize this ability, he would have to make several speeches as he moved from one department to another, tailoring different aspects of his speech to make sure that it applied directly to them. This would not only be a waste of John's time, but it probably wouldn't go over as well either. People like to hear grim messages from people they know and trust, not a person in management who is, in their minds, similar to the invisible man.

Action 2: Disciplining the Managers

At this point, John made a mistake. Although John did try to invoke some form of discipline with his managers, he was far too lackadaisical in doing so. In effect, all John did was the equivalent of scolding a child and saying, "I'm so disappointed in you." Professionals don't respond well to this type of discipline, and it can result in a small amount of resentment in some cases. Instead, in this case John should have disciplined his team by not only informing them of the problem, but also by suggesting ways that they could fix it and informing them of the potential fallbacks of not doing so. By enlightening his top managers of something they may need to know, he could cause a ripple effect that would trickle down to the lower rungs of the company and potentially cause even the newest employee to guard against such actions in the first place.

Susan

Susan's discipline strategy is similar to John's in that Susan took two very similar actions. She met with her team and then disciplined them. However, her methods were quite different.

Action 1: Calling a Meeting

Again, this is a good move. Just like her superior, she was able to call her team to one location and inform them all at the same time. Where she slightly differs from John is that she did this in an informal location, and that isn't an advisable practice. By disciplining a team in an informal environment, Susan may have inadvertently caused herself to be viewed as unapproachable by her employees. Disciplining from an informal location, such as the watercooler, can make you as a superior seem like someone who is at all times unapproachable, even in informal settings. It's the same reason that the military, business, and even academia have a dedicated place to hold meetings and discipline. That way, if you're in the "business area," you'll feel as if you're conducting business. If you're in a more relaxed area, you'll feel as if you can relax. And just as children will avoid the principal's office like the plague, employees will also avoid locations that they view as negative areas.

Action 2: Disciplining the Team

Susan performed this part admirably. She not only chose a punishment that would be difficult for the employees, but also crafted it in such a way that it will prove a valuable learning tool to both them and the company, potentially even informing her of other security situations she is unaware of. Nice job, Susan.

James

James made two crucial mistakes that we need to mention. First, he lost his cool, and second, he made working similar to a punishment.

Action 1: Losing His Cool

There is no single faster way to be viewed as a tyrannical disciplinarian than to lose your temper and scream at your crew. By doing this, James both intimidated several people and succeeded in creating an image of himself as a manager who is susceptible to temper tantrums and is highly immature. At all costs, avoid being emotional when you deal with your team—it can hurt your reputation.

Action 2: Making Work a Punishment

The best companies have been undone by this concept. Work is supposed to be work; it is not supposed to be a punishment. If you have to stay late at the office, it should be because something needs to get accomplished. Under no circumstances should you make someone "have to stay late" because you think they deserve it. It may sound harsh, but work isn't kindergarten. If you make work seem like a punishment, people will respond negatively—most likely by finding another place to work!

Sharon

Just like James, Sharon made some serious mistakes. First, she didn't call a meeting. And second, she chose a bad medium to discuss the situation. Lastly, she presented a half-cocked idea to her team formally.

Action 1: Not Calling a Meeting

Unlike the rest of her coworkers, Sharon decided not to call a meeting. From what we've discussed so far, this obviously wasn't a good idea, because she has almost completely removed herself from any personal ties to the event. This is especially illogical because she is essentially the person directly in charge of the area that was exposed. As a leader, there are going to be good times and there are going to be bad times. For Sharon, this is one of those bad times. The best thing she can do at this point is face the facts, treat the situation for what it is, and face her crew with the bad news. Not doing so will lose her a slight amount of reputation (as people believe she is embarrassed), and it could also potentially cause a great deal of paranoia as employees wonder how their manager feels on a subject.

Action 2: Choosing a Bad Medium

When something has gone wrong, it's never a good idea to notify people via an e-mail. E-mail is an impersonal communication method that is designed to deliver facts, reports, and information. It is not a device that is well suited to informing people of potentially serious problems or, worse yet, disciplinary issues. Imagine for a moment being an employee who is suddenly told that she is going to be demoted via an e-mail. It would not only be crushing to hear, but it would almost be insulting that someone didn't have the courtesy to tell her to her face. The same idea applies here. When delivering discipline, always do it in person.

Action 3: Presenting a Half-Cocked Idea

There are no such things as half measures in discipline. As the wise Jedi master Yoda once said, "Do or do not. There is no try." If you have to make a disciplinary action, you *must* make a decision and stick by that decision. Telling someone that a punishment "is coming" or "will be thought about" is not only cruel, but it also allows them to imagine far worse things than what you will do. It's also highly ineffective. It indicates to an employee that you are concerned about the problem, but not concerned enough to take a true action and are instead disciplining based on the fact that you believe it just "needs to be done," and not that it *should* be done.

Resolution

Tactic 1: Discipline in Person

Whenever you're dealing with an employee who needs to be disciplined, you should always do it in person. Call a meeting, schedule a time to talk in your office, or go out for a walk and grab some coffee, but do it to their face. By doing this, you will show them that you are a real person and that you have opinions, and you will also enforce that you are their superior and someone who is taking an active role in the leadership of your team. People almost always respond well to this method, even if they don't like being disciplined.

Tactic 2: Create a Fair and Effective Punishment

Punishments in the workplace are not designed to be labors that make you toil or suffer. They are designed to encourage good behavior and create a more positive work environment. Whenever you are punishing an employee, do it in a constructive manner and plan accordingly. If you approach someone with a punishment that is ineffective, tedious, or simply half-designed, employees will sense it and it will decrease morale. If all else fails, remember the words of Cicero: "The punishment shall fit the offense." It's almost always a good rule to live by.

Delegation

In any company's organizational structure, some positions will have certain authorities over others. Managers can watch over supervisors who could watch over shift leaders who can in turn watch over associates. Some larger companies can have huge corporate divisions that are broken up by department, branch, and even national divisions. Some companies, such as Exxon-Mobil, are so very large that they literally have thousands of managers who delegate their authority to tens of thousands of others.

In management, it's especially important that you understand what it is that you can and cannot delegate to other employees. In this scenario, I'll take a look a situation where a manager finds himself involved with a complex situation and decides to delegate his authority to several of his employees. Then, you'll see the logic that went behind the decision and whether or not it's a good idea, so you'll be ready when you find yourself in a position of authority after passing your A+ exam.

Scenario

Jim Thornton is an employee at a local retail computer store and has just been promoted to supervisor after passing his A+ exam. Having very little management experience, Jim is anxious to make a good impression with the store owner and has decided that he'd like to accomplish four tasks: reorganize the inventory, thoroughly clean the store, put out new sales tags, and then rearrange some of the marketing displays to better suit impulse buying.

Eager to start this process, Jim calls an employee meeting at the beginning of his first day and begins to go down his list of tasks. Unfortunately, Jim only has two employees at this early shift in the morning, so there will be more tasks than there are people. However, Jim has a plan.

At the meeting, he states to his two employees, Tom and Gina, that he will be assigning them duties based on their level of experience. Because Tom is the more tenured employee, he will be responsible for cleaning the store and putting out sales tags. Gina, on the other hand, will only be responsible for reorganizing inventory in the back room.

While his two employees are working on those tasks, Jim decides that he would be best suited to examining the layout of the store and experimenting with new customer layout ideas. This is not only a useful activity, but it is also the most enjoyable to Jim.

A few minutes later, Jim is surprised to see that he has already finished reorganizing the store layout while Tom and Gina are still working. Since he sees that they are busy working, Jim decides to take a break and makes his way down to the local pastry shop and gets a bagel. After returning to work, Jim discovers that Gina has now finished her work and is sitting down in the back room. Thinking this is OK because her work is done, Jeff allows this to continue.

Several hours later, Tom finally finishes the very heavy tasks of cleaning the entire store and putting out several hundred new sales tags. Exhausted, Tom starts to go to take a break when a customer interrupts him with a question. Tom then tells the customer that Jim is actually the manager and might be able to help better than he could. Jim, obviously seeing that this is just a trick for Tom to get out of work, quickly responds by saying, "No, that's OK, Tom. You can help him."

Background

The experience level of the individuals involved is fairly clear, but the most important point to note about the information we are given regarding these three individuals is that there is something that we are *not* told. We are not told whether Tom is more experienced than Jim.

Personnel are often placed in leadership positions above workers who have been with the company longer. It's one of those unfortunate facts of the business world that can cause a lot of grief and turmoil, but it is nonetheless something that you will regularly encounter in your career. Since this is the case and it doesn't have a tremendous effect on the outcome of this scenario, we can go ahead and assume for our purposes that Tom is the most senior employee, followed by Jim and ending with Gina (see Figure 6.1).

FIGURE 6.1   The experience hierarchy

Tom > Jim > Gina

Overview

This situation is particularly interesting for several reasons. The range of emotions, feelings, and interpretations varies widely and is different for each person. First, Jim is obviously feeling ambitious and anxious as he tries to make a good impression and prove himself as a solid member of the team. Second, Tom is most likely frustrated that he has a junior employee over him. Furthermore, he's probably quite angry at having to do such trivial work. Finally, Gina is most likely very uncomfortable when she sees Tom's reactions to the work and notices that Jim is unaware of those reactions. The workplace tension is very high and will probably only be eased by time and the resolution of the current leadership strategies being used. Let's explore those strategies and see if you can improve upon them.

Key Concepts

Delegation is a difficult concept for anyone to understand who isn't familiar with it or who hasn't had a great deal of experience with it. This is because it's a tactic that absolutely requires someone to understand how most people react to a task and when and where it is best to use said tactics. Although mastering delegation takes years of experience, you can easily take a look at Jim in this scenario and understand some of the mistakes that he made. This will help you avoid some of the primary pitfalls that most new leaders fall into and place you on the right track to becoming a successful manager.

Be careful when delegating trivial tasks. Workers who are assigned trivial work tend to have lower morale and can be easily angered.

Jim's Mistakes

Mistake 1: Expecting Too Much Too Soon

Jim's first mistake was ultimately fatal in that he expected far too much of himself far too soon. Although we all may want to become great speakers and leaders like Winston Churchill and Theodore Roosevelt, it doesn't happen instantly and it takes a lot of practice. As a manager or supervisor, you should always approach a new job position with the following question: "What do I expect my reasonable output to be?"

This is a very different question than "What would I like my output to be?" or "What is my goal?" The time for goals as a manager comes later. Once you've established yourself and gotten a feel for your organization, you can carve a niche for yourself that is well suited to your capabilities. And once you've done that, you can set another goal for yourself that is even higher. Just be careful not to expect to change the world overnight.

Mistake 2: Not Following Previous Procedure

After deciding to do much more than the previous manager had done, Jim placed himself in a losing position: Not only was he new to his position, but he was also trying a new approach. Unfortunately for Jim, that's almost impossible to do. The people you are with simply aren't familiar enough with you, as a new supervisor, to do what you expect of them. Simply put, they just don't trust you. Trust and confidence take time to inspire in a team, and the best way you can establish this is by looking at what has been previously done in an organization and following that process by the book for the first few days. After you've done that, not only will you be more familiar with the process, but the team will also be more familiar with you.

Mistake 3: Ignoring Seniority in Delegation

This action is probably Jim's single biggest mistake. Imagine, for a moment, Tom's perspective. You've been working at the same company for years and been doing pretty well. Suddenly, some young pup that just got hired got some fancy certification and now he's suddenly in charge of you, even though you know more about the subject and more about the company.

Needless to say, you're already a bit bitter. But now, things are even worse. Not only is the young pup bossing you around, he's making you do meaningless work. With the old manager, you never would have had to do anything like this. In fact, when you started with the company, the new manager actually had to clean the store himself. But the icing on the cake is that after you've done all the work without complaint, he has the audacity not to let you take a five-minute break and refuses to handle a customer for you. What a jerk.

If you remember nothing else from this section, remember this: Seniority is important. When someone on your team has been there a long time, treat them like it. They're not only a valuable source of information, but they're probably your *most* skilled worker (or, if not most skilled, certainly the most experienced). As a team leader, you need to understand the gifts each member of your team has and then capitalize on them. With very few exceptions, this is one of those assets that you can take to the bank.

Resolution

There are two tactics you can take when you are delegating to a team. First, you should do it in phases and, second, you should try your best to instill confidence as you do so.

Tactic 1: Take a Phased Approach

If Jim wants to be an effective new leader, he needs to take the three-phase approach illustrated in Table 6.2.

TABLE 6.2   Phased Implementation

1. New Management Strategy	2. Create Goals	3. Implement Your Plan
Establish yourself.	Define realistic and reachable goals for yourself.	Begin to realize your plan in a step-by-step fashion.
Understand your company, your people, and your goals.		
1–2 weeks	1 week	4+ weeks

By doing this, you create a system that is sure to produce results. In management, slow and steady wins the race.

Tactic 2: Instill Confidence

While implementing his three-phase strategy, Jim could begin to conduct several confidence and team-building exercises with his employees. While there is no one specific method for this, his team needs to be armed with some information that assures them that Jim both knows what he is doing and can lead the team to higher goals. Once he is sure they have seen this, he can begin to let his true vision for the company come to life.

Mentoring

Mentoring is a leadership practice that can serve you both as a leader and as an employee. The idea behind mentoring is that someone with much more experience in a field will begin to advise and counsel someone with less experience in order to enhance their capabilities and improve production as a whole.

Up until the past couple of centuries, almost all business was trade based, and this was the main system for training. If someone wished to become a blacksmith or a tailor, they'd become an apprentice to their master (mentor). While under the tutelage of this mentor, they would be paid a fair wage and taught the trade.

In modern business, this concept has changed in that people don't stay permanently attached to their mentors, but they certainly still require their advice and skill. The purpose of this scenario is to demonstrate some good managerial mentoring practices and how they can be used to enhance the quality of your team. Additionally, this scenario will show you how you can mistakenly upset people with your mentoring if you are not careful. By the end of this section, you should feel confident enough to identify mentorship when it is being given and understand its value in the workplace.

Scenario

Joshua Jameson has just begun his new position at the SuperComp tech support department today and he could not be more overwhelmed. Today, he has had to examine his company benefits, respond to already in-progress customer support calls, get to know his fellow employees, and also start to get to know his boss.

The day had started out on the wrong foot in that he'd woken up too late and had to rush to work. But now he's in a situation where he's totally lost and doesn't have any idea how to catch back up on the work that he has to do for the remainder of the day without staying until midnight. In his opinion, beginner's hazing is all right to an extent, but his situation is a little ridiculous.

Another employee at SuperComp is Catherine Darling. Catherine isn't in the same department as Josh, but she knows his business. Just like him, she started out as a Level 1 technician and worked her way up to her present position of a Level 3 Critical Support technician. While on her way to get a drink of water, Catherine makes her way past Josh's cubicle and observes him wrestling with some paperwork. She also notices that his phone is ringing and that he seems to have e-mails going off constantly in his inbox, indicating tickets that are already running.

Because she's been in that situation before, Catherine sits down at her own cubicle after getting a glass of water and opens up some of the tickets that Josh has remaining in the public queue. Without asking, she opens up some of the tickets and processes the more difficult ones for a Level 1 employee and then sets a "FLAG" on his phone line to busy, so he doesn't end up getting more calls.

Afterward, Catherine makes her way out of her cubicle and toward Josh's office, where he is still shuffling with his paperwork. Calmly, she speaks up and says, "Wow, you look busy."

Josh looks up frantically from the paperwork and says, "Oh yeah. Honestly? I'm completely lost."

Catherine kindly smiles and replies, "Sure, I was that way when I started too. Let me give you a hand."

For the next few weeks, Catherine begins the process of transitioning Josh into the company. She explains some of the nuances of their system, introduces him to new people, and gives him advice on his training homework. Quickly, the two of them become fast friends.

Background

One of the givens of this scenario is that Catherine has been in the company for a long time and that Josh has just recently joined the crew. Normally, this is the main prerequisite for creating a mentoring-style partnership. However, something that we should note is that while Catherine has certainly been with the *company* longer than Josh, nothing was mentioned about the amount of time that either of them have been in IT in general.

This is important to point out because mentoring doesn't necessarily always take place as a more experienced person takes on a less experienced person. There are often cases where someone with less experience will show a senior partner various aspects of the company they may not be aware of. For the sake of this scenario, however, we will assume that this is a purely perfect world–style mentorship and that Catherine has both more experience in IT and more experience with the company.

Overview

Situations like this happen in the real world every day. From the lowest to highest position on the company totem pole, everybody gets help from time to time. The best real-world example of when this occurs is in the changing of a large company's leadership. A case in point is Microsoft Corporation and Bill Gates.

Bill Gates served as the chairman and front man of Microsoft until he ultimately decided to end his career as the leading role in 2008. Obviously, his impact on the world was extreme and there have been very few businesspeople to equal his capabilities. However, because he isn't immortal, he had to leave his company in the hands of individuals who he viewed as not only capable but as people with whom the stockholders would feel confident. Because of this, he announced in 2006 that he would be mentoring two leaders to take his place: Ray Ozzie and Craig Mundie.

In doing this, Gates claimed that he not only would take them directly under his wing to show them the way he did business, but would also make sure that they were armed with the goals and values that he had set for Microsoft. Consequently, stockholders felt confident that Ozzie and Mundie could lead them to a positive future. As you review this scenario, you'll see how Catherine accomplished a similar role for Josh, taking him under her wing and transitioning him into a benefit to the company. Furthermore, the following section will explain some of the best tactics and approaches to use when fostering a mentoring relationship.

Key Concepts

 Mentor: A trusted teacher, counselor, friend, and guardian.

Guide, Don't Lecture

Whether you find yourself in the role of a mentor or a trainee, try to remember that your purpose (or your mentor's purpose) is to guide. It isn't to lecture. To succeed as a mentor, you have to understand that people generally don't respond well to someone who just gives them information. They respond well to someone who shows them a proper path.

A mentor is someone who involves him- or herself. The actual definition of a mentor is a trusted teacher, counselor, friend, and guardian. More than being someone who just teaches, a mentor is someone who cares about another person. They teach by giving examples and handling day-to-day challenges with their trainee until they feel that the trainee is up to the task.

Be a Friend, Not a Boss

Catherine and Josh don't have a relationship or situation in which Catherine can tell Josh what to do. Although she is a more experienced technician, she's not a supervisor and she has no authority over Josh. Instead, their relationship depends on friendship and mutual acquaintance. Once you step over the line of being a mentor to a trainee, you evolve into being more than a mentor. You're a superior.

However, it should be noted that sometimes mentors can be individuals in positions of authority. Although it is rare, some companies still to this day use a mentor/trainee relationship in which a senior supervisor fosters a younger employee in order to help them understand what they need to do to succeed in a company. In this case, the mentor becomes something more similar to the master in a master/apprentice relationship. They both shape you into what they want you to be *and* they call the shots.

Pay It Forward

After you've taken someone in and shown them the ropes at your company, it's a good idea to let them know that they're capable of doing the same thing with other people. Letting someone know that they're ready to mentor their own newly arrived trainees is a good way to show them that you've officially "passed the baton." They're no longer being mentored. They're mentoring!

This also has the added benefit of creating an environment within a company that reflects on the quality of personnel. It's a neat experience to walk into a company and say, "X was trained by Y, who was trained by Z, who was trained by Q." Not only does everyone know each other, but it also feels as if everyone has been in the same position. It feels good to be in a tried and true environment.

Resolution

Whenever you decide to foster someone as a mentor, you should do it in a four-stage process: evaluation, initiation, offering, and finally mentoring. It's a system that has been used many times in the past and is almost certain to achieve results for someone who both wants to be mentored and would respond well to it.

Stage 1: Evaluation

The very first thing Catherine did when she began to think about fostering a mentor relationship with Josh was evaluate his current conditions. Before she even begin to analyze, she had a bit of information:

- He was a new employee.
- This was his first day.

These two pieces of information alone are the single greatest clue that mentorship may be needed. However, there are some cases where people are new to their position on their first day and may have been in the business for a long period of time. Therefore, it's a good idea to accompany the evaluation period with a short amount of observation.

In this scenario, Catherine both observed Josh's behavior and examined his workload. Only after she'd both determined that he seemed to be overwhelmed and *confirmed* that he was did she intercede. This is a good rule to practice because if it isn't followed you can end up dispensing a lot of unnecessary advice that can get you into trouble. People resent being told things that they already know when they don't feel that they need to hear it.

Stage 2: Initiation

At this point, initial contact with the individual needing mentorship is begun. There are several ways to go about it, but usually just talking and asking leading questions helps. Leading questions are open-ended questions that probe for more information, such as:

- "So, are you enjoying the company?"
- "What does your workload look like?"
- "What do you think so far?"
- "How are you coming along with that project?"

If someone generally desires mentorship, they will normally respond by stating that they are lost, confused, or uncertain of a specific aspect of company policy. Depending on how much they are confused, they might just ask for help, but this isn't very common. Normally, it will be up to you to judge the person's response to your leading questions and determine if they genuinely need advice. If so, it's safe to proceed to the third sage: offering.

Stage 3: Offering

Offering is as simple as the name implies. When you are offering someone help, you are saying that you want to be of service to that person. You're opening up the doors of your knowledge and saying, "I've done this before and I'm willing to help you get through it."

Sometimes, this offer will be met with genuine acceptance, as was the case with Josh and Catherine. However, sometimes it will be met with resistance. This doesn't mean that the potential for a mentoring relationship is gone, but it does mean that someone is not at a psychological point where they feel they need help.

The most important thing to remember about this stage is to respect someone's boundaries and offer genuinely. Just go forward, plainly say that you can assist, and then see if your assistance is accepted. You shouldn't pressure someone into feeling that they must accept your help or back them into a corner. Instead, you should listen to their response and see if they feel inclined to accept. If they do, you can begin to mentor them. If not, you should respect their wishes and continue with your day-to-day affairs.

Stage 4: Mentoring

Once you've begun to mentor, there is no clear and set path. Mentoring techniques vary wildly and can run deep in terms of complexity. Remember a few golden rules: You're a friend, not a superior; try not to lecture; and always make sure that you're as positive as possible. If you feel lost along the way, try to remember that as lost as you may feel, the person you are mentoring is even worse off. This tends to help a lot.

Also, don't feel worried if you make mistakes. Everyone does. Instead, try your best to learn from your mistakes and remember that you will probably have a chance to mentor someone again if things go badly. Most people find themselves mentoring dozens of people throughout their IT career.

If you get lost and you've been mentored before, you can always go back to the person who taught you and ask them for help.

Fraternization

When most people here the word *fraternization*, the first thought that comes to mind is a scene from a college party, but that couldn't be further from the truth. To *fraternize* essentially means to associate with, or to call yourself friends with. In the workplace, fraternization occurs very frequently as coworkers have office parties or formal social events, or simply go out for a drink after work.

Fraternization is usually a beneficial activity for coworkers, and it is also a lot of fun. As a leader, you'll be placed in dozens of situations where you'll have the opportunity to fraternize with those beneath you in an organization. Employees will try to invite you to their homes or introduce you to their friends, or they might even simply ask you to go to a party. On the surface, this may seem like a harmless activity. But the truth is that fraternization with your employees can have a negative impact on your position as a leader. Let's consider a scenario involving a leader who has a well-organized team and chooses to fraternize with them. After the scenario, we'll explore the emotions of all the individuals involved and then outline some of the most important points to take away from the scenario and how you can resolve to correct yourself from falling into a similar situation.

Scenario

Suzie Andrews is the lead desktop support manager for the IT department of a medium-size business and has been working in her position for over seven years. During that time, Suzie has actively engaged in the hiring, firing, and training of her team in order to create a well-organized and balanced crew that works together very well.

This past year, Suzie's team's numbers were at an all-time high, and the president of the company sent her a personal note indicating how satisfied he was with her performance. In addition, he guaranteed Suzie that if she kept up her current high levels of performance she would be considered for a place in upper-level management within the company, possibly even as an executive.

Having just heard the news yesterday, Suzie walks into the office that morning in an extremely chipper mood, ready to face any challenges that await her. As she arrives, her team has gathered around for the daily tradition of early morning coffee and doughnuts. Hungry herself, Suzie grabs a doughnut and then delivers the news of the team's wonderful job and the possibility of a promotion and is met with great applause.

Later that day, Jim, a fellow coworker, approaches Suzie personally in her office and tells her that he'd like to celebrate by having a drink with her and the team after work. Thrilled by the idea, Suzie agrees and then plans her day to end fairly early in order to go out with the team to enjoy herself. It's been a long time since she's gotten to catch up with friends.

As they begin to leave the office, the team assembles outside the office building and asks who'd like to go. Almost everyone agrees to go, except for Sharon, who says that she doesn't feel up to going out for a drink and would rather get some sleep. Not put off by this, the rest of the team heads out to Barney's, their favorite local bar.

At the bar, things get a little wild. The new guy, Dan, has a few too many and begins to flirt with every woman at the company, starting with Suzie. Thinking it's pretty funny and taking it in stride, she tells him she's not interested and Dan moves on to the next person. Jim, on the other hand, becomes almost dead silent as he continues to drink himself into an almost silent stupor and admits later that he has to call a cab. All in all, it is a fun night and Suzie has a great time.

The next day, Suzie finds that the temperament of most people in the office doesn't seem right. Everyone is excessively quiet and seems to be avoiding her. Unsure why, she continues her tasks as normal, but the numbers for the IT department that week are their lowest ever. The next week isn't much better and things almost seem to be getting worse as people have ceased to communicate and are in some cases acting much lazier than they used to. And no matter what Suzie tries, she can't seem to rally anyone and is at a complete loss as to why.

Background

For the purposes of this scenario, the actual positions that Suzie's employees hold are not highly important; what is important is that the scenario indicates that Suzie has been in charge of the team for a long period of time—seven years. This means that Suzie is intimately familiar with the company and the people she works with. Also, we have to assume that Suzie has never gone out with her coworkers in a social situation like that before. While it's likely that they've been to company picnics and social events, what they were participating in during this scenario is a completely different thing. The last item you need to know about is that Dan, the "new guy," is someone who signed on with the company less than a week ago and is fairly new to the entire process.

Overview

For thousands of years militaries of all nations have had a common rule between them that simply states, "Officers are forbidden from fraternizing with members of lower rank." Their reason for this is that the military is put in life-threatening situations where an enlisted person could consider someone as more of a friend than as their commanding officer. This means that a soldier might think that they could disobey an order during an exercise or, worse, during combat, because an officer would allow them special treatment and exceptions.

In the business world, a similar theme exists, but with much more complicated reasons behind it. Business doesn't exist in such a clear patterned, structured, life-or-death situation as does the military. It is a living and breathing entity that adapts and adjusts itself based on the current situation But this doesn't mean that fraternization couldn't still ruin a team's organizational structure, because it certainly can, as you will see in a moment.

Key Concepts

Each of the individuals in this scenario was affected very differently by this situation. Some of these effects you may have been able to predict, but you should look through each individual's perspective so that you can better understand some of the views that people different from yourself may hold. By the end of this section, you'll get a good idea of how dramatically fraternization can affect an entire team.

Sharon

Sharon has a unique perspective in this situation because she is the single person in the team who decided not to go out. You might be asking yourself, "Why does she matter? She didn't come." And it's a very valid question. The reason it matters is because you have to think about *why* Sharon didn't go.

Think about earlier in the scenario when Suzie first learned that the team had done well and that she had possibly earned a promotion. She didn't just say that the team had done well, she also succeeded in telling her team that they had done well and she was going to gain because of it. It is entirely possible that Sharon may not have appreciated this.

Consider that we don't know from the scenario how long Sharon had been working at the company or what her relationship with Suzie is. Because she discussed her own potential promotion with the members of her team, she may very well have alienated one of them. From Sharon's perspective, not only does Suzie make more money and have more authority than she does, but she's going to be making even *more* money now and be even higher ranked!

For this reason, details about your own personal job situation should be kept to yourself and not shared with those beneath you. If you've had a recent success, a nice bonus, or a raise, it's not something you should tell the office about. If you're in charge of a team, you certainly shouldn't tell your entire team. The only exception to this rule is if the bonus, raise, or other promotional program is so public that everyone is aware of your progress. This way, it can be viewed as a team incentive. Otherwise, you're just rubbing your success into the faces of those less successful than you.

Jim

Think about Jim's situation for a minute. Could there have been a reason he asked Suzie to come to the party? Is it possible that he might have seen a way to take advantage of the fact that Suzie was becoming more successful? It certainly is.

Furthermore, it's reasonable to assume some other things. There's a possibility that the invitation was not platonic. Jim could very well have been attracted to Suzie and wanted to see her socially with his friends. In this case, Jim could be opening up Suzie to a liability that she wasn't aware of. Office romances or advances are never a good idea.

On a nontheoretical level, a lot of questionable actions are going on here. Most specifically, consider Jim's heavy drinking. Although there's certainly nothing "wrong" or illegal about it (assuming he was of age), drinking in excess could have seriously embarrassed Jim. He might have a serious problem with drinking and just now exposed it to his fellow coworkers. In fact, he may believe that Suzie, who happens to be his boss, now has some information that she can use to blackmail him with if he starts to become slothful at work. All in all, he's not in a good state.

Dan

Dan is in the worst situation of anyone here. Not only is he new, but he also made a complete fool of himself at the party. He didn't just get silly and ask a few random women out on a date—he asked out his boss. In his opinion, his boss now knows that he is attracted to her and would like to date her. Consider how that has to affect his work.

Now, whenever he walks by or glance at her, he'll wonder if she's going to view it as a sexual advance. It's not fair to him, but the workplace rules place almost all the authority on Suzie's shoulders concerning harassment policies. From now on, he's going to have to be constantly on guard. That's no way to have to live or work.

Suzie

Suzie has been affected by the situation more than anybody. While her intentions were purely innocent, she has crossed the line between being a friend and being a boss. That's a line that should never be crossed. What's even more difficult for her is that she has no way of knowing that. Most people don't just walk up and *tell* you what their problem is; they let it eat away at them.

Now, instead of heading toward the fast track, Suzie's department is heading toward the gutter. The reason? Because she decided to go have some fun with a few friends from work and things turned bad.

Resolution

The best way to avoid a problem with fraternization is by not fraternizing in the first place. Remember the following few rules.

Rule 1: You're Their Superior, Not Their Friend

Never forget that there is a big difference between being someone's superior and someone's friend. For that matter, there's a great deal of difference between being someone's friend and someone's coworker. You will find some advocates who claim that people who are friends can work together, but it is very rare that you will find someone who will claim that people who are close friends can work together in an employee/employer relationship. Take my word for it—it's best not to try it.

Rule 2: Don't Expose Yourself to Unknown Variables or Questioning

Whenever you are in a position of leadership, it's important for you to maintain an almost unassailable position. CEOs stay in separate offices from the rest of the workplace. Generals don't sleep with the common soldiers. IT managers and supervisors don't go partying with the rest of the crew. You should always endeavor to place yourself in a position that does not expose you to any unknowns. If there isn't a control mechanism to maintain a structure, you shouldn't involve yourself. By staying separate and in control of your own environment, you will set yourself up to succeed.

Rule 3: Work Is Work, Fun Is Fun

Work is work. Fun is fun. The two don't mix. The best way to succeed at any company is to have an active social life outside the company. You should look forward to going to see your friends and family, not your coworkers, outside of work. Most likely, you'll be seeing your coworkers and office for over 40 hours a week. Make way for a change in your life and look for something better!

Rule 4: It's Never Worth It

No matter how fun it may sound, no matter how neat the people may be, it is never worth it to find yourself fraternizing with your employees. You will only succeed in making them uncomfortable and ostracizing yourself from your team. Or, if you don't, you will certainly lower your standing in their eyes. Take your role as the leader seriously and be content to just be the leader. After all, it's far cooler than just being a friend.

Micromanagement

The easiest trap for any manager who cares a great deal about their work to fall into is micromanagement. Micromanagement is a process that involves management overseeing a project down to such minutiae that they are essentially creating the entire project by themselves. The reason this trap is so easy to fall into is that, as was discussed earlier, delegation is a difficult process. When you couple delegation with the fact that most humans feel that they can do the job better by themselves than someone else can, it can quickly lead into a micromanaging nightmare.

In this case, we're going to look into a case of micromanagement that starts off with best-laid plans and ultimately develops into a terrible case of micromanagement. Afterward, you'll see a real-world example of micromanagement and then note some key tactics that can be used to avoid micromanagement in the future.

Scenario

David is the team lead of OmniCorp Computer, Inc. and has been working with the company for nearly two years. David started out in quality assurance, where his job was to make sure that every part OmniCorp put out was tested and ready for shipment before the customer received it. It was a stressful job, and David took it seriously, showing his excellent attention to detail and care for the product as his faulty shipped units numbers were at an all-time company low. This earned him a new position as quality assurance team lead for the branch in San Diego, where he currently lives.

Last week, David received a letter from OmniCorp's corporate office in New York City, where the CEO claimed that from now on quality assurance would be responsible for the final assembly of all computers and accessories before they hit shipping. This would include such parts as plastics and stickers. Upon hearing this, David goes to work on his team.

While on the line, David tells his team the new policy and instructs them on the correct procedure to assemble the final units. Sarah, his newest team member, is new to the entire operation and finds this all a little confusing. While the rest of the team begins to immediately adapt to the extra part of the shipment process, she is having difficulty assembling the final parts and shipping the product in time to keep outbound levels to a reasonable minimum.

Seeing this, David approaches her and asks if he can help. Sarah thanks him and says, "Thanks, David. I'm having a problem with this front panel. How does it hook up to the case?"

Smiling, David says, "Yeah, it's a bit tricky. Take a look here, there's a part that you have to pull out on the front of the case. It's so it doesn't slip during shipment."

Laughing, Sarah pulls out the part and the front panel snaps in. "Oh, that was easy! Thanks, David."

"No problem," David says. "Why don't you continue the rest of the procedure and let me look over how you're doing things?"

As soon as Sarah agrees, David notices that she is not attaching the side panel in the most efficient manner. It would be better to slide it in on the left side first and then the right, because the left side fits in and holds more easily. Thinking it's something she should know, David interrupts.

"It's a bit better if you do it left side first. It goes in a lot easier."

"Oh?" Sarah asks while finishing the fastening on the side. "I can do it this way pretty quickly. Are you sure it's faster?"

"You bet it is," David says. "Try it next time."

David then walks Sarah through the rest of the process. He notes that she is placing the computer into the box at an angle that has the potential to cause components to shift, but that her approach is much more expedient. Personally, he by far prefers the more secure method that makes sure nothing slips, but it takes several extra minutes. He then explains this to her.

Over the course of the next several hours, David walks Sarah through every step of the process as he would like to see it done. By the end of the day, Sarah is almost a walking, talking, working copy of David in nearly every way and looks fairly exhausted.

Upon taking his attention away from Sarah, David makes his way back to the rest of the assembly line and discovers that almost every other worker has been doing things similarly to Sarah. Thomas, Davian, and even Bill, the most senior employee, are all doing things inefficiently. Not missing a beat, he notes down on his task list that he'll need to speak to each of them individually to make certain they can do things the proper way from now on.

Background

One of the most famous, or perhaps *infamous*, micromanagers of all time was Bernard Ebbers, the CEO of MCI WorldCom. Bernard "Bernie" Ebbers was a legendary miser and was known as being an extremely hands-on CEO who directed his company in such a fashion that he oversaw every detail. Currently, he is serving a 25-year sentence in Louisiana for both conspiracy and fraud.

While Bernie Ebbers had very little to do with IT or engineering (he was once quoted as saying, "I know what I don't know. I don't know technology or engineering"), he is an excellent case of someone who conducted not only unethical business but true micromanagement. In fact, Ebbers was so famous for micromanagement that he once personally ordered employees to stop receiving free coffee at work because he believed they were stealing it. He even went as far as to oversee the customer service department and negotiate contracts that he had more specialized staff to take care of. He was universally disliked by almost everyone in the company and has probably the worst reputation of any CEO to ever walk the face of the earth, challenged only by the team at Enron.

While David here is by no means as far gone as Bernie Ebbers, he is suffering from the same sorts of problems. He's involving himself in too much in detail and too little in the abstract. Let's now examine some of the main causes of micromanagement and then see how to avoid it.

Overview

Sarah may be new to the company, but it's pretty likely that she's not new to computer work. Most people in IT have already had a lot of experience, and it's safe to say that she's been around the corporate block a few times. Or, if not around the block, she's most likely A+ certified and very familiar with how to assemble a computer.

Something else we need to note in this scenario is that David has only been with this company for two years. Although that may seem like a long time, it isn't long enough to have a good feel for how to manage people or an organization. He is relatively new and is bound to make a lot of mistakes in the future.

In your corporate career, you are going to be dealing with a lot of new managers, and it's likely that you'll be in the position of being a new manager yourself. It's a difficult place to be in, and it's easy to fall into the same trap David did.

Key Concepts

Unlike a lot of leadership concepts, there is no gray area with micromanagement. It is simply something that should be avoided at all costs. What makes this difficult is that it's so easy to fall into a pattern of micromanagement and cause a negative effect to traverse through the entire department. Here are some general traits of someone who suffers from micromanagement.

Obsessive

Most micromanagers are extremely obsessive over every aspect of their work. That's not to say that being obsessive over *some* of your work is bad, but micromanagers take it to a new level. They care about every nook, cranny, and pothole in not only their product but also their people, process, meetings, parties, and anything else that can be organized.

Don't be confused; being a little obsessive can be good. Steve Jobs, the successful CEO of Apple, was once quoted as saying, "Quality is more important that quantity. One home run is much better than two doubles." Obsession has something to do with that. The key point of no return when it comes to management is when you spend more time obsessing over the actions of the members of the team than you do managing the project.

Uncompromising

Compromise is one of the key important factors in all business. If you don't compromise, you're going to end up with a product or service that isn't as good as it could be. While many people might have great vision and are able to conduct their business in such a way that it achieves great things, it is a certain fact that their vision isn't as great as it could be with the different interpretations of others.

When trying to avoid micromanagement, remember that part of your duty as a manager is to work with your employees. Their opinions matter, and the fact that you care about their opinions matters to them. No one wants to work for someone who has the mentality of "my way or the highway."

Authoritative

As I mentioned in the earlier scenario on "Authority," at a certain point you can have too much authority in a project. Micromanagers succeed at doing this in spades. If there's one key habit they all have, it's that they will make sure everyone knows that things are to be done in their fashion, at their time, and at their convenience.

This sort of attitude has a detrimental effect on the morale of a crew. No one likes to hear that they can't be innovative, and no one likes to work for someone who constantly reminds them of their position of authority. Avoid this attitude and not only will you succeed in creating content employees but you'll also open the door to unlimited potential in terms of employee feedback and ideas.

Resolution

Since you understand now that micromanagement is something that you should avoid at all costs, I'll avoid the long description repeating of why it is a bad idea. Instead, I'll provide you with some key goals to keep in mind when managing people.

Goal 1: Think in the Abstract

If you've ever read any business books, you've probably heard the expression "think outside the box." And as cheesy and trite as it is, it's unfortunately true. People who don't think about managing and leadership in a general way can manage to confine their crew. Consider this: If you tell someone to mow the grass, they will probably mow the grass. If you tell someone to tend to the front lawn, they may very well mow the grass, trim the hedges, and even pull some weeds!

Goal 2: Have Confidence in Your Crew

This is something that most micromanagers struggle with. After all, if they had complete confidence in them, they wouldn't monitor their every action. Instead, they'd simply give them a direction and let them go. Have confidence in the people you work with. Every company worth its salt has a strict hiring process and will choose from a large pool of applicants. If someone is there, they are probably well suited to the position and capable of handling responsibility; you just have to trust them.

Goal 3: Relax

It goes without saying that while you're working, you should relax. Don't worry about tomorrow; just be calm today. If you are constantly thinking about every detail of every project and never stop for even a brief moment to breathe, you're probably going to end up pulling your hair out. Even if you don't pull your hair out, you'll certainly end up causing your team a lot of grief as they deal with your stress levels.

Goal 4: Don't Be Afraid to Mess Up

Mistakes happen, especially in management. Micromanagement tendencies whisper in our ear that if we aren't in charge of every aspect of something, then nothing bad will happen. This isn't true. Everyone makes mistakes. By making yourself aware of the truth, you'll find you're a lot calmer and easier to work with. Remember, if you're ever worried about making a mistake when it comes to management, realize that it's entirely possible that you may very well hit rock bottom in your career. Bad things can happen. The benefit is that once you're there, you can only go up! And, inevitably, you will most likely rise further after your downfall than you thought you would in the first place.

Feedback

Although many people may try to deny it, just about everyone has a small thought called "doubt" lingering in the back of their head. Personally, whenever I'm working on a project I like to know how the person I'm working for feels about it. Am I doing a good job? Is there a possibility that I can do better? Is there something important that I am missing? These are all questions that flood into the back of my mind.

The purpose of feedback is to provide answers to those questions so people know how they are progressing. It is a way for managers, supervisors, and upper-level leaders in a company to constructively and formally inform members of the organization of their status within the company and what they can do to improve. In this scenario, we're going to discuss a feedback situation from two perspectives. First, we'll look at feedback from the perspective of the person receiving it. Then, we'll examine it from the viewpoint of the person giving it. As a leader, you're going to need to know how to deal with both.

Feedback: Spoken or written communication designed to formally evaluate progress and work status.

Scenario

Today is the first anniversary of Natasha Pierson's arrival at Tornado Entertainment as a junior-level technician in Atlanta, Georgia. Natasha has been happy with the company and has made a great many friends in her time at Tornado. Since passing her A+ exam, Natasha has distinguished herself by also achieving Linux+ and Security+ certifications and is currently working her way toward achieving a Server+ certification, which will place her two certifications ahead of any of her coworkers. She is proud of what she has accomplished and is looking forward to another great year.

Because of her one-year anniversary, Tornado manager Samantha Thompson has recommended that Natasha meet with her at 11 o'clock to receive an evaluation. Fairly confident of her accomplishments, but still a little anxious, she sits down and waits outside Samantha's office at 10:55. After a few minutes, Samantha asks her to come in. Samantha greets Natasha warmly with a smile and asks her to sit. Natasha returns the smile and the evaluation begins.

Samantha begins the evaluation by giving Natasha an idea of what is going to occur. She informs her that she will first review Natasha's high points, indicating the benefits that she's added to the company and where she sees her in the future. Next, she will go over Natasha's low points and see what areas can be improved. Lastly, she will give her an overall rating.

As Natasha expected, the interview starts off well.

"I see here, Natasha, that you have managed to achieve three certifications since you began with us and are on your way to attaining a fourth. Congratulations! That is a monumental achievement."

Natasha smiles, pleased. She then says, "Thank you, Samantha. I've been trying very hard to set myself apart from the rest of the group."

"I can see that," Samantha says. "So much so that I can see what might be causing what I see on this next page. Apparently it says that you don't spend much time around your coworkers and that you choose not to participate in company events."

Natasha frowns. "Why is that a problem?"

"I wouldn't describe it as a 'problem,' Natasha," Samantha responds. "But I would classify it as a concern. We like to view ourselves as a large family, and when people don't choose to associate with the family it feels to some of us like there might be something wrong."

Hearing this upsets Natasha. In truth, she just wants to be able to do her job in the morning and then leave at night. She doesn't want to be a part of the social network.

"Well, I don't understand," she says. "I work harder than any other two people here and you're yelling at me because I'm not the most popular person in school? I'm an IT technician, not a socialite."

Samantha's eyes widen. "Well ..." she falters. "You should work on that!"

Background

Most real-world companies have a formal interval when evaluations occur and feedback should be given. Once you begin work as a technician, you'll find that most medium to large companies are good about systematically sending you updates. However, one thing that goes almost without saying is that you have to learn to be prepared for these situations.

More often than not, you're going to hear something in an evaluation that you are not going to like. It's never good to hear that you're doing something an employer doesn't want, even if you think that you are doing a bang-up job. Be prepared; the real world can be a downer sometimes. But don't be discouraged; companies always give you both the good and the bad, and the great news is that the bad can be easily dealt with.

Overview

Two things bear mentioning in this scenario before we begin to discuss anything else. The first is that, as I've mentioned previously, feedback *will* happen at any place of work and it is not always good feedback. However, feedback does come in several forms and fulfills several roles. In the following section, we'll examine some of these different forms and try to begin to understand the impact that feedback can have on personnel in the office.

Second, as an IT professional, you need to be aware that you are probably going to receive feedback at your position several times during your career and there is a strong possibility you may one day be giving feedback. Pay close attention and try your best to be understanding of some of the key tactics presented in the sections that follow.

Key Concepts

Negative Feedback

Negative feedback consists of two parts. First, it involves giving someone negative information or a negative review; second, it requires that information to be given in a negative manner. For example, a negative comment could be something akin to saying, "Your performance is terrible and it doesn't seem to be improving." Not only is it a negative comment, but it is reinforced in a negative manner and doesn't provide any sort of hope for improvement. In general, this sort of feedback isn't advised in the workplace and can seriously decrease morale.

Positive Feedback

The goal of all feedback is, or at least should be, to achieve the title of "positive feedback." Positive feedback not only succeeds in telling someone about a piece of information they need to be aware of, but also reinforces that there is room for improvement. Here are some good examples:

"Your performance hasn't been very solid compared to previous years, but I believe we can work on that."

"You look very strong in your technical area, but I see room for improvement in your customer service rating. This period, I'd like you to shoot for a rating of 5.0."

Samantha's Mistakes

Before we talk about Samantha's mistakes, lets first begin by discussing what she did correctly:

The feedback she gave was positive.   Samantha's feedback was all positive. She encouraged Natasha by letting her know that she could improve in a lot of her areas and by acknowledging the areas that she was most strong in before she began to address her weaknesses.

She was extremely professional.   Every comment Samantha gave was conveyed with courtesy. She made Natasha feel welcome and tried her best to show that anything she said was for Natasha's own benefit.

Now, let's examine her mistakes:

She obsessed over detail.   When giving feedback, you should try your best to look at the big picture. Samantha did not do this. Don't find yourself concentrating on minutiae; instead, try to let minor things slide. It's not important that someone receives a 100 percent; it's important that they receive an A. By concentrating on the fact that Natasha "wasn't social," she succeeded in making Natasha feel overall like she hadn't accomplished anything.

She lost control of the situation.   By saying, "You should work on that!" Samantha completely lost the professional tone that she was shooting for. Not only did Samantha violate their professional relationship, but she made herself look bad by losing her temper.

Natasha's Mistakes

Because Natasha is new to the situation, it's a bit easier to concentrate on what she did incorrectly over what she did correctly.

She was not receptive to criticism.   Natasha walked into this meeting thinking that she was going to pass with flying colors and, unfortunately, that is not always the case. You should always be prepared to hear constructive criticism in any evaluation.

She argued.   You should never argue with someone in an evaluation. Although you may not agree with what someone is saying, you can voice it in another way. For example, you could say, "I didn't realize I was doing that. Have I done it on more than one occasion?" Or more simply, you could say, "Do you think we could discuss why you believe that?" and receive more clarification.

Resolution

The resolution for giving feedback is fairly simple from the point of view of a leader, and the resolution for receiving feedback is extremely easy.

From the point of view of a leader, all you have to do is remember two things:

Your goal is to improve the performance of your employee.   This does not mean that you are given a license to criticize—it means you are given the privilege to help. View yourself as someone lending aid, not someone disciplining.

Be extremely professional.   Consider your action as more of a business transaction than a personal one and it will lead you to success. Don't view this as something between you and the particular person. Instead, think of it as something between you and a set of facts. X is lower than Y and thus must be corrected.

From the point of view of the person being evaluated, all you have to remember is that you need to maintain your professional behavior, and keep in mind that the evaluation isn't designed to poke holes in you as a person—it's designed to strengthen you as a worker. Differentiate the person you identify as yourself from the worker that you are and you will succeed marvelously.

Bonus Questions

When you take the A+ exam, chances are that you'll see very few questions on leadership. However, this doesn't mean that it's something you shouldn't be prepared to see on the test. CompTIA has a wide variety of questions that it relies on and occasionally it chooses to implement questions based on real workplace skills, such as leadership. Accordingly, this section has been added so you can have some review on this topic, but more importantly, be prepared for different types of questions in general.

Bonus Question 1

Here is a good example of a type of question you would see on professional behavior and feedback:

1. Which of the following would be the best way to response to criticism from an employer?

    A. Maintain silence and make no comments, concentrating on their opinion.

    B. Give your own opinion on the criticism and debate it.

    C. Briefly comment and consider what you can do to improve.

    D. Ask for the comments in writing.

Answer A: Incorrect. Part of receiving criticism is to comment and acknowledge that it has been given. You shouldn't maintain complete silence.

Answer B: Incorrect. You should never debate or argue with a superior.

Answer C: Correct. Whenever you receive criticism at the office, you should first try to evaluate the merit of it. However, you should also do your best to comment on the criticism and ask what you can do to improve.

Answer D: Incorrect. Asking for the comments in writing is not only unnecessary, but it could also cause a lot of annoyance on the part of your supervisor.

Bonus Question 2

Here is a good example of a question you might ask about how to deal with authority in the workplace from the perspective of someone who has just passed the A+ exam:

2. Which of the following concepts can be the most destructive to an office environment?

  A. Frequent evaluations

  B. Customer approval

  C. Employee resentment

  D. Schedule conflicts

Answer A: Incorrect. Frequent evaluations can strengthen the resolve of a team and greatly assist in productivity.

Answer B: Incorrect. Customer approval is not a destructive force at all. Be careful; the A+ exam tends to offer answers like this that are very obvious, but they can sometimes be coupled with words like "not," making them seem correct if you read through the question too quickly.

Answer C: Correct. Employee resentment is a destructive force in an office environment and should be avoided if at all possible.

Answer D: Incorrect. Although schedule conflicts can be destructive forces, they pale in comparison to employee resentment. In fact, schedule conflicts can result in more productivity as time is managed more effectively.

Summary

I'd like to wish you luck on your A+ exam and, more importantly, on your IT career in general. The one thing that you can be sure of as you begin your time in the workforce is that your path in technology is going to be both challenging and rewarding. If you take nothing else from the scenarios presented in this book so far, remember that communication is going to be your single key to success, no matter where you go.

As you advance, you'll find yourself presented with dozens of opportunities, promotions, and possibilities that will allow you to become even more of a technological expert than you already are. However, these opportunities, while wonderful, can only be truly realized to their full potential as you discover how best to communicate. Communicate not just with your customers, but with your coworkers, consultants, and eventually employees that you lead in your organization. The goal of every leader and every professional is to be understood. The trouble is that it's just not an easy thing to do. It takes a lot of practice and, above all, experience. Fortunately, that experience will come with time.

I'd like to thank you very much for taking the time to read this book. I hope you've enjoyed reading it as much as I've enjoyed writing it and I always encourage feedback. Please feel free to send me an e-mail at sjohnson@preplogic.com. God bless.

Chapter 7

Communication in the Real World

This chapter varies slightly from the other chapters in this book in that the events described here actually occurred in the real world, although the names have been changed to protect the identities of the parties involved. The reason this chapter has been included is because most scenarios that you encounter in the real world don't perfectly fit into the communication issues that I've discussed up until this point. In fact, they tend to be very muddled and contain a variety of events in different configurations. I hope that while reading this chapter you will find that you have a firm foundation in what you've learned so far. After all, the goal of this book has been to familiarize you with the major communication issues that you face at work.

This chapter breaks down into seven scenarios that will vary slightly from what you've seen thus far. The scenarios will contain only three sections. The first section describes the actual event, and the second section, Key Concepts, evaluates the event and explains what was and was not done correctly. Finally, there is a section that summarizes what you can take away from this situation. The seven scenarios are as follows:

Scenario 1: Plugged In
Scenario 2: Being "CAT"ty
Scenario 3: Dialing Out
Scenario 4: Persuasion
Scenario 5: Administration by Majority
Scenario 6: Packet What?
Scenario 7: Spies Among Us

Plugged In

One of the oldest problems in tech support communication is simply not understanding the customer's setup. We do a lot of things to make sure that this doesn't occur. We have the customer describe the working environment, use keywords to reference their items of ownership, and sometimes even go as far as to look up their particular order to see what exactly they were given. In fact, some companies keep highly regulated (and proprietary) databases of customers' inventory, service tags, and model numbers to more quickly expedite the support process.

Joshua, a tech support representative with Moheco University, started out the day in a good mood. Because it was Good Friday, the university decided that it would be nice for the 24-hour customer support office to be open for only half of the day. Thus, Joshua's 8-hour shift would be only a 2-hour short furlough before he returned home with pay. It was looking like today was going to be really nice. Unfortunately, he then received a call from a student at the university trying to get a computer set up, and things went downhill from there.

Joshua answered the phone. "Good afternoon and thank you for calling tech support. This is Josh; how can I help you?"

There was a slight pause on the other end of the phone and then a sweet-sounding female voice answered. "Yes, I have a problem with my computer. I can't get it to turn on."

Knowing that there was a power outage in the Climrock dorm this morning, Josh thinks to cut off the problem. "Ah, I see. Can I get your name, ma'am?"

"It's Jenny. Jenny Thompson," she responded.

"OK, Jenny. Before I begin working on this problem, may I ask if you had your computer on during the power outage that occurred earlier this morning at Climrock?"

"Power outage? We didn't have one. I live in Clemret," she said, sounding confused.

Realizing the problem was more advanced, Josh jumped into gear. "Oh, I see. Well, can you tell me the problem?"

"Sure, sure," she said. "I actually just got this computer at the store and I plugged it into the wall. But when I turn it on, it's just blank on the screen. It's not doing anything."

"So the monitor isn't displaying?" he asked.

"That's right, it's not displaying. But the thing is that I hear it on. It's making a loud whirling noise."

"Is this noise out of the ordinary? Does it sound louder?"

"No, not really. It just sounds normal."

Turning to his own computer, Josh looked at the standard procedures for campus issues involving nondisplaying monitors. Under the sheet, it simply said:

Step 1: Check to see if the user has plugged the monitor in correctly.

Thinking this could very well be the issue, Josh asked, "Jenny, before I go any further, can you verify to me that the monitor is plugged in correctly?"

"Oh, yes, I made sure it was plugged in," she said.

From that point on, Josh tried almost everything he could think of to solve the problem. He asked her to reboot the computer, unplug components and plug them back in, change jumpers, reseat the video card, and even completely unplug the CPU from the computer and then place it back in (hoping that might lead him to something), but all to no avail.

Eventually, Josh decided that he needed some help. Accordingly, he called another member of the support team to the line; it was now way past their quitting time. The other member of the team introduced himself and began to try a few more tricks, such as unplugging the mother-board from the power supply and testing the monitor for the "test" screen. But still the two of them couldn't fix the problem.

As time went by, the problem started to gather more attention. Off-duty members of the help desk came in on the phone call, offering solutions and suggesting measures, none of which seemed to work. With more than five technicians on the line, they couldn't solve the problem. Until Josh asked one question:

"OK, Jenny. Could you tell me what the back of the monitor looks like? Could you describe if it's missing something?"

Jenny sighed. "Sure, but this is getting really frustrating." They heard her maneuvering the machine and reorienting herself.

"Ok," she said. "The computer has a white back with a lot of slots on the back and a cord hanging down, plugged into the wall."

Josh paused, stunned. "Did you say 'a' cord? There aren't two?"

"No, just one," Jenny said.

It turned out that at the very beginning of the conversation, when Josh was qualifying that she had in fact plugged the monitor into the wall, he hadn't asked about the VGA cord—she had actually forgotten to plug the VGA cable into the video card on her machine. At the end of the day, five technicians had spent many hours on one problem that could have been fixed in less than five minutes because of one single communication issue.

Key Concepts

Let's now examine Josh's mistakes and his correct actions in a bit more detail, starting with what he did correctly.

What Josh Did Correctly

Josh certainly did a number of things right. In addition to eventually solving the problem and doing his very best to help the customer when she needed, he did the following:

Josh was very patient.   He went through all the right steps. He was calm, put together, and even stayed hours longer than he needed to make sure that her problem was taken care of. That's simply great customer service worthy of recognition. Everybody should endeavor to be that dedicated.

Josh thought abstractly.   Josh tried everything here. He thought of new concepts, called in other team members, and tried to do everything he could to make the system work. This is something you have to do a lot when you work in tech support, because you never know what might be prohibited or helpful in your particular environment. Furthermore, sometimes the only way you can discover the problem is by following some strange procedures.

Josh's Mistake

This isn't to say that Josh didn't make mistakes—most importantly:

Josh didn't qualify his customer.   Before the problem was even fully presented, he began to think he knew the solution. This can be a real detriment to your workflow, because not properly qualifying someone before you start diagnosing can (obviously) lead to misdiagnoses and actually introduce more problems than you prevent or cure. It's an easy trap to fall into because sometimes you will face a similar problem literally dozens of times in one day and have the desire to categorize this problem along with all of your others. It's very important that you *not* do that. This is because *no* two problems are exactly alike. Whether you realize it or not, every situation is different and you need to treat each with the respect it deserves (even if it seems kind of silly at the time).

Resolution

Just as Josh learned in this situation, you have to realize in your own work that every step, no matter how minor, is important in the process of solving a problem. Procedures are there for a reason, and in a world of miscommunication and imperfect mediums of conversation, ideas can be easily misinterpreted. So when you are faced with a situation where a teleprompter, manual, or instructional tool tells you to do something that you find to be absolutely simplistic, don't be so harsh. Sometimes the simplest issues can save you both a lot of time and a lot of effort.

Being "CAT"ty

A few years ago, back in the days of Y2K and the legendary era of information technology, Daniel Pirch was at the right place at the right time. At the turn of the millennium, literally thousands of companies were looking to upgrade their now aging computer networks running at now antiquated speeds to the latest generation of switches and routers, in some cases increasing their bandwidth over a hundredfold.

Furthermore, Daniel had been smart enough to realize that the place to be in the industry wasn't necessarily sales or installation but configuring these systems. Consequently, Daniel only had to spend one or two days at a business as he arranged their networks and servers to be set for a solid configuration, instead of the months-long process of totally installing a network from the ground up.

The only unfortunate part of this situation was that Daniel was only called out to the scene toward the end of the project. He wasn't involved with the wiring, the topological decision making, or even (for that matter) the objective setting of the project. His role was strictly isolated to his field, in which he was an absolute expert.

One day, Daniel received a call from a large company that had just spent a great deal of money installing new wiring to support their fully integrated network. Because of the extremely high demands of their information infrastructure, they had arranged at a high level for everything to be channeled through a networking closet that supported the absolutely amazingly fast speed. And they knew that Daniel would be the one to make it happen.

More than a little excited about the fresh high-tech install, Daniel made his way to the company as quickly as possible, just so he could get a look at the fresh new hardware and play around with the system before planning his full configuration. Upon his arrival, he was absolutely shocked. It was everything that they said it was. The company had probably spent hundreds of thousands, if not millions of dollars, on all of this equipment and it was all truly revolutionary. Without hesitation, he began to work.

Halfway through planning his main configuration, Daniel thought it might be a good idea to get the jump on the installation early. Some of the installation could be done in phases and, since he was a pretty honest guy and this was a repeat client, he figured he could save them a little money on his bill—it wasn't like he was short of work. So he began to hook up the components.

Oddly, as soon as he started the installation he noticed something was wrong. All of the cable coming through to this location was Category 3, not Category 5. Figuring it must be for some other part of the installation, Daniel chalked it up to the wiring not being quite completed yet, so he went to speak to the project manager, Greg.

"Hey, Greg," he said.

"Hey, Dan, what's going on?" Greg asked.

"Well," Dan began, "I was just about to begin my configuration for your main router when I noticed that all of the cable running into the networking closet is Cat3. Is the wiring not done yet?"

"Cat3?" Greg asked. "What's Cat3?"

Dan smiled, figuring Greg must be more of a businessman than a tech guy. "It's a type of wiring that's used for slower-speed installs. With this network, it'll need to be run on Cat5. I don't see any Cat5 in the closet."

"They told me all the wiring was done," said Greg.

"Done?" asked Daniel. "Well, I think we might have a problem."

"Are you telling me that they screwed up the wiring?" asked Greg, looking alarmed. "I'm not entirely sure yet, but I think so," said Daniel.

"Well, do you know or not?" Greg nearly screamed.

"I know that the wiring that you have in the networking closet is insufficient for the type of network I need to design. I am not sure of much beyond that," Daniel said cautiously.

"Damn it!" Greg exclaimed. "This is going to put the project back at least a week. Why didn't you come sooner? I thought you were the best!"

Daniel frowned. "Greg, it's not my fault that they wired it incorrectly. I wasn't involved with the meeting."

"Yes, but you were a part of the process. Why didn't you double-check what had been done up until this point?"

The conversation went on for a while, but Greg's mind placed the fault entirely upon Daniel. It wasn't until three days later, when Daniel had completed the contract and fixed the wiring issues caused by the other contractor in addition to his standard workload, that Greg came to his senses and realized that Daniel was not the person to blame for the incident. Fortunately, the contract was eventually completed, but Daniel went away from it with a sore feeling in his gut and a bit aggravated. At the end of the day, however, the job was done and his reputation remained intact.

Key Concepts

Both Greg and Daniel took some correct actions, which I'll point out in this section. Each of them will be listed next, along with the reasons their behavior was good and/or bad.

Greg's Actions

In this scenario, Greg was unquestionably rude and unprofessional. This type of behavior is unfortunate, but it presents itself often in modern office environments. Sometimes, when things go wrong, people need someone to blame. They're angry and they need a way to both channel and fuel that anger to make it appear that someone besides themselves is responsible, whether or not that is true. In the real world, you should do your best to have as little exposure to people like Greg as possible. They are dangerous and they tend to not care about anyone but themselves.

Daniel's Actions

Daniel's actions can be described by two overarching themes: courteousness and making clear and concise statements.

Courteous   Daniel was fair, informative, and patient. He was also able to resolve a situation and inform the company of a mistake that wasn't his responsibility. Ultimately, this didn't serve him well, but his actions and ethics were in the right place.

Clear and Concise   Just like in the A+ objectives, Daniel was extremely clear and informative. He didn't use excessive jargon and he even went as far as to explain things to a businessman without using excessively technical terms. As an IT technician, Daniel made all the right moves. As a professional, Daniel also made the right decision by staying calm and allowing the customer (in this case, the manager) to vent all he wanted.

Resolution

When faced with a situation like Daniel's, it's best to follow his example. Don't let your emotions get in the way. Instead, remember the lessons you have been taught on professional behavior, even if others are displaying them. Whether or not you're right at the moment, you'll be right in the long run when people look back on how you behaved in a difficult situation and find your actions admirable and just.

Dialing Out

After recently jumping into the field of IT, James Stanbert landed a job with one of the single biggest PC providers in the country. He was new to the field and excited to be there, and was now connected to one of the fastest-growing industries in the world. It was truly the place to be. Unfortunately, a large portion of the job (actually, the *only* portion of the job) was dealing with very low-end customer service support issues. This wasn't necessarily a bad thing, but with this particular company, it could be very trying.

One day, toward the end of his stint with that portion of the company, James received a phone call from a user who had an issue with her computer. The exact words of the conversation aren't recorded, but parts of it were very similar to this:

Customer: "Hello? Support?"
James: "Yes, this is support. How can I help you?"
Customer: "I have a problem with my Internet."
James: "OK, could you tell me what the problem is, ma'am?"
Customer: "It doesn't work."
James: "All right, ma'am. Are you able to get online?"
Customer: "No."
James: "Does your computer appear to be dialing the number?"
Customer: "No."

James: "OK, could you tell me what seems to be happening?"

Customer: "It won't work."

James: "I see. But does it appear to be trying to work?"

Customer: "I don't know."

James: "Ma'am, could you tell me a little bit more about your situation?"

Customer: "I don't know. It just won't work."

The conversation actually went on like this for about an hour. No matter how he phrased his question, he just couldn't get the person on the line to give him more details. He ultimately had to resort to asking yes or no questions and simple phrases like "Press the big button in the middle." Eventually, the call led to this:

James: "OK, so it appears that your computer is trying to dial out and there is no dial tone. Could you check and see if the phone line is attached?"

Customer: "The phone is in the other room."

James: "Yes, ma'am. I understand. But the computer is attached to the phone line, correct?"

Customer: "No."

James: "The computer isn't attached to the phone line?"

Customer: "No."

James: "Is there a jack in the room?"

Customer: "No. I only have one phone jack in the kitchen and I'm using it."

It turned out that after all his efforts the customer simply had no phone from which to dial out. Once he was clear on what had happened, James was able to inform his customer of the requirements for using the Internet and helped her get this issue resolved.

Key Concepts

Talk about an awkward situation to be in! I think this takes the record in terms of miscommunication and lack of understanding. Let's take a look at James's correct actions and mistakes and see if we can learn from them.

What James Did Correctly

James did a good job of maintaining a professional manner and tone of voice, even over the phone. He also did a surprisingly good job of asking leading, open-ended questions and trying to use abstract ways to reach the customer. Unfortunately, the customer didn't respond.

Sometimes this happens. Life doesn't work like a textbook and sometimes people who call for tech support don't want tech *support*; they want tech solutions and they don't want to work toward them. When situations like this occur, it's best to do as James did and be patient and encouraging, and help the customer understand the situation.

James's Mistake

James really made only one mistake in that he assumed far too much from his customer.

Assumption   Someone once told me, "Assume your customers are the dumbest people on the earth, and it will help you serve them!" And although I in no way agree that customers are the dumbest people on earth, I have to admit that there is a lot of merit to that statement. By appealing to the lowest knowledge level and making sure that every step is covered in your procedure (just like Josh did in the first scenario of this chapter), you can present yourself as nonintimidating and understanding, and will be able to identify and correct any mistakes.

Resolution

Remember, when you encounter someone who isn't talkative, go back to one of the basic tenets of tech support: even if they're quiet, they still want help. Quiet customers, like the one discussed in Chapter 1, just have a different mind-set than other customers who aren't quiet. It doesn't mean that they're strange. It just means that they approach things in a different manner.

Also, remember some of the rules from Chapter 6 and the tactics James used here:

- Ask leading questions.
- Be encouraging.
- Ask open-ended questions.

These will not guarantee your success, but they will certainly help you along the way.

Persuasion

While some of the topics I have discussed may provide adequate or reasonable benefits, such as advancing your career or perhaps ensuring your likability in the office, there is no other topic that will serve you quite so well over the course of your entire life as mastery of the art of persuasion. Like many of the topics discussed in this book, persuasion is not a skill that is easily attained. It must be practiced and pondered, at first as an impediment to your workflow and only eventually, after many years, resulting in a useful skill.

As you begin your career as an IT technician, you may find this frustrating. It's not easy to try to succeed and to persuade someone toward your point of view and then fail. It's inevitable that you will stumble and fall along the way, but it will ultimately be a learning experience. Although there's no way anyone can truly prepare you for a situation involving persuasion, I can show you a real-world scenario in which someone was able to persuade an entire nation to fight on in the worst of times. When I think of the minor tasks I sometimes have to accomplish in IT, I ponder this event and it helps me to carry on. And while you as an IT technician may never be faced with a task quite so daunting in your office, it is a good idea to learn from the master.

In 1940, Britain was facing the greatest enemy the modern world had ever known—the German army under the command of Adolf Hitler. Germany was an unstoppable, unyielding force of titanic power that slammed against England day and night, sending wave after wave of Nazi bombers and planes against a country that was in no way prepared to fight.

After just a short time, much of England was ready to give up. The ceaseless attacks that they underwent, combined with the massive tolls of death and destruction that they were exposed to throughout every day, were too much for most of the populace. Then, on June 4, something changed.

It changed when Winston Churchill, the prime minister of the United Kingdom, appeared before Parliament and his nation and delivered a riveting speech, causing the entire nation to rally. Among many other things, he was quoted saying:

> We shall go on to the end. We shall fight in France. We shall fight on the seas and oceans. We shall fight with growing confidence and growing strength in the air. We shall defend our Island, whatever the cost may be. We shall fight on the beaches. We shall fight on the landing grounds. We shall fight in the fields and in the streets. We shall fight in the hills. We shall never surrender, and even if, which I do not for a moment believe, this Island or a large part of it were subjugated and starving, then our Empire beyond the seas, armed and guarded by the British Fleet, would carry on the struggle! Until, in God's good time, the New World, with all its power and might, steps forth to the rescue and the liberation of the old.

To this day, Winston Churchill is cited as being one of the most inspirational and persuasive speakers of all time. Much can be learned by reading through his works and reviewing some of the tactics he used. The most amazing thing about him as a person is that he was not necessarily special. He was fairly short and chubby, and had a slight lisp that made him difficult to understand.

What this tells you about persuasion is that you don't have to be particularly amazing to succeed at persuading others. You just have to be right and deliver your point correctly. Regardless of what you are, it doesn't change what you do. When you're persuasive, you're simply persuasive. If that isn't encouraging, I don't know what is.

Key Concepts

Churchill's speech is much longer than the portion presented here; in fact, it went on for nearly 20 minutes. However, you can learn a lot from this short section by simply looking at his actions.

Churchill's Actions

Churchill's actions are of particular interest to you as an IT professional because they point out three concepts that are required in order to properly persuade someone:

- Clarity
- Conciseness
- Repetition

Clarity

When you're trying to persuade someone, you have to be abundantly clear. It doesn't matter whether the person is a customer or a coworker, a friend, or an employee—you just have to get the message across. Many people become confused by this because they think more about how to deliver the message than what the message actually is. Consider, for a moment, that if you're trying to persuade someone that something you really believe is a good idea, chances are it's actually a pretty good idea.

Borrowing again from the wisdom of giants, Cicero of Rome was once quoted as saying, "There is no better way to convince others than first to convince yourself." If you concentrate on what your idea really is, convince yourself of its merit, and then deliver it clearly with that sort of confidence, you are going to move someone. Chances are, you'll probably convince them. Just remember that you can't jump the gun on persuasion. Define your purpose, understand it, believe it, and then deliver it.

Conciseness

If you look at Churchill's statements, you'll see that they are not elaborate. Most of the sentences are around seven words long, but the words hit home. They are strong and purposeful, just as yours should be. As you deal with your coworkers, choose your words and choose them wisely. If you communicate in a way people cannot understand, you will isolate yourself from them. Instead, you have to pick a language that everyone speaks.

A good rule of thumb to follow when you're speaking or trying to persuade in any manner is to run the "could it be confused" check. This basically means that you take the statement and you run it through over and over again in your head, checking to see if there is any possible way that it could be misinterpreted. If there is, rephrase. But in all this, you need to keep the length of your statements short. When you think about it, you'll find that most statements or points are not very complicated; they are just simple phrases waiting to be unlocked. The trouble is that only you can find the key.

Repetition

If you've ever heard the expression "repeat, repeat, repeat," there's a reason! First, it's listed earlier in the book. But, on a more serious note, when you're trying to get someone to do something, it's a good idea to reinforce the concept in their head. In the office, we can do this by simply repeating ourselves or rephrasing the procedure. Instead of constantly repeating something like "move the watercooler," we can say "rearrange the watercooler." Here's an example:

"Do me a favor and move the water cooler to the corner. By rearranging it to the corner, we'll clear the hallway."

In the case of Churchill, he did this by repeatedly telling the British people that they would fight under any circumstances, on the streets, in the air, in the fields, and so forth. By reinforcing this idea, he both planted it into their brain and rallied them to the idea. Any additional reinforcement just resulted in further motivation and encouragement.

 Although repeating is good, you should never repeat exhaustively. This can just cause trouble as you begin to annoy people. If you begin to see someone look frustrated or generally hostile, it's probably a pretty good queue to stop repeating!

Resolution

Classically, the method of persuasion breaks down into two distinct parts:

- Persuasion by emotion
- Persuasion by reason

When you're persuading by reason, you're appealing to the logical part of people's brain that controls decisions concerning facts and figures. Commonly, most logical persuasions involve the use of facts and figures as you present a logical argument.

 Logical argument: An argument created to reach a conclusion by persuading with common assertions.

On the other hand, appealing to emotion is much broader. Persuading by appealing to emotion involves looking to someone's feelings, beliefs, values, morals, or ethics in order to assert a point that is valid. For instance, if you wanted to argue that Bill Gates was evil to a misogynist, you could say that Bill Gates was actually a women's rights activist. This way, because of their (very narrow) beliefs, they would most likely now dislike Bill Gates.

Administration by Majority

Returning now to the first half of the 1990s, the early days of file sharing and system administration were a pretty interesting time. IT concepts like TCP/IP and IPX/SPX were not necessarily "new" technologies, but the world was still getting used to them. Most businesses didn't have a huge network of computers and a server room that maintained most of their data. Instead, a large majority of business transactions were still done via phone and paper.

At the same time, file sharing hadn't quite been perfected to the level that it has been today. There were huge policy issues, and IT had a hard time confirming whether users were connected to share a file, much less sharing the file in the first place. This made for a lot of, shall we say, "interesting" situations when it came to organization and verification, as users and IT tried to determine whether something was new, or whether it had been changed, or who had control of what.

With that background in mind, this brings us to our friend, Nelson Couper, a general networking contractor. Just as in a couple of earlier scenarios, Nelson was one of the early adopters of technology and had made a name for himself in the IT world early on. He was smart, well spoken, and seemingly untiring, and he did quality work. Companies were lining up outside his door to claim some of his time.

One week, during Nelson's daily routine of calling some of his contacts and arranging his schedule for the following week, Nelson received an offer from a large banking association to resolve a minor DNS issue they were having. It was a small call, but the pay was pretty good and it looked like it could mean more leads. So Nelson accepted and showed up the following week.

At the site, Nelson was impressed. They had numerous desktop systems that were supported by several administrators and desktop technicians (such as your future self). Their organization was also divided up in such a way that they could easily transfer data between systems and let others see important information at incredible speeds. This again was a good thing, but as Nelson began to look into the situation, he noticed something odd.

It seemed that all of the shared files were placed in one folder that had over 3,000 subfolders. Within these subfolders, users would place important information, such as business documents, and install files for important company software. They would also trade notes back and forth and just generally conduct business. What was odd about this arrangement was that the subfolders seemed to overlap. Some folders would have tax information that could be found in another subfolder. And some high-level folders would be identical to subfolders found beneath them. It was a huge mess.

What made it worse was that it didn't seem to have any rhyme or reason. There were just files everywhere! In Nelson's opinion, it was the absolute worst administrative nightmare he had ever seen—so much so that he brought it up to the general contractor, Bob.

He said, "Bob, what is with all of the files here? They seem to be in complete disarray."

"Yeah, I know," said Bob sadly. "I tried to set it up in a more organized fashion, and no one liked it, because they couldn't understand it easily."

Nelson paused for a moment. "Bob," he began, "are you sure that's a good idea?"

"Well, I'd like it to be another way, but people give me too hard of a time."

Nelson chuckled to himself a little, but didn't say anything more on the subject. Instead, he just finished up the job that he'd been paid to do.

Now, skip to the modern day, ten years later. Nelson is still in IT and is working on a completely different job. While he's at this new job, he's speaking with a coworker who asks him if he has any funny stories.

"You know, I do!" Nelson said. "I once worked with this idiot over in a contract in Piedmont, North Dakota, and he was in charge of this huge array of servers back in the '90s. Oddly enough, he let the users dictate folder policy! It was the most hilarious thing. The guy actually let people tell him, the administrator, what to do. What a dope."

"Wait a minute," she said. "Piedmont? I used to live there. What company was it with?"

Nelson laughed. "No kidding? It was Commucorp, Inc. Do you know anybody there?"

His coworker blinked. "Yes, my husband. He's the system administrator."

Key Concepts

Nelson was really in a bad spot in this situation. It's not only unbelievably ironic and a cruel twist of fate that he happened to be speaking to the worst person at the worst time, but what he was trying to say was also meant to be humorous. However, it does go back to some of the key ideas in communication you want to keep in mind.

What Nelson Did Correctly

Nelson made a few right moves. First, he kept quiet when he was dealing with a coworker who was doing something improperly. Second, he paid attention to what he was in charge of and left the rest of the administration up to the person who was in charge of it. This reinforces the idea that you should keep your business to yourself and make sure that you don't become the type of employee or coworker who reports on the actions of others just for your own self-benefit. If you need to brush up on your workplace communication, refer again to Chapter 5.

Nelson's Mistakes

I feel like I almost don't need to point this out, but Nelson violated a cardinal rule when he spoke ill of a colleague. Do yourself a favor, and never, ever insult a colleague, coworker, customer, or friend. It's just not good business and it can get you in trouble!

Resolution

The best way to stay out of situations like Nelson's is to remember an overriding theme in this book: business is business. When you're fraternizing with an employee of your equal rank, you shouldn't divulge information that could possibly come and bite you in the behind. It's not smart, because you never know what might bother someone or what might cause tension between you and a colleague.

Packet What?

One of the funniest stories in all IT (at least that I have ever heard) involved a technician working in a third-party company for a larger company that didn't have any IT support. The company had been in business for a long time, but simply didn't have the need or meet the requirements for a full-blown IT department. Instead, they would just consult this friendly third-party company when they had the need.

What complicates things is that the two companies used wildly different technology. The company that needed the issues resolved used NetBIOS, Windows machines, and only one central server. The assisting company used TCP/IP, Linux machines, and multiple servers. So, consequently, whenever the third party had to come out to assist with the large company's IT situation, there would be a lot of technological incompatibility issues. The technicians were accustomed to operating on different machines, the users had different demands, and even the managers had different ideas of what the computers should and should not be able to do.

Regardless, the problem came down on the head of Glenn Thompson. Glenn was the technician at the third-party company and was pulled in to assist with the main company's IT problem. And, despite the extremely complicated communication and technology issues, after three hours Glenn was able to nail down the issue by looking at the topology of the company. In fact, the problem was very broad, but it essentially boiled down to an excessive amount of NetBIOS packets causing the network to bog down, and it could be fixed by removing one computer that functioned as a router.

Unfortunately for Glenn, the main company didn't believe this. They had installed the computer themselves and were convinced that it couldn't be the reason.

"There's no way," the head of the team said. "You're absolutely nuts. It isn't that computer, it's the one in server room B."

"No, I'm sure of it," Glenn said, emphasizing his point with a few technical facts.

"That's baloney. Are you sure you know what you're talking about?" he asked.

"Yes, I'm sure," Glenn said. "If you'll just let me explain ..."

"I don't really have time for this. Time is money, and I'm certain it's not that computer that's the problem, it's the one in server room B. Come up with another explanation," said the manager.

"But, sir, I am sure this is it," Glenn said.

This conversation went back and forth for over an hour. Ultimately, the company still did not believe Glenn and had him remove the computer they thought was the problem: the one in server room B. Glenn then said, "OK, I'm going to prove to you beyond the shadow of a doubt that it is not this computer that is causing the problem."

He then unplugged the machine from the wall, disconnected it from the network, and placed it in the middle of the room. He then went back to one of the machines connected directly to the network and monitored the traffic. Sure enough, there were still NetBIOS packets being broadcast all around. It turned out, after all their arguing, that Glenn had been right, and he had just proved it.

Key Concepts

Fear and technology are two things that go hand and hand. As discussed throughout this book, it's a good idea to make sure that people are fairly familiar with a certain technology and what you're going to be doing with that technology before you do it. Granted, you might be asking yourself who was afraid here. The answer is that almost every action made by the main company was done out of fear: fear of a technology department, fear of implementation issues, and even fear of a solution.

What Glenn Did Correctly

Glenn did an excellent job of informing the company of the problem with their current situation and properly informed them of how to combat and resolve it. Unfortunately for Glenn, he had bad luck in that the company he was working for didn't want to hear his opinion.

Glenn's Mistakes

Although he did inform them of the situation, Glenn did a poor job of informing the company of exactly *why* he was making the decision that he made. It's not enough to just say what the solution is and then suggest that you implement it. You need to suggest a solution and then give the reason behind it.

Furthermore, Glenn went a little overboard with the display of unplugging the computer from the wall and placing it in the center of the room. The people at that company already knew that if it was unplugged, chances are that it was not going to be affecting the environment around it. If anything, this weakened Glenn's credibility slightly and made him appear a bit overbearing.

Resolution

When you're faced with a fearful customer, try to remember that the best thing you can do is remind them of the words of Franklin D. Roosevelt: "The only thing we have to fear is fear itself." Part of your job as a technician is to smooth concerns, carefully transition changes, and smooth out any difficult process for a user. It's a benefit both to them and to you because the more comfortable you make them feel, the more willing they're going to be to listen to you.

Spies Among Us

In the early 1990s, Joseph Peterson was at the top of the proverbial IT game. Because he began his career in computers a long time ago and proved to be a valuable addition to the computer staff since then, Joseph was promoted to the primary access controller of a major oil and gas company that, at the time, had one of the single largest arrays of supercomputers, workstations, and storage area networks in the world.

Because of his success, Joseph had become a little lazy and began to let things slide. He had moved to a position of such a high level that he spent most of his day-to-day routine simply checking people in and out of the computer room and just making sure they had access to what they needed.

Early one morning, Joseph received a phone call from a buddy he'd had from college named David. David and Joseph were roommates for two years, and David had gone to work for another energy company in a similar position. Happy to hear from him, Joseph and David immediately began catching up on old times and talking about the way things used to be.

It's important to note that at the time, certification had just begun to come into play. Major vendors were releasing such complicated hardware that they needed qualified people to manage and maintain it. Consequently, David informed Joseph that he'd actually begun to take on a new position with a training company that familiarized people with the "new" Novell server equipment. And because he knew that Joseph was in charge of a major server room, David asked if Joseph would mind him sending his students on a tour of the facility.

Joseph happened to be out of the office on the day of the tour, but he said that he could allow them access to the computer room at 8 A.M. and then have someone there by around 8:20 to give them a guided tour of the facility. Happy to hear this, David agreed and they set up the meeting.

The day that Joseph was out of the office, the person in charge of the server room for that day, James, walked into his office at 8 o'clock and found the following memorandum on his chair:

> Hi James,
>
> I wanted to let you know that I agreed to let a classroom come through the server room this morning. I figured you wouldn't mind giving them a 15-minute tour, so I hope you don't mind. They should be waiting for you when you come into the office this morning. Thanks a bunch!

A bit frustrated that he wasn't made aware a bit sooner, James sighed and then moved to the server room to give the visitors a proper welcome. When he arrived at the server room, not only were they "at" the server room, they were inside. And not only were they inside, they were crowded around one of the terminals. And even more strangely, they all looked as if they were not speaking any English.

Knowing that this was a serious problem, Joseph burst into the server room and yelled, "What are you doing!? You can't be on the main server! That has access to everything!"

Little did Joseph or James know it, but the so-called "students" of David's were actually from a foreign government. Without their knowledge, the energy company had unknowingly exposed their network to a foreign power for nearly half an hour, and potentially lost a great deal of their secrets and possibly even financial information. It was a classic case of social engineering—and they had become the victims.

Shortly thereafter, James informed the chief of technology of the incident and passed a request to change the root passwords for the server and change some important filenames, minimizing the chance that unauthorized personnel with privileged information could access it sometime in the future. Within just a few hours, their system was up, running, and secure once again.

Key Concepts

This scenario is more complicated than some of the other ones we've discussed in that it concentrates on two people's actions that played a critical role in this scenario and created a potentially huge security disaster. Now, let's take a look at both Joseph's and James's decisions.

What Joseph Did Correctly

Unfortunately for poor Joseph, he did almost nothing right. The one thing that you could give him credit for is that he tried to be a good friend to his former colleague. But, unfortunately, that doesn't get you very far in the professional world.

What James Did Correctly

On the other hand, James made a lot of great decisions. He stopped the event, used the chain of command, and contained the situation:

He stopped the event.   Without hesitation, James jumped on this situation. He knew that the people involved were not allowed to have access to the server room, and he stopped them cold. While his actions might seem a bit harsh, you have to remember that security is *very* serious stuff. A company's entire existence can depend on the quality of its security policies and personnel, so it's best to treat every situation as if it is of the utmost importance.

He informed the correct personnel.   James made another great move in that he went to his superiors and he informed them of the problem immediately. Because the situation was so complex and James's role in the company is not clearly defined, we can't chastise him for not immediately going to the authorities. However, in other situations, you should know that if a situation is serious enough you may need to get the authorities involved. Remember, though, you should only do this if you are *absolutely convinced* that there may have been a serious enough infraction that you should alert the authorities. If you are uncomfortable in the slightest, it's best to inform your superior and let them handle it. In fact, many companies require this.

He prevented escalation of the problem.   By stopping the situation early, informing the right personnel, and suggesting the right course of action, Joseph put a lid on a serious situation and made something that could have turned into an international incident into just an interesting story.

Joseph's Mistakes

While Joseph did nothing right, he did not lack at all in terms of mistakes. In particular:

He was lazy.   If Joseph really wanted to show his friend and the class the server room, and he had the authority, he should have done it on his own time or made accommodations. It's not a good business practice to toss duties like this to other personnel.

He didn't use the correct medium.   While Joseph could have sent an e-mail, made a phone call, or personally told James about the situation. Instead, he just wrote James a physical memorandum and let him discover it after the event had already begun. This goes back to knowing that for every communication situation in the office, there is a proper channel, as was discussed in Chapter 3. For issues of importance, you need to know which method of communication to use!

Resolution

Although not everyone gets a situation in their career that's quite as exciting as this one, it's important to recognize what a huge role IT communication can play in an organization's security. In a worst-case scenario, the possibility exists that some of these individuals may have been truly malicious entities from a foreign government and intended to steal trade secrets in order to compromise corporate or national security as a whole. When you're faced with a situation like this one, follows James's lead. Be quick to respond, appropriate in action, and informative in delivery. This will ensure that the right people know the right information at the right time.

Summary

Throughout your career you'll be faced with many situations that may or may not be similar to the ones in this chapter. While some of these may have seemed funny or amazing (and some of them really are), they all teach valuable lessons. In the real world, you're going to be face to face with scenarios that involve everything you've learned about communication and more. And no matter how much you prepare, you won't be prepared for everything that comes your way. But I sincerely hope that after reading this book that you are more prepared for when these inevitable situations do come your way.

Should you need a bit more practice than what I've been able to provide, I highly suggest that you pick out a friend or partner and role-play some of the examples that have been discussed in this book. Try being a quiet person, or a really angry customer. It's not only fun, but it provides real-world experience as you change from approach to approach, depending on the people involved. Lastly, I wish you good luck, Godspeed, and hope for the best in your IT career. Welcome aboard!

Index

resolution, 33
scenario, 30–31
intelligence, assertive, 15
background, 15
exam skills, 17
key concepts, 16
overview, 16
resolution, 16–17
scenario, 15
intent, listening for, 64–65
interoffice phone conversations, 77
background, 77–78
exam skills, 79–80
key concepts, 78–79
overview, 78
resolution, 79
scenario, 77

J

jargon. *See* slang and vernacular

L

lazy workers, 38
background, 38
exam skills, 41
key concepts, 39
overview, 38–39
resolution, 40
scenario, 38
leadership
authority, 140–143
delegation, 149–152
discipline, 143–149
feedback, 166–170
fraternization, 157–160
mentoring, 153–157
micromanagement, 161–165

lecturing
to angry customers, 4
in focusing distraction, 58
in mentoring, 155
legal issues
in ethics, 84
in sexual harassment incidents, 37
liability issues
in ethics, 84
in security, 95–96
listening
to callers with accents, 76
to criers, 61–62
to offensive callers, 64–65
logical arguments in persuasion, 184
lying as trust issue, 42

M

majority, administration by,
184–186
managers
apologizing to, 136
involvement in discipline, 146
working with, 44
background, 44–45
exam skills, 46–47
key concepts, 45–46
overview, 45
resolution, 46
scenario, 44
meaning, listening for, 64–65
meetings for discipline, 146–148
mentally disabled customers, 20
mentoring, 153
background, 154
key concepts, 155
overview, 154
resolution, 156–157
scenario, 153–154

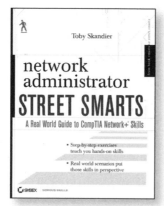
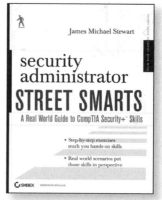